Songlines and Fault Lines

GLENN MORRISON

Songlines and Fault Lines

Epic walks of the Red Centre

MELBOURNE
UNIVERSITY
PRESS

MELBOURNE UNIVERSITY PRESS
An imprint of Melbourne University Publishing Limited
Level 1, 715 Swanston Street, Carlton, Victoria 3053, Australia
mup-info@unimelb.edu.au
www.mup.com.au

First published 2017

Cover design by John Canty
Typeset by Megan Ellis
Printed in Australia by McPherson's Printing Group

National Library of Australia Cataloguing-in-Publication entry
   Morrison, Glenn Andrew, author.
   Songlines and fault lines/Glenn Morrison.

   9780522870985 (paperback)
   9780522870992 (ebook)

   Includes index

   Travellers' writings, Australian.
   Aboriginal Australians—Northern Territory—Alice Springs (NT)—Social life
      and customs.
   Central Australia—In literature.
   Alice Springs Region (NT)—Description and travel.
   Alice Springs Region (NT)—History.

For Ian and Willa

Almost it was as if my steps had strayed
Into some strange old land or unknown isle,
Where time itself, with drowsy hand had stayed
The shadow on the dial …

Ernest Favenc

FOREWORD

'My eyes were in my feet', observed the novelist and poet Nan Shepherd beautifully in 1945, reflecting on forty years spent wandering the Cairngorm mountains of north-east Scotland. For Shepherd, walking was a means of knowing, not in the weak sense of 'getting to know a place', but rather in the full, fierce sense of knowledge being *grown* along the way via movement on foot—of knowledge as subtly site-specific and motion-sensitive.

Glenn Morrison's eyes have been in his feet for decades now, and in this remarkable book he walks his way at once into the landscapes of Central Australia and into their contested histories. What the mountains were to Shepherd, so the desert is to Morrison: a place where—in Shepherd's phrase—you can slowly 'find your way in', without ever believing yourself to have arrived at a vantage point of total vision.

Landscapes are layeredly complex, and they require layered and complex forms of address. Over six chapters, Morrison builds up a geological structure of porous strata, whereby each succeeding chapter is percolated by its predecessors. Patterns emerge, preoccupations echo, reverberate and modify one another: home and frontier; footstepping and path-following; blindness and insight; pace and rhythm; wires, lines and bees; and the prejudice often exercised against flat landscapes in general—and the Red Centre in particular—as a kind of *terra nullius* or void-space.

Morrison's writing restores the desert's intricacies. This, to my mind, is one of the political activities of good place-writing: to resist sly smoothings-out and easy emptyings, to represent all landscapes as entangled and ruptured. Yes, the desert is awesome in its scale and austerity, so much so that it has been repeatedly seen as exo-planetary and alien. But it has also long been a home to Aboriginal peoples—as well as to an extraordinary array of non-human life. Fantasies of the desert as an otherworldly realm or as a self-similar wasteland are prime examples of the durable 'wilderness delusion'. This is, of course, a terrain densely criss-crossed with print-trails—many of which Morrison has followed both through the landscape and through the archive.

Among the several qualities I admire in this book is its alertness to 'song' as well as to 'fault'. It can be easy when dealing with histories so grotesquely traumatic as the Falconio murder or the settler massacres of Aboriginals to exclude as improper any response of wonder. How can one legitimately experience beauty or amazement in a landscape where so much darkness has seethed? But to disallow the possibility of what might be called the grace of place is to crush another kind of life from it. Morrison is as politically sensitive a companion as one could wish on these paths, but he is also alert to the invigorations of rough rock under hand or sun on skin—and to the dreams as well as the horrors that the desert has incited.

Walking is both our oldest means of motion, and a cutting-edge contemporary technology. Ecologists, for instance, still rely on what is called the 'foot transect' as a means of gathering data in a landscape; archaeologists refer memorably to 'ground-truthing' as a way of authenticating data gathered by remote-sensing instruments. For many writers and artists too, walking remains creatively and philosophically indispensable. *Songlines and Fault Lines* superbly re-proves this, for this is a book that could not have been written by sitting still.

Robert Macfarlane, March 2017

CONTENTS

AUTHOR'S NOTE

Visiting Mparntwe that first time in 1998 was like coming home. Doubtless you know the town by its European name: Alice Springs, capital of the Australian Outback, heart of the Red Centre. That was all I knew. But that would change.

Shrugging off my bags at a motel room, I stepped outside to views of the MacDonnell Ranges and breathed the not-so-dry desert air. It was October. Daytime temperatures hadn't climbed to the sizzling heights of summer and conditions were pleasant. Rain had fallen that morning, and the air was heavy with a fragrance like fresh-turned soil, sweet and somehow closer than I'd imagined. There was a breeze.

A six-week contract lay ahead with a touring band booked for the opening of a new Irish-themed nightclub. We were due to appear that evening to coincide with the start of the Masters Games, a biennial sporting event for over thirty-somethings. Six thousand would-be athletes and other visitors had followed us into town: 'Sport with a twist of lemon', I would dub it for a magazine piece due the next week. Even so, and despite a list of urgent must-dos, my first urge was to go walking.

The object of my peripatetic desire was the bare rock hills dominating the view from my balcony. They were part of a much longer main range, a jagged spine of geological chaos bisecting the town from east to west that had been easily visible from the plane coming in. Its tumbled rocks were calling me, or so I imagined. The fact remains, even nowadays, I don't feel comfortable in a place until I've walked it. Later that afternoon, scraping and huffing to the top of a giant slab of granite and quartzite that was a great deal steeper than it looked—eventually someone told me it was called the Heavitree Range—I wondered why on earth a working-class white man from Sydney might get such an inexplicable sense of homecoming. Seemed to me Aboriginal people had walked these hills for generations. Surely it was *their home*?

The feelings of home stayed with me. In 2001, tired of the city and its traffic jams, my fiancé and I packed a Hilux utility and drove from the coast to the centre of Australia. I took a job as a reporter with the local newspaper and she started a business in massage and yoga. With surprising swiftness for a couple used to the bright lights, we settled right in. Over time, my responsibilities at the newspaper grew, as did the inevitable stresses of raising a family. Sometimes, fit to burst, I did what I have always done and took to the hills for a 'tonic of wildness'. Most of all I wanted room to breathe, and in the deserts of Central Australia, finally, there was enough. Time not to have to think, so much as feel my feet drum against bare rock, quadriceps quiver at the base of a scree slope, the desert broil against my skin. The space to ponder my relationship with the Australian landscape, which had puzzled me since roaming the sandstone banks of the Georges River in Sydney's south-west as a boy. In the deserts of the Centre, any similarly intimate relationship seemed implausible. And yet I felt something physically tangible—geographers call it the *affect* of a place—and it felt right.

Between editions of the newspaper I read those who had walked the Centre before me, which soon sparked an interest in Aboriginal ways of seeing landscape. That's when I discovered *The Songlines* (1987) by Bruce Chatwin, and walking took on a whole new range of meanings thanks to the somewhat pretentious British travel writer, who had visited Central Australia for just nine weeks during two trips in the 1980s. More than a simple path to reverie, walking, I came to see, was a cultural, even political act.

By 2009, fed up with climbing the newspaper ladder, I resigned as editor to go freelance and reclaim my life. Since Dickens and earlier, it has been popular for writers to walk a city or place to take its pulse and write about it. The aim is to find out what really goes on in a town's back lanes and lesser-known bars, to upend the normal flow of life that crosses and re-crosses its geography within boundaries sketched in around cultural norms.

I began to walk over, beside and around Alice Springs. I door-knocked its Aboriginal town camps as part of my work in community engagement. With my wife—we married at the Alice Springs Desert Park in 2003—we camped sections of the world-renowned Larapinta Trail, a 'desert-wilderness' trek winding 223 kilometres west along the MacDonnell Ranges from Alice Springs to Mount Sonder. The peak is a popular climb, not far from Glen Helen Gorge and upriver from the old Lutheran mission at Hermannsburg. At Glen Helen Homestead, the deeply cragged and broken geology of the Finke River also begged to be climbed. And soon enough, way above the world's oldest water-course and dangling my legs over a cleft in the rock, my gaze fell to the old cattle station-turned-tourist oasis, where I still play music from time to time.

Whereas people once explored or traversed cities and towns on foot, most now travel by train, tram, bus or car. Transport networks in modern cities and towns are built to cater for them. As a result, the dedicated pedestrian in need of a warm welcome often finds themselves in need of a jacket. For me, sauntering through a town or cityscape offers a more human vantage point from which to view the shape of things, which, as a result, become easier to define. And the pace of walking is important; time seems to dilate at its more human tempo.

Less frequently, authors have walked the 'city' for literary ends in Australian country towns, such as in *The Songlines* and Robyn Davidson's *Tracks*. Alice Springs has changed a great deal since Chatwin's controversial nine-week tour, which left many in the town upset by his blow-in ethics. He describes Alice Springs as a town where 'men in long white socks were forever getting in and out of Land Cruisers', and later, 'a dreary Americanised strip of travel agents, souvenir shops and soda fountains'. *Tracks* author Davidson calls it a place of 'architectural ugliness ... a discomforting contrast to the magnificence of the country which surrounded it'. Yet, by her second year, Davidson developed not a love for Alice Springs, but something she describes as 'a passionate hatred [and] an inexplicable and consuming addiction'.

Home to 28,600 people, of whom roughly one quarter are Aboriginal, Alice Springs is the Northern Territory's third largest town and a regional supply hub for Central Australia. About 200 kilometres from a notional geographic centre of Australia, the Red Centre's informal capital is 1533 kilometres by road south of the Territory's actual capital,

Darwin, and lies north-west of the sand dunes of the Simpson Desert on the fringe of the Lake Eyre Basin. Up to 2000 more people live within a 500-kilometre radius of the town, spread across cattle stations, remote Aboriginal communities, the regional centre of Tennant Creek, mines and outstations. More than 75 per cent of those living remotely are Indigenous. In fact, Alice Springs services all of these populations, and several others in Western Australia and South Australia, including the Anangu Pitjantjatjara Yankunytjatjara (APY) lands.[1]

Originally, the Aboriginal language group called Arrernte inhabited what is now called Alice Springs. Its name Mparntwe (pronounced em-barn-twa), means 'backbone of the river', and actually pertains to only part of the town, and denotes one estate group of the Arrernte. Two more Arrernte estate groups—Untoolya and Irlpme—are indigenous to nearby areas, with other language groups inhabiting neighbouring country. After rain, the Todd River runs through the town's CBD and is called Lhere Mparntwe, the features on its banks and beyond springing from the deeds of ancestral creation figures of Aboriginal storytelling.

Recently best known as a 'frontier' town, Alice Springs was crowned the nation's 'Outback Capital' in 2002 then soon after dubbed the world's 'stabbing capital'. Media portrayals of the region focus largely on violence, alcohol abuse and racist attitudes, depicting a place where, as *Age* journalist Russell Skelton writes, 'remote and mainstream Australia ... collide, with savage and unpredictable consequences'. But there are good stories of Alice Springs to be told, stories that seriously query its representation as a town divided.

Chatwin's philosophical 'novel' and Davidson's pilgrimage across the western deserts led me to other walking narratives of Central Australia, which remain some of the region's most popular reads. Before long I found myself opening the explorers' journals, T.G.H. Strehlow's *Journey to Horseshoe Bend*, and other non-fiction travel and anthropological tomes from Central Australia's extensive nineteenth- and twentieth-century literature. The more I looked, the more stories of walking I found. Throughout the literature, I was reminded again and again of the 'labyrinth of invisible pathways which meander all over Australia and are known to Europeans as Dreaming-tracks or Songlines', as Chatwin so eloquently describes them.

My bookshelves filled and a project aimed ostensibly at finding the meaning of home soon became one of literary and anthropological research. Some might think that means hiding from your fellow human beings in a dusty corner of a university library. On the contrary, many lively conversations about the work were conducted on walks of the hills surrounding Alice Springs, in cafés, at libraries, while camping in Central Australia, on the phone, on Skype or around dinner tables. And many spirited fellow travellers guided and encouraged me in my quest, for Alice Springs is alive with inquisitive souls ready to share their ideas, often as not with complete strangers.

At the broadest level, *Songlines and Fault Lines: Epic Walks of the Red Centre* is the story of Central Australia since precolonial times, as told by six souls who walked its magnificent undulations and measured its challenges through their feet. Drawing on anthropology, cultural theory, journalism, politics and philosophy, the book traces perceptions of the places and spaces of the Red Centre through those who have walked it. What emerges is something of a biography of the songlines, and an exploration of their cultural and political fracture under European settlement. My aim has been to probe the fault lines running through Australian culture, while nevertheless sketching the region's many attractive qualities for those who haven't been there. But it is also, I hope, something more.

A serious challenge for Australian writers and journalists has been to find ways to allow the various histories of their country to percolate together and inform each other. Each story in this book helps to put into perspective a slice of our history. For the first time ancestral journeys of the Dreaming tracks are situated alongside Western walking narratives to tell of the various ways Australians and others have imagined and reimagined the Centre of Australia. For on some days in Central Australia, it can seem as if all of these imaginings—past and present—are alive and operating all at once on its streets and in the canyons surrounding. And in each story of the Centre there is also a building block, not only of who we are as Australians, but importantly, of who we might yet be.

In Australia's pursuit of a settler identity, a commonly heard aphorism is that Aboriginal people have 'close ties to the land'. I am told

Aboriginal kinship itself comes out of the country, from the Ancestor beings, and in the five years since I began researching this book, popular interest in Aboriginal culture, and in particular the songlines, has grown rather than diminished. But has settler understanding of an Aboriginal sense of place advanced in the process? If so, why is the pejorative 'walkabout' still so prevalent? And can literature help? Reading and analysing Aboriginal stories from the Dreaming can most certainly help, and this book is a first attempt to do so, viewing the ritual walking of the songlines as an act of pilgrimage, and the story resulting from the journey as a pilgrimage narrative.

Six historical phases frame the essays, each phase portraying a particular era: a precolonial era up until the first European crossing of the Centre in 1860; an exploration era from 1860 until control of the Northern Territory was handed to the Commonwealth in 1911; an interwar period finishing roughly at the end of World War II; the so-called Menzies era of the 1950s and 1960s; the Land Rights period of the 1970s and 1980s; and finally a post-Land Rights phase, including the late 1990s and beyond, herein called the Intervention era.

But this is not a book of history, and I am no historian. Rather, it is six literary snapshots of the way we think about Central Australia and how that has changed over time. It represents the Centre as a palimpsest, a metaphor used widely since its inauguration by Thomas de Quincey in 1845. In particular, it explores ideas of home, the place where you belong, where—in the best of all possible worlds—you feel safe and secure. It also explores ideas of an Australian frontier. For if home is primarily safe and secure, then frontier implies all that is unsettled and in conflict, a place defined by turmoil.

Walking is something we share, Aboriginal and settler. It defines us as humans. By examining stories of where we have walked, I hope to emphasise the characteristics we share, rather than the differences so often touted. Revealed is a great deal of cultural exchange between black and white throughout Central Australian history, something our popular imagining of the Centre as a frontier—where there is an imagined clear divide between us—conceals. For one has only to wander Alice Springs' main street on any day of the week to hear half a dozen uniquely Australian languages being spoken in addition to English. Or to walk the Centre's hills, visit a remote Aboriginal settlement, spend a little time in its cafés. There you will find simmering a melting pot of Australian stories and histories, one life informing the next, a unique sharing writ large and plain in the Centre's red soil and on the faces of a diverse and extraordinary people who call it home.

Glenn Morrison, April 2017

Ywerreleperle

Alekarenge

Barrow Creek

Ti Tree

Northern Territory

Queensland

Alice Springs Telegraph Station

Alice Springs

Uramerne (Ooraminna)

New Crown

Finke

Stuart Highway

Oodnadatta

Lake Eyre

Coober Pedy

Marlpwenge

South Australia

Lake Frome

N

0   100   200 km

Port Augusta

1

MARLPWENGE

In dry years, the grasslands of the Barkly Tableland are a rich blend of browns and reds. The hills are low and the sky enormous over a tumbled spread of rocks and soil, Mitchell grass and acacias. In such a landscape, it is easy to imagine an Australia of before: before Europeans, before the frontier, before the Australia we know today. But it is also a landscape holding close its secrets, of terrible deeds played out across an ancient topography since the nineteenth century.

Nevertheless, the sunsets are glorious, and in the south passers-by can sometimes be found sipping a beer and watching from the veranda—slightly in need of repair—of the Barrow Creek Hotel, some 280 kilometres north of Alice Springs on the Stuart Highway. The roadside stop marks, roughly speaking, the broader Barkly region's southernmost fringe. Here detectives, reporters and sightseers gathered time and again from 2001 to puzzle over their theories regarding the disappearance from a lonely stretch of nearby highway of British backpacker Peter Falconio.[1]

Last time I visited Barrow Creek, a group of Aboriginal men and women had gathered in the shade of a gum opposite the hotel: the men, skinny in checked shirts and jeans, cowboy hats and boots; the women in floral-print dresses, patterns obscured here and there by grime. They stood but a stone's throw from where colonial surveyor

John Ross had sited the Barrow Creek Telegraph Station in 1871. The historic settlement is one of several repeater stations originally designed to boost the strength of Morse-coded signals on the Overland Telegraph Line from Adelaide to Darwin then via undersea cable to Britain via Singapore.

Hard to come by throughout the region, water at this spot has proven particularly unreliable, though surprisingly, early plans to move the station some 40 kilometres to the north were never enacted. Off-white tuck-pointing still binds the well-crafted stone of the station's huts, which seem to rise from the earth itself. From time to time, a car would pull off the highway and a road-weary tourist would emerge to stretch their back, walk uncertainly around and peer into the huts. One or two read the interpretive signs placed by Parks and Wildlife Commission NT, which manages the site.

Even for those aware of its history, the names of the dead of Barrow Creek and the places they were killed seem to ring out from the stone of the huts. For newcomers, it can be quite a shock. John Millner: sheep-herder, killed by Aboriginals in 1870. Telegraph station master James Stapleton and linesman John Franks: speared during an attack in February 1874 by a local Kaytetye group, the traditional inhabitants of the area.

The deaths sparked revenge killings by the settlers, and as many as 90 Aboriginal men, women and children died in reprisal attacks, many of whom had little or no connection to the original incident. At Coniston in 1928, dingo-trapper Fred Brooks was murdered, reportedly by a Warlpiri man whose wife had been staying with Brooks. Again, a posse of police and settlers rode out, this time killing an estimated 105 Warlpiri and Kaytetye alike.[2]

I didn't know the Aboriginal people gathered in the shade at Barrow Creek that day. Likely as not they were Kaytetye. Perhaps one or other of the older members of the group might have had a relative who lived through Coniston as a child. Kaytetye still live on country around Barrow Creek, which they call *Thangkenharenge*. Their neighbours are the Anmatyerre language group to the south, the Alyawarre to the east, Warlpiri to the west, and Warramungu to the north around the town of Tennant Creek. The impact of the Overland Telegraph Line on the lives and culture of Kaytetye and the others along its route was profound and should not be underestimated.

Nonetheless, the results of Australia's colonisation were also occasionally humorous. At a Land Rights meeting in 1999, a story was told of an old Kayetye man who encountered the 'singing wires' of the Telegraph Line for the first time. As he listened to the humming of the wires, he thought bees were alerting him to honey inside the poles. But when he chopped down the pole, he found only iron inside, which, according to the story, made a pretty good tomahawk.[3]

The good humour in the retelling of the old man's story suggests strength and resilience. Indeed, there are Kaytetye who still speak their traditional language or use a well-developed form of signing. But the truth is there are fewer and fewer each year. Some tell the old stories of the journeys of the Ancestors, travels that reach deep into neighbouring lands and across the continent along the songlines.

One such Kaytetye is elder Tommy Kngwarraye Thompson, a father-of-five thought to be in his seventies, a man widely respected around Barrow Creek as a storyteller. Among the stories Thompson tells is that of the Aboriginal Ancestor Marlpwenge, who walks from Central Australia south to the present-day location of Port Augusta in South Australia and returns, a round trip of some 3400 kilometres. Thompson's retelling of Marlpwenge's remarkable journey and the lessons learned along the way is published as 'Artweye erlkwe Marlpwenge: A Man from the Dreamtime', part of a collection of stories called *Growing Up Kaytetye* (2003).[4] The collection grew out of research by Sydney University linguist Myfany Turpin, who in 1996 had begun work in the region on a dictionary project for the Kaytetye group.[5]

Like most Australian Aboriginal languages, Kaytetye is in danger of disappearing as its older speakers pass away. With them go the stories that give the language life and body. Thompson is one of only a handful of Kaytetye speakers left and, importantly, only some of the stories that might help sustain Kaytetye culture have been passed on to the younger generations. Clearly, the need to record such stories is of some urgency, for with respect and support from the broader community they stand a strong chance of survival. But respect for Aboriginal culture has long been in short supply.

North of Barrow Creek, for example, is a group of granite boulders named Karlu Karlu, a Kaytetye Dreaming site that settler Australians call the Devil's Marbles. For Kaytetye, these impressive-looking boulders are the eggs of the Rainbow Serpent, an Ancestor that passed nearby on its journey during the Dreamtime. Nonetheless, the cultural significance and related stories of Karlu Karlu were roundly disregarded when one of the boulders was removed in 1953 and transported 400 kilometres south to mark the Alice Springs grave of Dr John Flynn, founder of the Royal Flying Doctor Service. The rock was returned, amid great controversy, in 1981.

Many collections of Aboriginal stories and myths from Central Australia have been retold and collected over the past 150 years, and the number appears to be growing. Alongside contemporary narratives, memoirs and journalism have emerged traditional Dreaming stories, still often collected by outsiders such as anthropologists, but for which demand is likely to increase as literacy rates climb among groups of remote Aboriginal people. Dreaming narratives and songlines journeys have also reached popular forums. As linguist Christine Nicholls of Flinders University argues, even though the narrative journeys of the Dreaming Ancestors were sung or spoken, they represent a significant body of oral literature, comparable with other great world literatures, including the Bible, the Torah, the Ramayana, and the Greek tragedies of Aeschylus and Sophocles.[6]

While the non-Indigenous world is now familiar with stories from the Dreamtime, only a handful realise their true significance. The forebears of the Kaytetye, for example, once walked the arid inland following the paths set down in narratives that were told, sung, danced and performed around campfires and at tribal gatherings and ceremonies over many generations. Such tales are much more than the simple children's fables many non-Indigenous people are wont to dismiss them as. For the Kaytetye and other groups navigated neither strictly by the stars nor by instruments, but rather by remembering and repeating their stories and songs, the words telling them which way to go and the locations of food and water along the route. The Eaglehawk songline, for instance, stretches from Heavitree Gap near Alice Springs to Byron Bay at Australia's easternmost point, connecting the Arrernte to the Euralayi people.[7] And while stars were not strictly considered a tool of navigation, they were nonetheless enlisted to remind travellers of the songlines stories, especially when travelling at night.

By following the songlines, Aboriginal people could make journeys across thousands of kilometres of desert, safe in the knowledge that each footstep had been traced already by an Ancestor, and retraced over and over again by generations of Aboriginal groups since. In fact, oral stories and songs of Aboriginal journeys and ceremony are not unlike Chaucer's *The Canterbury Tales*, in which a group of pilgrims travel together from London to the shrine of Saint Thomas Becket in Canterbury. In structure their tale is similar to *The Decameron* by Giovanni Boccaccio, in which a group gathers each night to tell a part of a story. Both *The Canterbury Tales* and *The Decameron* convey a great deal of the life and culture of the fourteenth century, even critiquing political, social and religious circumstance.

But Aboriginal songlines and navigation are not well documented and writing down an oral story is complicated. Some knowledge is secret, and enforced by traditional Law, and so anyone recording and translating traditional stories must carefully tread a line between the parts of the story that are 'open', and parts that are culturally sensitive.[8] Delivering an oral story might use speech, song or dance; the words come with intonation, facial expression, physical gestures or a particular tone: lively, excited, quiet and so on. When talk becomes text, the condition of the words is different from their condition in speech or performance and so any printed tale risks being distorted. There may be special knowledge owned by men but not women (and vice versa) to be considered. Perhaps trumping all of these important issues, however, is that there is a pressing need to preserve the oral wisdom of Aboriginal elders before the older generation, the keepers of the culture, 'pass on without passing on their stories'.[9]

The story of Marlpwenge is an open and published version of the retold journey. While lacking the depth and secret detail of the original version, we may use it, nonetheless, to interpret how Kaytetye related to the places they lived and travelled to on foot. Aboriginal pathways across the dry inland were determined by the location of drinking water sources: rivers and creeks, waterholes, lakes and springs. The trade routes along which people travelled criss-crossed thousands of square kilometres of mostly arid country connecting different language groups. Such routes mapped not only a travelling economy, but also what I have elsewhere called a 'geography of survival', plotting a safe route across a dry land.[10] In fact, walking underscored most aspects of precolonial Aboriginal life and culture, of which the ritual walking of the songlines was but a part. To suggest, therefore, that such activities are comparable to acts of pilgrimage is to seriously challenge settler Australian preconceptions of Aboriginal journeys, which so often demean the practice through the use of the pejorative 'walkabout'.

The expression 'gone walkabout' remains firmly entrenched in the Australian vernacular, and is defined in the *Macquarie Dictionary* as 'to wander round the country as a nomad … especially of Aborigines'. In some quarters the expression is co-opted as a colloquialism for a freewheeling mode of travel by settler Australians. Used to refer to Aboriginals, the phrase implies a sense of misplacement and being lost, along with degrees of laziness and unreliability.

However, a deeper understanding of walking the songlines soon reveals that Kaytetye and other Aboriginal groups were anything but lost. Exactly why this misunderstanding persists, and conversely, why these stories are so important to Australian culture and literature, even a national identity, can be answered by better understanding Marlwenge's story and others like it. During a lengthy journey on foot, Aboriginal relationships to Country become readily apparent from the routes and practices of walking the songlines. What emerges is a foundational layer in the palimpsest of Central Australia, a base stratum of 'Aboriginal home'.

~

One day, a wind arrives. Carried on the power of the Dreamtime, the wind brings a message, a plea for help from a language group called the Arabana, who live far to the south of Kaytetye country.

'Down there in the south they are eating each other,' says the message, 'one of them is a devil eating everyone.' On hearing the message, the Ancestor Marlpwenge decides to help. But to do so he must walk all the way from Central Australia to Arabana country near present-day Port Augusta.

A Kaytetye man of middle age, Marlpwenge is married to Nalenale, a young girl. She will walk with him on the journey. As Myfany Turpin writes by way of introduction to Marlpwenge's story, it shows how 'today's marriage practices were established during the Dreamtime'. Though Marlpwenge and Nalenale are married they are of the wrong skin.[11] Skin names are part of an Aboriginal kinship system, which delineates how people relate to each other, their roles, responsibilities and obligations and whom they can marry. From the outset, the relationship between the pair is flagged as crucial to the narrative's purpose. However, exactly why it is significant remains, as yet, unclear.

The couple's journey begins not far from Barrow Creek at Ywerreleperle, near Alekarenge (Ali Curung), about 350 kilometres north of present-day Alice Springs. This is Kaytetye country, from which the couple will trek 1700 kilometres south, passing through the Alice Springs district on the way to Arabana lands. Marlpwenge makes the forward trip in the company of Nalenale, then follows the same route in reverse to come home.

The events take place during a period that in English is called the Dreaming or the Dreamtime, when the world was, and continues to be, created. The Dreaming is a time both long ago and now, anthropologist Bill Stanner's term 'everywhen' being perhaps the most accessible interpretation.[12]

As Marlpwenge and Nalenale depart, they are said to 'leave their Country'. Marlpwenge's Country, his home, is a region defined by the reach of his language, and for a short time he will walk within its boundaries. But soon enough he will arrive at borders with neighbouring language groups, where different words relate to a different topography, different plants and animals, new songs and a separate (but nonetheless related) body of stories.

The idea of a home territory stretched far and wide in Indigenous Australia. Travelling back and forth over such a territory was, nonetheless, a part of everyday life, in addition to being a dimension of ceremonial life. In Western understanding, the idea of home is taken to mean 'a place, region or state to which one properly belongs'. Put simply, it is the place one feels 'at home'. The French philosopher Gaston Bachelard compares the home or 'nest' with the shell of an invertebrate, suggesting a human being likes to 'withdraw into his corner'. Importantly, in either culture, home may gain its meaning only when one leaves it, by taking a journey away.

For Kaytetye and other language groups, tribal territories were linked by clearly defined paths between language groups. Each group enjoyed property rights as well as hunting and food-gathering rights for their territory, including any permanent waters and mythological sites. The groups would communicate by smoke signals, and visitors were obliged to announce their arrival, with certain rituals prevailing whenever such an event occurred.

But home also had a sense of mobility. The Pintupi of the Western Desert are a good example, because they were able to set up a *ngurra*, or camp, anywhere on Country within a few minutes—and with all the comforts of home. This feeling of being at home anywhere within a bounded territory relied on the Pintupi having created a universe of meaning in the totemic features and stories of their highly mythologised Country. Under such conditions, broad empty space could easily become a known and welcoming place. The result, in the words of anthropologist Fred Myers, is that the Pintupi were 'truly at home as they walk through the bush, full of confidence'.[13] Here, Culture and wild Nature were one.

Conversely, many still think of Aboriginal people as nomads, even though they are really quite territorial. For 'Country' is bounded space, a home base. A better description of Aboriginal people might be 'restricted nomads', a people belonging for generation after generation to a particular territory, but who may both leave and return. This raises a question as to how the spaces at the centre of Australia became so highly mythologised. Settler Australians, who cling largely to the coast, see their vast inland as an Outback wilderness. How did such wide open spaces become a region named and intimately known by a people travelling only on foot?

For most of the past 100,000 years, Australia, Tasmania and New Guinea were joined, forming a single continent separated to the north by a stretch of ocean from the neighbouring mainland, which comprised present-day South-East Asia and various aggregated islands. Current research suggests Aboriginal Australians originally migrated from Africa, as was the case for all human populations. Splitting off from the main migratory group, however, they descended from South-East Asia to Australia some time between 47,000 and 55,000 years ago.[14]

Sea levels were more than 100 metres lower then, and land bridges now submerged were exposed above the water all along the route. Climate change had been forcing a shift in living conditions across Europe and Asia in such a way that much of the water in the earth's oceans had become tied up in ice sheets and glaciers. Even so, any migrant descending the Indonesian archipelago at that time would have met a final hurdle, nearly 100 kilometres of ocean blocking a route to Australia's Top End.[15]

Human groups of the time were still of the Stone Age, with some 30,000 years to go before anyone would seriously contemplate an ocean trip abroad. Yet Aboriginal stories from the Gulf Country and elsewhere trace changes in sea level over the period since, and some even speak of ocean journeys by canoe. Some commentators suggest Aboriginal people may have arrived in canoes or perhaps even on bamboo rafts. They may have set out from the Indonesian islands (then part of a broader land mass) such as Flores or perhaps Timor. Others put the crossing down to the result of a mishap, such as becoming lost at sea and swept south.

Whichever way Aboriginal people managed the crossing, it wasn't all that long before they ventured even further south and settled the inland. Previously it was thought the Centre had been settled only after the last Ice Age. But the recent discovery of artefacts and fossils at Warratyi in the Flinders Ranges of South Australia shows that Aboriginal Australians settled the arid inland some 49,000 to 46,000 years ago, about 10,000 years earlier than previously estimated.[16]

Could it be that Marlpwenge is one of these earliest Australians? Or is he a mythological protagonist, acting in the service of allegory? In a Judeo-Christian creation mythology, perhaps Marlpwenge would be akin to a precolonial Adam, and Nalenale his Eve?

In an Aboriginal worldview, people today are descended from totemic Ancestors such as Marlpwenge, who created the landscape and laid down the Aboriginal Dreamtime Law. Commonly, such Ancestors are non-human creatures such as a caterpillar or snake. Others may be part-human, or human, as in the case of Marlpwenge. The totemic Ancestors may also relate to phenomena such as rain or sunshine.

During the Dreamtime, the Ancestors emerged from the earth, travelled across its empty plains and created hills and valleys, rivers and soakages as they walked. Kaytetye Ancestors, for example, 'awoke' to the empty space of the world and set about adorning it with places and people. The Ancestors produced topographical features, 'sometimes calling them into existence by naming them'.[17] In the sense that Dreaming stories are often creation stories, Marlpwenge is perhaps more a god than an Adam of God's creation.

And yet, such stories walk the same path as European ideas that humans 'produce' their lives and the world around them, creating spaces and, in turn, being created by them. For example, we construct a library as a space in which to read and behave quietly, the city street as a conduit for travelling from office to café, commerce and back.

In the living of our lives there is a feedback loop between self and world, such that the spaces we produce constrain our future activity in them. In the same manner, the creation stories of the Aboriginals invoke a close and personal relationship between language, mythology and place, one that steers an Aboriginal lived experience of the world.

In 'The Birth of Kaytetye', a creation story from Turpin's 2003 story collection, we come to understand how 'Everything was established in the Dreamtime. The Dreamtime laid everything out like a blanket, even the Kaytetye people'. Gum leaves, for instance, were laid out as if they were groups of sisters, 'related as aunts and nieces to each other'. The leaves were girls from the Dreamtime. They told each other stories with the power to create, and 'From these stories, the Kaytetye language and people were born'.

Also laid down during the Dreamtime was Aboriginal Dreamtime Law, which governed the lives of Kaytetye born into these spaces, right down to 'the way children might play the game of cubby houses'. Place and space were tightly entwined with notions of family and totemism, and all were mirrored in the language of a land often referred to as a living being. Marlpwenge's story betrays this same governing politic, when he tells us very plainly that 'The Dreamtime laid the way'.

Political geographies in every respect, Aboriginal lands were sub-divided regionally, each region hosting a major totemic site that governed Law and identity. Each zone had its own ritual, poetry, music and art. People were created partly through conception from ancestral spirits that continue to reside in the most important totemic sites; a person's 'conception site', for example, where a mother first determines she is pregnant. Such sacred sites link to the totemic Ancestors, but importantly, and especially for navigation, they may also function as geographic markers of Country.

It follows that a person's identity was established partly through their association with a particular totem or totems. When an Ancestor returned from a journey on foot, from calling the world into existence, they would go back to the earth, to become a *tjurunga*, a sacred item of wood or bone or stone. It isn't difficult to imagine just how important a *tjurunga* might be; some are powerful, in the wrong hands, even dangerous. Unsurprisingly, the location where an Ancestor returns to the earth is of great significance, and commonly known in settler parlance as a sacred site.

Kaytetye, and in fact all other Aboriginal groups, are defined by this intimate sharing of sacred sites and stories, identity and landscape. A Westerner might think of it as a different way of seeing, a perspective anchored in a complex web of signs that dotted the landscape, each sign pointing beyond any particular individual to a greater spiritual meaning.

The scale and sophistication of the Aboriginal cultural achievement can only be fully realised once we consider that the entire Australian landscape, right across the continent, was similarly segmented into totemic regions, or Country, each defined by a central totem.

～

Marlpwenge and Nalenale begin their journey southwards, walking beyond the bounds of their language group and deep into the desert where an entire universe is evoked—of which settler Australians know little. With each step in their journey, the couple defines a map of sorts, in the form of a story that will guide future generations of Kayteyte across a vast landscape dotted with mythic features.

At Alekarenge the couple stops at 'newborn puppies', topographic features created by an Ancestor, likely boulders, perhaps related to this or another Dreaming story. They see *ahakeye*, plum tree, but 'the fruit is not ready' and they leave it for later. A soakage 'has water in it' but they do not stop to drink.

At several sites like this the travellers pause, while at others Marlpwenge hurries them along: 'Leave those puppies,' he says. 'Let's keep going south.' When Marlwpenge and Nalenale arrive at Arntwatnewene, or Bluebush, they find bush plum and later record the location of two important soakages (where precious groundwater is known to be close to the surface).

In the desert, a working knowledge of the location of reliable food and water supplies meant the difference between life and death for a traveller on foot. In the arid zone, Aboriginal people relied on various sources of food and water, which, unlike in the humid zones, were spread thinly over vast areas and sensitive to rainfall uncertainties ruled by El Niño oscillations.

Each of the topographic features recounted in Marlpwenge's tale is visible 'evidence' of the travels and actions of the Dreamtime Ancestors as they follow and further create a Dreaming track. Each tree, rock, river and valley recounted in the story is an important signifier of the travels of the Ancients and their legacy, to be told and learned and retold across generations of Kaytetye.

Subsequent walkers would maintain the Dreaming track, perhaps using fire, or by visiting sacred places to perform ceremony, dance and sing songs, or to ritually dig important water holes and soaks. Elders taught their young the locations, routes and ritual practices required for maintenance, all embraced in a code of behaviours in which knowledge of such routes and their stories was earned progressively with age and ceremonial initiation.

Sometimes, however, Marlpwenge and Nalenale seem to stop at a site merely to pay their respects. Their story traces a mythic geography of Aboriginal Dreamtime Law, a landscape in which there is a reverence for particular sites, and an understanding that some sites are more significant than others. There is also an understanding that operating at large in this vast dry landscape is a degree of sorcery.

When the wind approaches Marlpwenge, for instance, we are told it is 'just like today when you write a message on a piece of paper and send it, but in the Dreamtime the wind blew it'. Here is mystery, indeed, Marlpwenge's receipt of the message invokes another world, another plane of existence, a space more spiritual than material.

Some Aboriginals are sorcerers or medicine men, said to 'cure the sick, conduct inquests, accompany the kaditja revenge expeditions … and act as mediums'.[18] Such spaces are the realm of the *ngangkari*, or Aboriginal spirit doctors, who are healers, but also sometimes claim to travel through the air. *Ngangkaris* west of the MacDonnell Ranges were said to assume the form of eagle hawks to fly long distances at night to the camps of other tribes and cause illness and death. Nonetheless, much of their work relates to healing, and *ngangkaris* still practise in Central Australia, doing valuable work in Aboriginal health, especially mental health.

The landscape is the embodiment of the *ngangkari's* spiritual power. For the Ancestors through their activities had sewn this power into particular sites in the landscape; the spirits of Kaytetye children, for example, to be born again and again to successive generations. People in such a landscape are linked to their creators, who still 'slumber' in sacred sites dotted across the spaces of the Centre.

But such power must be renewed, through the ritual re-enactment of the Ancestors' deeds, through ceremony and journey undertaken generation after generation by living persons who walk the songlines, performing and telling the stories of Kaytetye. Songs were sung at each named site celebrating the Ancestors' deeds, and importantly, by being sung in the correct order, the songs mapped the location and nature of each site, linking water to water for survival. As a consequence, the heroes of the Dreamtime stories and those following in their footsteps were guided and constrained by paths taking the shortest distance between water and food sources.

Naturally, Aboriginal people travelled for reasons other than ceremony, such as survival, or to maintain family relationships and attend social events. Moreover, the routes travelled were also highways of trade, along which many goods were exchanged and distributed, including ochre, spinifex gum, myths, corroborees, song and dance, all given and exchanged according to supply and demand. Some travellers sought a marriage partner, groups moved with the seasons, or left a well-hunted area fallow. Many of the rites and practices characterising such travel can be seen as a form of pilgrimage, and the comparison is an important one.

On a pilgrimage, emphasis is given by the pilgrim to the place towards or over which they travel. On the hajj, for example, pilgrims journey annually to Mecca in Saudi Arabia, an act considered a religious duty for Muslims. In his essay *The Idea of Pilgrimage*, Hilaire Belloc elevates place to a destination towards which one is impelled by the experience of sacred things, or 'a personal attraction affecting the soul'.

With Marlpwenge's pilgrimage in mind, a special link to place may also derive from knowing the places of one's predecessors and acknowledging the stories of the past. Anthropologist Tim Ingold suggests, in fact, that it is only such deep knowledge of the past that can allow us to follow the footprints of our ancestors in the present. This was ably demonstrated on a 2006 walk of Spain's Santiago de Compostela (or Camino Trail), when Australian diplomat Tony Kevin described how he was 'walking at the interface of two radically different worlds, separated by technology and hundreds of years: through two overlaid maps of Spain, the medieval and the modern'.[19] The time of a pilgrimage may be present or past, or even both in the way Kevin describes. Kevin's journey pursued several personal and religious goals, such as tracing his roots in Catholicism, and other issues material and spiritual that he wanted to understand. But what of Marlpwenge? What might have been the greater purpose of his journey?

Part of the answer is to pass on the 'geography of survival' to young Kaytetye in a story that is clearly allegorical. This is particularly evident in the power demonstrated by the Ancestors. When Marlpwenge and Nalenale arrive near the site of present-day Alice Springs, for example, they make a gap in the MacDonnell Ranges and travel through. This is Emily Gap to the east of the present town, a topographic feature 'created' by the Ancestors, and now a popular tourist and picnic site. The couple then camps nearby at Ooraminna, now a tourist homestead.

Before whites settled the Red Centre, a great many Aboriginal people travelled the route taken by Marlpwenge and Nalenale, and were able, with knowledge of the stories, to use the many 'soakages that were all along the track', as Thompson's retelling of the story has it. The route is clearly set down, and even more detailed information of the route would have been given in any closed version of the story to an initiated Kaytetye. For this was a busy route. People coming from the south would use the track to come to Oodnadatta, travelling naked and on foot.

When the 'early white people asked the Aboriginal people to show them their track' they were shown 'all their soakages', for Marlpwenge knew them all. As a result, the white people took 'horses and camels to the soakages to get water', which highlighted increasing conflict over resources between Aboriginal and settler during the colonial period, especially regarding sources of water.

Navigating across the desert by way of storytelling in the manner of Marlpwenge is sometimes called 'wayfinding', to distinguish it from methods using an independent or global set of coordinates, such as a sextant or Global Positioning System. The traveller follows in the footsteps of Ancestors, remembering the stories and songs. Knowledge of a region comes from the historical context provided by previous journeys made.

In settler Australian culture, however, ideas of wayfinding have become lost in the confusion created by use of the term 'walkabout'. The term earned its place in common usage from pastoral managers concerned at the sudden disappearance of an Aboriginal member of the workforce. Two meanings of 'walkabout' arose. The first is of travel in a traditional manner, commonly applied to the lay-off season in the northern cattle industry; the second, an abandoning of responsibilities by Aboriginal people as seen by others.

The once popular Australian periodical *Walkabout Magazine* provided a third meaning, as 'a racial characteristic of the Australian Aboriginal who is always on the move'. This Aboriginal is a nomadic primitive, a misrepresentation still widely accepted. On the other hand, there may be an element of purposeful rebelliousness in the actions of Aboriginal people who do not let anyone know when they intend to leave, perhaps in order to deny an employer control of their lives.

This confusion between walking the songlines or aimless walkabout harks back to a sense of timelessness imparted to the Dreaming, an association that links Aboriginal people to the noble savage of Rousseau's imagining and Romantic primitivism, a figure living in a timeless and unchanging Eden. The effect is to trivialise Aboriginal cultural practice and emphasise the superiority of settler culture.

The result is to widen the perceived differences between the two cultures, and so deepen any imagined frontier. Aboriginals emerge represented by Nature, primitive and ancient; the settler by Culture, civilised and modern. Lost, is the beauty and sophistication of Aboriginal culture's geography of survival.

Perhaps as a result, relatively few pilgrimage routes of the songlines of Central Australia and elsewhere have been documented.[20] Anthropologist Isabel McBryde has mapped Aboriginal journeys in east Central Australia along routes skirting the Lake Eyre Basin to the east of the Simpson Desert and joining the Red Centre to the Flinders Ranges. On similar paths to Marlpwenge's, ceremonial and exchange links stretched from the Arandic groups of Central Australia to the Arabana of the southern Simpson Desert and the Nullarbor. The journeys trace routes of trade and pathways to mine ochre, but also delineate roads along which travellers fulfil ceremonial obligations and educate young initiates to manhood.[21]

And such Aboriginal trade networks were far flung. There was a roaring trade in the highly prized narcotic *pituri* from the Simpson Desert region, for instance. A psychotropic plant that contains nicotine, *pituri* was grown in south-western Queensland and Central Australia. The plant's stems and leaves were dried, broken into small pieces, packed in special net bags and traded as far as 900 kilometres from their source across a region of some half a million square kilometres.[22] As for the Arrernte, they were known for the hardiness of their spears, and pearl shell from Western Australia is reported to have travelled further than perhaps any other traded object.

We may think of the pilgrimage journey along a songline as travel between linked nodes, each place being of special value, as well as being a trade route, or a means of safe passage across the desert. Poetically, the pilgrim on such paths is a traveller. But there is also a much more serious business afoot, for the pilgrimage journey has special significance for the pilgrim, who, after all, journeys a long way to a sacred place as an act of devotion. The pilgrimage journey comprises three elements: a sacred place and a particular way to reach this place; a distance to be covered and a road to go along; and a certain number of religious acts before, during and after the trip. Importantly, however, the pilgrim must also step away from normal living and into a liminal space, where some transformation may take place.[23] Which begs the question, what kind of transformation was Marlpwenge destined to undergo?

Marlpwenge arrives with Nalenale to Arabana country, far to the south of Kaytetye lands and near to the present-day location of Port Augusta. Though the local Arabana warn against it, Marlpwenge lights a fire, risking 'that the devil will come out and eat us'. Fortunately, the couple survive the night.

Next morning, Marlpwenge prepares to battle the monster. He rubs red ochre over a hair-string belt, puts it around his waist and ties it on. The boss of Arabana country arrives to reiterate his reasons for requesting Marlpwenge's help.

'We need a good hunter to kill it,' he says. 'Maybe you from the north, from far away, can kill it.'

Bravely, Marlpwenge laughs at the beast, walks boldly to its cave and kills it without fuss. In the eyes of the Arabana, Marlpwenge is a fearless killer, a brave hero. The devil's head rolls north to a place called Elkertelke, north-west of present-day Barrow Creek, along the very same Dreaming track. The Arabana are finally safe.

It is not made clear in the narrative exactly who or what the beast is. It may be a mythical creature, or indeed one of the Arabana's own bent on cannibalism. Or the beast may reflect a part of the story that is not open to the public, a common enough factor. Or there is another possibility we might consider: that the nature of the beast is less important than the identity its killing helps to impart to Marlpwenge.

In retelling her journey along the Ngintaka songline of the Western Desert in 'An Anangu Ontology of Place', anthropologist

Diana James notes dancers who perform the Ngintaka songline *become* the Ngintaka, the Lizard man, the Ancestor who gives Anangu mistletoe berries and other edible grass seeds.[24] Place is *performed*, through storytelling, singing and dancing at each site along the creation Ancestor's routes as they criss-cross the continent. Anangu, the people of the song, are 'created by and actively co-create *Tjukurpa* by singing and dancing place alive ... the ontology of place is expressed in the songs of the living being of place'. The Dreaming, or Tjukurpa, is and has always been.

Other acts of pilgrimage reflect a similar re-enactment of a journey along a predetermined path, as in the Muslim hajj, or even the ritual walking of a labyrinth. As a Catholic walks the Stations of the Cross, for example, he or she 'becomes', or at least closely identifies with, Christ.

So too the Aboriginal walker of a ritual pathway *becomes* the Ancestor. And just as the dancers of the Ngintaka songline become the Ngintaka, the reader of Marlpwenge's journey—perhaps a young Kaytetye listener—becomes the hero Marlpwenge. By such reckoning, Marlpwenge's bravery is pure allegory, his construction as hero demonstrating to the reader that those who walk the track may assume the identity of the Ancestor who forged it.

Stories like Thompson's 'A Man from the Dreamtime' are central to the way Indigenous society represents and educates itself. Songs and stories of the Ancestors, and heroes like Marlpwenge, were and remain a pillar of Aboriginal culture and represent the link between people and Country. But linking story and identity is not exclusively Aboriginal; it is a trait shared by settler Australians who also construct identity through narrative.[25] Importantly, however, there remains another form of identity implied by the journey south, suggesting still more to the songlines journey than a mere tracing of the geography of survival or a moulding of Marlpwenge as hero.

When Marlpwenge receives the message on a wind, he is bound to act. The conceit of the narrative is established: he must set forth in order to help his countrymen. There is no question over this, no weighing of options. In addition to being a simple narrative conceit, then, this is also a lesson of Law.

For as well as the close link between Kaytetye and their Country, there is this other bond, or obligation, to other language groups living along the same Dreaming track. Later, when the pair turns for home, Thompson tells us: 'Aboriginal people would come back on that track, on their Dreaming track, northwards. Those two Kaytetye people followed that line. They are all relations along that track. Countrymen'.

The term 'countrymen' refers to groups living along the same songline, the track being walked in this Dreaming story. In this close relationship between language groups along defined paths, a way of being is shared across language boundaries and along the songlines. While borders may divide one stretch of country from another, each with its own language, stories and traditions, there is nonetheless another link between language groups, a relational sense of attachment stretching down the songline. What this says about the nature of Aboriginal borders is significant.

A tribal identity born of country does not invoke a frontier in the way that settlers would later come to understand the notion. There was a sense of sameness or homogeneity (accepting the various totemic and language differences) across such borders and along the songline, each Country contributing to a cultural mosaic of stories, identity, traditions and obligations related through an economy of the walking journey.

We might think of this sameness as a degree of insider-ness, a commonality of purpose between the groups. Aboriginal borders to Country might be called 'porous', in that a way of being is shared, an understanding common, across the divide. Ultimately, however, Europeans would introduce 'non-porous' boundaries to the Red Centre, a culturally impermeable dividing line between different ways of being, between Aboriginal and settler life worlds. On one side of such a boundary was the home of precolonial Aboriginal people, Country and the songlines; and on the other side, space valued for its potential resources, a backdrop for the spread of Enlightenment values and progress. This was the colonial frontier.[26]

A non-porous colonial frontier provided settlers with a way to demean the Aboriginals, to represent them as primitive and unsophisticated in line with a staged history of European progress and development that was to be commonly portrayed from the Enlightenment onwards.

Of course, conflict still occurred across Aboriginal boundaries. Violence was a common enough result in a landscape where group territories existed with boundaries transgressed on penalty of death. Anthropologist Herbert Basedow notes both intertribal and intra-tribal violence, and a study in Arnhem Land reveals intertribal war-fare accounted for 200 deaths in a group of 800 over twenty years. Ethnographers Baldwin Spencer and Frank Gillen observed that follow-ing a disagreement between groups—perhaps over a woman or an act of sorcery—an avenging party called *atninga* might be formed.[27]

But the boundary was not the sort of divide between Nature and Culture that Australian boundaries would later become under colo-nialism. Even so, we can detect a tracing of the colonial frontier in Thompson's retelling of the Dreaming story, which changes subtly under the influence of colonisation. In the apparently timeless Dreamtime land-scape of Australian mythology, a number of postcolonial place names are used: Wagon Gap, Adelaide Bore, Snake Well, even the controversial Bungalow at Alice Springs Telegraph Station.[28] When they went to 'New Crown Station', Thompson tells us, they 'travelled along where the rail-way is today—that track of theirs where the white people put the railway line down. Before that people used to take camels along that road'.

With the coming of the Europeans, new objects and encounters appear in the Kaytetye landscape and so are included in the story. All of which seems to work against any idea of a 'timeless land', or even a culture that is unchanging and static. Embracing such 'new' elements of the landscape suggests a culture adaptable and dynamic.

Another noteworthy aspect of Thompson's narrative is that his per-spective shifts occasionally from ancient to modern times, first discussing events long past, then shifting to the now and talking of 'the old days'. Dreaming stories and songs often exhibit this shifting perspective, in which the singer is sometimes inside and sometimes outside the story. In Central Australian Aboriginal love poems, for example, the singer some-times sings about ancestral events and at other times participates in them. Subjective and objective experience are fused, wherein humans are both products of the Dreaming and participants in it. For the Dreaming exists in the past as well as the present, the shift in perspective further reinforc-ing the notion that the performer or storyteller becomes the Ancestor.

~

The Arabana build a fire in the cave of the beast and kill the devil's babies. Later, they offer Marlpwenge gifts of food as a mark of thanks for killing the monster. But Marlpwenge is eager to start for home, and sends Nalenale to the Arabana women for a firestick while he prepares for the journey. Here, with their mission's completion in sight, an event takes place without Marlpwenge's knowledge that will shift the entire emphasis of the journey, and finally explain the mystery of Marlpwenge's real purpose in such a pilgrimage.

The Arabana women grab Nalenale. They rub her in red ochre and swap her for another girl, whom they send back to Marlpwenge. She is a replacement for Nalenale, and brings the requested firestick. In 'Our Way of Life Told by the Dreamtime Women', an earlier tale in Turpin's 2003 collection, it is noted that when a girl is ready to be married, the mother-in-law brings a firestick to the girl, after which they go together to her promised husband. The mother-in-law gives her daughter to the husband to return with him to live as a married couple.

Both of the girls in 'A Man of the Dreamtime' have been rubbed in red ochre for the exchange. Notably, red ochre appears widely in the story of Marlpwenge's journey, a device anthropologist Philip Jones identifies with the sacred blood of Ancestral beings, important to Aboriginal ceremonial life. In proximity with the red ochre, then, the trickery of the Arabana women is of ceremonial significance.

Marriage in traditional Aboriginal groups is determined by many factors, including kin, country, ritual and historical relations. Certain taboos prevail, including avoidance of in-laws, all within a complex arrangement of obligations to kin. Any deviation from the norm attracts attention from the group. That Marlpwenge and Nalenale are of the wrong 'skin' is of such significance.

An assigned skin name denotes the status of a person in relation to the wider language group and beyond. Skin names are part of an Aboriginal kinship system, and strict adherence to the skin system was vital to maintain genetic diversity among tribal groups that were often small in number. The system delineates exactly whom you could marry. In defiance of the system, however, Marlpwenge and Nalenale had lived together.[29]

Travelling was important to exogamous Aboriginal marriage, as a means of arranging partners in order to keep group numbers at strength. As well as stipulating whom you could marry, skin names also helped to identify potential marriage partners. In 'A Man from the Dreamtime', the skin-name mechanism bears fruit: the Arabana women recognise Nalenale as not the right skin for Marlpwenge, and so act to rectify the situation for the greater good of all. In colloquial terms, the narrative is a 'skin story', and all is made well by Marlpwenge travelling a long way to where he finds the right partner.

For her part, Nalenale disappears from the story at this point. After the pair's encounter with the Arabana, her role is fulfilled. Of the wrong skin for Marlpwenge, Nalenale's fate is to be replaced by a woman of the 'right' skin. And so, in the company of a new wife, Marlpwenge turns for home. Thompson tells us: 'That's as far as the Dreaming track goes. All along that track live Aboriginal people who are Kaytetye relations'.

Marlpwenge's story teaches not only a 'geography of survival', a safe route through the desert, and constructs Marlpwenge as a popular hero figure, but also explains the importance of the skin-name system, the right way to conduct the marriage relationship according to Dreamtime Law. And so it is that Marlpwenge and his new wife reach Alekarenge, where they find a cave fit to live in. And all appears to be well.

For a time life continues, until one day Marlpwenge's new wife wants to return to her previous home in the south. The old man consents and the girl begins her journey. But it is not long before she meets several 'aunties'. They tell her to go back to the old man. They rub themselves with fat and name the girl with their skin names: *Petyarre*, *Kemarre* and the girl's name, *Ampetyane*. Because of the naming, the new girl is enabled to return to live with Marlpwenge with the full support of Kaytetye Law. When the girl sees Marlpwenge once again, therefore, she is glad, and stays with him for good. Thompson describes the moral of the story:

> That old man Marlpwenge married a woman from far away. That's why people travel around and get married to people from far away today. It's how it was in the Dreamtime and still is today. A single man travels a long way, gets a wife from another country group and brings her back with him. The Dreamtime laid the way.

The skin story of Marlpwenge is but one example of why Aboriginal people travel. And though it is from one particular region, the principles have broader reach. The anthropologist Jeremy Beckett notes that people in New South Wales, for example, also have 'beats' and 'lines' along which live kin who will give them hospitality, thereby affording convenience of travel and the opportunity of spouses. Research by anthropologist Nicolas Peterson regarding the circumcision journey reinforces that the Aboriginal journey is a pilgrimage, a 'rite of passage'. In fact, in the 'Myth of the Walkabout', Peterson describes initiation journeys of the past as being undertaken on foot over several months.[30] Other studies show these networks reached even further. As John Mulvaney notes, it was possible for a man who had ferried pituri from the Mulligan River and ochre from Parachilna also to own a 'Cloncurry axe, a Boulia boomerang and wear shell pendants from Carpentaria and Kimberley'.

Indeed, with help from 'camels, horses and even bicycles', the journeys of the songlines continued by such means up until the 1960s, when the car began to intercede. Despite poor government policy and the effects of the welfare state, journey practices from pre-settlement days still persist and remain only 'lightly transformed', though now most journeys are driven.

But a journey's underlying purpose remains. In *Aboriginal Tribes of Australia*, Norman Tindale describes a 1933 circumcision rite in the north-west of South Australia.[31] Undertaken when Aboriginal lads reach puberty, the rite begins with the boys being beaten violently by female kinfolk armed with digging sticks. The women encircle one or more of the boys around dusk, then prod and beat the youngsters until they become 'half stupefied'.

Everything thereafter is about disorienting the youngsters and estranging them from the tribe, both physically and mentally. Tindale records the importance of the initiation ceremony as a 'break' in life; by temporarily banishing the boys from their mothers and sisters their 'childhood outlook' is disturbed, reconfiguring each of them as 'an outcast', at least for the duration of the ritual. Later, a boy sits with head bowed. He waits for the 'mysterious abduction' that befell his older brothers, and which 'in some mysterious manner ... transmuted them into men'.

On a pilgrimage, the emphasis is on the journey as a life-changing event. Imagine the manhood initiand. He fears the coming ordeal, and yet simultaneously desires to become a man. The walking narrative of 'A Man from the Dreamtime' teaches Marlpwenge the right way to marry. Both journeys are forms of pilgrimage. Both teach elements of Law. By the end of the ritual journey, the circumcision intiand can say 'Whereas previously I was blind to the significance of the seasons, of natural species, of heavenly bodies, and of man himself, now I begin to see; and whereas before I did not understand the secret of life, now I begin to know'.[32]

By the end of Marlpwenge's journey, he understands the true significance of the skin-name system. To call such ceremonial and Dreamtime journeys 'walkabout' is to trivialise an important Aboriginal cultural practice that continues today. A ghosting of these precolonial trade and ceremonial routes remains both evident and active: in fact, as Peterson has shown, the number of Aboriginals who drive the initiation routes and other traditional tracks is increasing.

The songlines are a living presence, a culture of the now. Co-opting the practice of walking them into the Australian vernacular for a settler identity of freewheeling nomad only hardens a frontier between black and white. The ramifications of songlines journey practices are far-reaching, having implications for contemporary Aboriginal land tenure, for portrayals of identity and for constructions of nation. And narratives such as 'A Man from the Dreamtime' might just help to keep the songlines tradition alive. At the same time, they help to explain why Country, and the network of related places spread out along the songlines, together comprise an Aboriginal sense of home.

2

STUART

It was still dark when we arrived at Jim's Place. Otherwise called Stuart's Well Roadhouse, the stop is about 90 kilometres south of Alice Springs towards Adelaide on the Stuart Highway. As my headlights swung across the front office signage, I joked we might buy a BBQ pack and ice for our walk. But the cabins, campground and nearby camel yards were silent as I parked the ute to the north of Jim's shop and elaborately rooved fuel bowser. The bare dirt of the camping area adjacent was dotted with white-trunked gums, which under the stars seemed to hover and glow over its flat red expanse.

Four other members of the Central Australian Bushwalking Club scampered from the car, zipping jackets against the cold and grabbing backpacks from the rear tray, each pack jammed with an assortment of nuts and fruit, water and various sandwiches for the day ahead. The start of our route lay in scrub to the east of the highway. From there we would strike north across the James Range following in the footsteps of the explorer John McDouall Stuart, who passed this way in 1860. As the first European to reach the centre of Australia, Stuart brought with him the colonial frontier, and many Central Australian Aboriginal people were confronted with white Europeans for the first time.

I had met the owner of the roadhouse, Jim Cotterill, many times. With his white beard and neatly combed grey hair, he was a familiar

Stuart
1860

Northern Territory

Western Australia

Queensland

South Australia

Attack Creek

Tennant Creek

Davenport Range

Central Mt Stuart

Strangeways Range

Mt Hay
MacDonnell Ranges
Brinkley's Bluff
Jim's Place
James Range
Hugh River

Alice Springs

Finke River

The Stevenson

Good Country

Oodnadatta

Lake Eyre

Chambers Creek

Lake From

Lake Torrens

Port Augusta

N

0   100   200 km

sight round the Centre; his wife Mardi had sold Fiona and me our house in Alice Springs. Always with a story to tell is Jim, part of a pioneering family who arrived amid the 1952 drought, which is when they established the business. Back then, the country was all red sands. Now, tourists dropping by are often curious as to where the 'Red' in the Red Centre had gone. Lost under a shroud of scrub and trees since the 1970s, Jim tells them.

Last time I lunched at Jim's, my daughter Hannah and I swam in the pool out back while Fiona lounged in the sun. But we climbed out quick smart after Jim net-scooped a deadly snake from the filter box. Fast asleep on the pavement nearby, Jim's singing dingo 'Dinky' hadn't batted an eyelid. In more wakeful moments, however, Dinky's 'act' earned him fame world-wide. Fans from near and far would gather at all hours of the day or evening to watch him stomp up and down the keyboard of an old and alarmingly out-of-tune piano inside the pub, all the while wailing his peculiar desert 'blues'. It was a sad day for all when Dinky finally passed.

Hair falling to his shoulders and shot through with a streak of white, the lean shape of poet and bushwalking club president Michael Giacometti emerged from the darkness. We would be five walkers in all. Quietly spoken as a rule, Michael gathered the troops without fuss and we fell in behind. There wasn't a great deal to say at this hour anyway, near-on dawn, temperature still below zero. Alice Springs was headed for a maximum of only 19°C in the second coldest July on record, five consecutive nights below −4°C.

In 2008, Michael had completed the first and only east–west crossing of the Simpson Desert from Bedourie in Queensland to Old Andado Homestead, to the south of our location and east of the Finke River. Solo, unsupported and on foot over 450 kilometres of sand dunes, he dragged his supplies and equipment on a two-wheeled cart, which, when he started, weighed about 165 kilograms.

If pressed, Michael admits the journey was 'mad'. But he had wanted to make a statement about water usage. In the Centre, many residents still use groundwater as if it is inexhaustible. Michael used only 2.5 litres for each of the twenty-four days he walked. He remains an intense and determined gent and I like him immensely. Earlier in the week we had swapped a few thoughts on Stuart's journal, from which Michael plotted the route for the day's walk using the explorer's descriptions and bearings.

We crossed the Stuart Highway from Jim's, through the ubiquitous buffel grass and followed a path of sorts, a mix of weather-beaten cattle tracks and none.[1] Pretty soon any sign of even this meagre trail petered out, and we picked our way between boulders and up the steep slope of the range without guidance. Ankles trembled and quads shook as I strode (or at least tried to stride) into the uneven grade.

Matters soon worsened among the rocks and balance became paramount—although at times near-impossible—and an all-consuming pursuit. Any idea of a 'walk' quickly devolved into the more familiar pattern of almost-falls and near-spills that characterises off-track walking in the Centre. Rather than take in the view, one's gaze is focused ever downwards. My body pivoted at times on only the tiniest sliver of shoe leather where it met with the thin edge of some rock or other. Life and limb poised precariously on this most tenuous of fulcrums, my frame would teeter on the brink of disaster, until, just in the nick of time, my other foot would land—thankfully, and more by good fortune than skill—on the next available balance point.

In such ungainly fashion, we reached the sandstone crest of the James Range in time for dawn. I looked back to Jim's Place, south to the Hugh River, and after a few minutes' breather turned north under Michael's lead into what was, for most of us, unknown country.

~

John McDouall Stuart arrived at the same juncture 152 years and a couple of months earlier, on 9 April 1860. He reached the range's highest point to find, according to his journal, 'a very thick scrub of mulga' and a range composed of soft red sandstone, with 'long blocks of it lying on the side'. To the east, he reports, lay red sandhills, beyond which were seen the tops of other hills to the north-east. To the north-west, his view was intercepted by a 'high, broken range' and he spied two bluffs around its centre, which would be his guide. Eventually, he would name the northern feature the MacDonnell Ranges after the Governor of South Australia. It was towards the eastern bluff, the higher of the two, that Stuart directed his course.

Stuart's journey is described in *Journal of Mr Stuart's Fourth Expedition—Fixing the Centre of the Continent, From March to October 1860*.[2] His traversal of the James Range that day was split between flats of grass among sandhills broken at points by gum-shaded creeks, and jumbled passes collapsing into surprisingly deep ravines. About 10 kilometres in, the Hugh River turned north towards a very rough range that Stuart has a tough time crossing, parts of which he describes as 'nearly perpendicular—huge masses of red sandstone on its side'.

In the adjacent valley Stuart finds 'old native camps', and after following the range for some 3 miles (about 5 kilometres), at last finds a place to cross the Hugh. Here the scrub was so dense that Stuart and his men could 'scarcely get the horses to face it', their way intercepted by the 'deep, perpendicular ravines'. On our leisurely day walk, the same ravines were an obstacle dealt with simply by stopping for a cup of tea and a snack. But with the horses, Stuart was 'obliged to round [them] after a great deal of trouble, having our saddlebags torn to pieces, and our skin and clothes in the same predicament. We arrived at the foot nearly naked'. By sundown, after having made only 8 miles (13 kilometres) more, Stuart and party came to a large gum creek with a broad expanse of water over a gravel and sand bottom. He ends the day with a brief note in his journal: 'Camped, both men and horses being very tired'.

By early in the nineteenth century, the map of Australia had evolved into the familiar outline of modern-day cartography. But for Europeans like Stuart, the nation's interior remained devoid of detail, uncharted, mysterious and dark. An 1840 expedition north from Adelaide by Edward Eyre had left many convinced that country north of the Flinders Ranges was a wasteland. Indeed, Melbourne's *Argus* newspaper in 1842 called the vast and unknown inland region a 'hideous blank'.

Against this background of a great unknown, tensions simmered between the states over who should host the route for an Australian communications line to join a new telegraph cable from Java to Europe. South Australia was keenly interested to bring the line overland from the northern coast, and for some time the government had offered a reward of £10,000 for the first to cross the continent from south to north.

Stuart was no stranger to the inland, having spent seventeen months between1844 and 1845 with Captain Charles Sturt following the Murray River to its junction with the Darling and beyond in an attempt to reach Australia's centre from the east. Turned back by the sands of the Simpson Desert, Sturt gave up the popular notion of finding an inland sea, and was eventually forced to return to the coast. He remained keen to return, however, later writing of his unflagging desire to be 'first to place my foot in the centre ... and ... raise the veil which still shrouds its features, even though, like the veiled prophet, they should whither the beholder'.

Several expeditions helped change settler thinking on the inland from 1856, and in particular to soften Eyre's bleak perspective on South Australia's north. The change came as a result of journeys by Benjamin Babbage, Peter Warburton and Augustus Gregory. Babbage and Warburton discovered what Warburton describes in his journal as 'bright green mounds rising out of a saltpan'. As it turns out, the mounds of water had long been recognised in Aboriginal society as highly valued features of their trade routes through and about the region. In part, the mounds are associated with the pilgrimage route of Marlpwenge, and proved key to Europeans successfully traversing the north.

Stuart staged three exploratory journeys north from Adelaide between 1858 and August 1859, each of which failed to reach the Centre. On the second he turned back only 100 kilometres short of the current South Australian border with the Northern Territory for want of horseshoes. On the third, he scouted the area to the west of Lake Eyre, where he discovered artesian springs, mound springs and soaks, some of more than 1700 individual springs that form part of twenty-three complexes within the South Australian portion of the Great Artesian Basin. The springs, sighted earlier by Warburton and Babbage, enabled all further northward travel for the next 150 years.

By the time Stuart reached the James Range in 1860, it was his fourth trip inland, this time in search of a route for the South Australian government's proposed Overland Telegraph Line. As he travelled, he had in mind the best places for river crossings, sources of timber for telegraph poles, and water supplies. After the earlier expeditions, Stuart had taken up a pastoral lease at Chambers Creek, which became his staging point for exploration of the inland. It was the furthest settlement north of Adelaide, 'the last point of civilization Stuart passed on his way out, and the first he touched at on his return'.[3] And so it was from Chambers Creek that on Friday, 2 March 1860, Stuart had started north on his fourth expedition with two men and thirteen horses.

Stuart brought with him a trusted companion from the third expedition, William Darton Kekwick. Prior to March, Kekwick had been south for the provisions, horses and men needed for the fourth journey. A Londoner, Kekwick was a quiet and trustworthy man with experience of mining, but who had become insolvent as a storekeeper. Aged thirty-eight when he joined Stuart's third expedition, he came with a knowledge of botany, though no formal scientific training, and much useful experience. He would become known on subsequent journeys as the 'shepherd of Stuart's flock'.[4]

From his venture south for supplies, Kekwick had also returned with Benjamin Head, born in Cornwall. At the age of twenty, Head had come to South Australia, where he found work as a rail-truck shunter, surveyor's chainman and stock keeper. By all reports Head was a bear of a man, perhaps 16 to 18 stone (100–115 kilos) by age twenty-five, and with clear-cut features. Head's size in itself would prove troublesome, however, with Stuart having to reprimand him on occasion for eating more than his share of the group's precious rations.

Stuart was Scottish, born in Dysart, Fife, in 1815. A civil engineer, he was educated at a naval academy in Edinburgh and emigrated to South Australia in 1838 where he worked with a survey party from the following year. Contemporaries characterised Stuart as tough, resilient and selfless, a man of 'true real grit'. Short in stature, his face long and thin, he sported an enormous beard and tended to remain silent on his journeys. But in town, says one newspaper report, he was 'affable and communicative'.

Stuart had the admiration and complete trust of those he led, remaining cool and cautious in adversity and retaining a tremendous strength of purpose. Conversely, some argue he was an alcoholic, but there seems little to support the claim, though he was widely known to imbibe heavily whenever he returned to town. Still, the geologist Charles Chewings would later refer to Stuart as 'made of iron,' the 'noblest of all Australian explorers'.

The trio camped their second night out from Chambers Creek at the Beresford Springs on Saturday, 3 March 1860. There they found evidence of a fight, 'the remains of a body of a very tall native lying on his back. The skull was broken in three or four places, the flesh nearly all devoured by the crows and native dogs, and both feet and hands were gone'. Numerous tracks and 'fires still alight' gave Stuart cause to believe the site had domiciled a great number of natives. On the banks were winter habitations and nearby a native grave of circular form up to 22 metres in diameter, composed of sand, earth, wood and stones.

Hot, damp conditions persisted through the first week of Stuart's journey, but by 10 March it had started to rain, and next night they were flooded with water and forced to shift camp to a nearby hill. This was not unusual for the latter half of the nineteenth century, when good rains were more frequent than after 1895. As a result, Stuart saw the landscape under the best possible conditions for survival. Still, the wet conditions hampered his progress throughout the month. On 12 March at Milne Springs, for example, Stuart writes: 'The country is so boggy that I cannot proceed today'.

While Stuart acknowledges the continuing rain meant good feed and water for the horses, he nonetheless suffered badly in the difficult and boggy conditions. Indeed, crossing the swollen Peake River required several attempts between 15 and 16 March, and Stuart's notes become more detailed around the loss of a horse, 'Billy', in the strong flow. The party must camp in heavy rain and on 18 March there is a 'sad accident' when Stuart's plans are submerged while crossing a creek on horseback.

The plentiful rains of 1860 contribute to an adversarial understanding of Nature from Stuart's journal, one based on the physical challenge of the wet ground underfoot. Boggy conditions and flooding creeks yield a representation of the explorer as Romantic hero pitting wit and strength against the wilderness. Here and throughout Stuart's record, Nature is to be conquered, a theme since common among writers of the

Northern Territory, who liked to emphasise the hostile and threatening. Indeed, journals such as Stuart's helped fashion Central Australia as a proving ground for European masculinity, and the explorer as an enduring symbol of courage. For Stuart, persistent acts of courage were a necessary part of 'knowing the Centre' and achieving the 'progress' his journey hoped for.

Nevertheless, the wet conditions of March cost Stuart dearly: inestimable delays crossing swollen rivers, a day to repair a damaged sextant, the life of one horse and a great deal of their dried meat provisions spoilt. The need to cross creeks continued through coming days, but to a lesser degree than before, and abated further as falls of rain diminished and the month wore on. But by 28 March Stuart faced another challenge: thick mulga scrub, through which he could 'barely see one hundred yards before me'. Fortunately, the scrub eventually broke to reveal the 'best grass I have ever gone through' and several 'splendid reaches of water', with evidence of extensive native habitation.

Stuart's fortunes, for the moment at least, seemed to have turned, and next day he comes upon another fine creek, which he names the Stevenson after a friend. The courses of water here are 'spread over a grassy plain a mile wide' and the waterholes 'long and deep', with plants growing along the banks, where wild oats grow more than a metre high. In the waterhole are fish, mussel shells and small crabs. Unfortunately, problems with Stuart's eyes, which had plagued him on the third expedition, return, and on 1 April he writes: 'I find today that my right eye, from the long continuation of bad eyes, is now become useless to me for taking observations. I now see two suns instead of one'.

Undaunted, Stuart continued across good country until on 4 April the party reaches another 'favourite place for natives to camp', where he reports parrots, black cockatoo and numerous other birds. He names the river the Finke, after the expedition's sponsor.

Stuart's journal from March had recorded 'very few signs of natives visiting this part of the country' (26 March). In fact, it was not until the West Neale River that Stuart notes 'numerous tracks of natives in the different creeks, quite fresh, apparently made to-day' (28 March). Stuart's indigene *in absentia* seems to support later criticism of his apparent 'reluctance' to communicate with Aboriginal people. But then on 6 April, the group encounters a 'black fellow among the bushes', the first living Aboriginal Stuart has come across. Crossing a small gum creek of quick sand south of what he would later name the Hugh River, Stuart notes that 'When we were nearly across, I saw a black fellow among the bushes; pulled up and spoke to him.

'At first he seemed at a loss to know from whence the sound came, but when he saw the other horses coming up he took to his heels, was off like a shot and we saw no more of him.'

Stuart's experience of Aboriginal people was mixed. On his first expedition of 1858, Stuart brought an Aboriginal guide and at first followed the man's directions. But the explorer quickly records his dissatisfaction with the fellow. Encounter with other Aboriginal people is absent from the 1858 journal, evident only as grisly remains and forgotten implements left near abandoned camp fires scattered on the banks of creeks and waterholes. A type of representation in itself, this was to become a pattern in Stuart's later journey texts. Yet his effort to speak to the fellow at the gum creek would seem to counter criticism that he did not even try to communicate with Aboriginal people.

On what was an all-round noteworthy day, the group also spied a hill that Stuart records as looking like 'a locomotive engine with its funnel', a feature he named Chambers Pillar after his benefactor. An unusually prominent landmark, the 350-million-year-old eroded sandstone pillar is called Itirkawara by Aboriginals, after the gecko Ancestor of the Dreamtime who turns to stone there after marrying a girl from the wrong skin group. The site is now a 4WD and camping destination, while the girl wrongly married forms another pillar to the north-east, about 500 metres away, popularly called Castle Rock.

From time to time on the journey, Stuart enjoyed botanising, as did Kekwick. Evidence of it abounds in the journal. Later in the month, for example, Stuart 'discovers' a new tree and the seed of a vegetable, which 'we have found ... most useful; it can be eaten as a salad, boiled as a vegetable, or cooked as a fruit'. Later still, Kekwick brings back 'a new rose of a beautiful description, having thorns on its branches, and a seed-vessel resembling a gherkin'.

The settlement of Australia coincided with the heyday of natural history. Much walking of the 'new' Australian landscape was for its scientific appeal, the emphasis being on all things taxonomic, corresponding with recent developments in the field. Joseph Banks started the fascination with Nature on arrival in 1770, inspiring many botanists and enthusiasts who followed. And Australia provided ample opportunities for the amateur naturalist, with thoughts of botanising often prompting a walk.[5]

But as a first-time visitor to Central Australia, Stuart was an outsider; in fact, he was more of an 'incidental outsider', for whom the places traversed are mere background for more important activities. Several things demonstrate Stuart's status: his lack of knowledge of flora and fauna, unfamiliarity with sources of water, and the consequences of these issues for the health and stamina of his party. Even so, it was at the Finke River that Stuart's outsider-ness is most evident.

At Finke River natives were scarce, Stuart reports, even though he spied tracks, wurleys, fish weirs, shields, spears and waddies. In contrast, when pioneer A.H. Elliot arrived in the vicinity of the Finke River in the 1870s only shortly after Stuart, it was to 'large camps of laughing niggers' at 'every permanent waterhole on the Finke'—so Elliot told the anthropologist T.G.H. Strehlow in 1933, which led to estimates of up to 1000 people living and hunting on foot in the Finke River Valley around the time of Stuart's passing through. Based on Elliot's report, Strehlow later describes the Finke around that time as 'a broad band of clean white sand, studded with reed-fringed permanent waterholes'.

'These waterholes', Elliot reports, 'were filled with fish brought down by floods from their breeding grounds in the deep pools situated in the gorges of the Western MacDonnells; most of these gorges and their waterholes were inviolable sacred sites, and hence constituted game sanctuaries as well'.[6]

While Stuart acknowledges good country and wildlife, he nevertheless records a very different viewpoint. The creek came from the west over a sandy bed for 2 miles (3.2 kilometres). After travelling a further 9 miles (14.5 kilometres), bearing 329 degrees, Stuart 'passed over a plain of as fine a country as any man would wish to see—a beautiful red soil covered with grass a foot high; after that it becomes a little sandy.

'At fifteen miles [24 kilometres] we got into some sand hills, but the feed was still most abundant,' he writes. 'I have not passed through such splendid country since I have been in the colony.'

Stuart remains fixed on his mission: find pastoral country, strike a route northwards for the Overland Telegraph Line, map it. For pasture, Stuart has a keen eye, but to edible species that might feed his expedition he is largely blind. Stuart's gaze is linked to intent: grasses will provide feed for the horses and future cattle, a concern ever on his mind. But such pragmatic observation lacks the nuance that longer exposure to a landscape can bring. Stuart's ability to 'know' the Central Australian landscape is constrained by his lack of geographic familiarity, the pace of the journey and the urgency and primacy of his imperial mission, as well as an unrelenting need to find water and feed. Had he known, Stuart might have availed himself of ample supplies of kangaroo, wallaby, giant goanna, snakes and bush vegetables, which, according to Strehlow and his informants, were present in abundance.

After the well-watered respite of the Finke River, Stuart makes to cross the James Range after leaving the Hugh River on 9 April, but finds the going tough and notes a 'great degree of difficulty'. Walking the very same route more than 150 years later, it is easy to imagine many detours, dismounts and searches on foot for a better way ahead during the day. As Stuart reached the crest, he would have been forced to pick his way through the hills and canyons. It is from this point on that Stuart really begins to encounter trouble. The following day his saddlebags are damaged, and the next he discovers 'my poor little mare, Polly, has got staked in the fetlock joint, and is nearly dead lame; but I must proceed'.

Throughout this period Stuart scales hills and peaks on foot to get his bearings and scout for water. On 10 April, he ascends a sandhill to spy 'a large number of native encampments ... rushes are growing in and about the creek: there is plenty of water'. In this fashion Stuart comes to rely on two things: a high vantage point from which to observe the landscape, and, increasingly, the presence of Aboriginals as a signifier of water. A high vantage point was an essential tool in the explorer's kit, and certainly provided Stuart a commanding position, in the sense of a militaristic power of occupation over and above that of the indigene, as well as a point of view mimicking that of the map—in other words, the God-like position.

In Central Australia, the physical strain of attaining this God-like position by walking the rugged terrain conspired with the lack of knowledge of an alien land to put the explorer at odds with the environment. The walking sectors of the journey take their toll and it soon becomes clear these are the toughest on the explorer, physically and mentally. This struggle of man against wilderness reinforces a dominant myth of national identity and later constructions of Stuart as a nineteenth-century Odysseus. All owe a debt to these episodes of walking.

Stuart's struggle with Nature also serves to hide his expropriation of Aboriginal land. For Stuart's gaze is that of the imperialist whose aim is to conquer an untamed wilderness for the purpose of development, concerned most of all with the ownership of space and knowledge. In this respect there is hubris in Stuart's writings, for as his struggles mount, his objectivity is revealed as a thin veneer. The explorer becomes what historian Paul Carter has called both 'the knight of romance and of the empirical sciences', an ambivalent creature serving masters both Romantic and scientific.

Perhaps it is inevitable to find an identity-forging bravado pervading Stuart's account of his fourth expedition. But it is important to remember also that for Europeans, the arid conditions were hostile and threatening. Even after Stuart had crossed the continent and the Overland Telegraph Line was complete, explorer and former Victorian postman Ernest Giles almost perished on the edge of the Gibson Desert to the west in 1874. Giles had given his companion Gibson his own horse after Gibson's died, along with instructions to follow their tracks back to seek help. As a result, Giles was forced to walk to safety, alone and carrying a keg of water. He started out 'bent double by the keg, and could only travel so slowly that I thought it scarcely worth travelling at all'.

'I became so thirsty at each step I took, that I longed to drink every drop of water I had in the keg,' Giles laments, 'but it was the elixir of death I was burdened with, and to drink it was to die'.[7]

The passage demonstrates perhaps more acutely than at any time in Stuart's fourth journal just how ill-equipped Europeans were for the desert environment. If Stuart or Giles had communicated with Aboriginal people and learned what resources the landscape might have offered them, all of this may have been very different.

From a gum-creek camp in the James Range, Stuart's battle with Nature continued as he made slow progress towards the MacDonnell Ranges. With pessimism now characterising his journal entries, Stuart records on 11 April that 'I hoped to-day to have gained the top of the bluff, which is still seven or eight miles off, and appears to be so very rough that I anticipate a deal of difficulty in crossing it'.

The next morning Stuart set out for the bluff, naming it Brinkley's. Brinkley's Bluff has since become a significant milestone and beauty spot on the Larapinta Trail. Attesting to the area's high aesthetic value are the words of a fifty-nine-year-old Melbourne hiker who suffered a stroke climbing Brinkley's in 2009. While waiting to be rescued, the stranded man nonetheless remained calmed by the beautiful view: 'I was thinking this is a pretty serious situation but what a beautiful view', he told reporters. 'It was a surreal thing.'[8]

As for Stuart, he had difficulty enough reaching the base of the climb, forced to cross and recross the Hugh River, which took him all afternoon. So it was not until the following morning at sunrise that Stuart ascended the bluff alone and on foot, taking an hour and a half to reach the top, which in his journal he records as 'the most difficult hill I have ever climbed' (13 April).

Unlike the stroke-afflicted hiker, however, Stuart made little of the view, remarking only that it was 'hazy' and 'not as good as expected'. Stuart's journal entry concerns mainly his relief as leader, for he had 'been enabled to decide what course to take'. Here is Stuart's explorer's gaze writ plain, for both explorers and settlers read these journals and the country they depict with a particular end in mind: colonisation. But Stuart's hard work was not over, for he then had a terrible job getting down the bluff, where 'one false step and I should have been dashed to pieces in the abyss below; I was thankful when I arrived safely at the foot'.

~

For Stuart, like all of us, walking is an act of discovery. To walk is to know space, for it traces a particular geography in the mind and, through the feet, onto the earth, a visual representation in memory of the objects we find and the various others we encounter. It is only to be expected that the desire of the explorers to penetrate the geographic interior of Australia on foot was strong and irresistible.

Many of Australia's first settlers brought with them from Britain a well-developed walking culture. Diaries and letters from the period reveal some walked purely for leisure, going for picnics, or day trips in the 'woods'. In Britain, rambling with a small satchel, perhaps staying overnight at an inn and taking in the countryside and rural air, had become commonplace. Walking was a popular way to think, discuss or philosophise; it spawned a growing literature celebrating the benefits of taking to the outdoors to become freed by and in Nature.

From the Romantics such as Jean-Jacques Rousseau and William Hazlitt to US transcendentalist Henry David Thoreau, walking was an opportunity for reverie, and for poet William Wordsworth, an aid to literary creativity. But for the Australian settlers, walking in the Great South Land was not at all like walking at home. For the colonists of Sydney, walking was, generally speaking, a form of work, bearing in mind that only six horses were brought to Australia on the First Fleet. Even on horse-mounted expeditions such as Stuart's, at least some members of an explorer party usually went on foot.[9] In rough country where the way forward was difficult, those at first mounted would frequently find themselves walking.[10]

In Aboriginal culture, place is constructed in part by ritual walking, a form of pilgrimage that is recounted in stories like Tommy Thompson's, the retelling of the journey of Ancestors Marlpwenge and Nalenale, through a network of known locales joined by walking paths. Such paths linked important water sources along the songlines, many of the soaks, wells and waterholes being sacred sites. Stuart's walking was fundamentally different from this, defined by both the means of travel and his intent. For Stuart, the desert—later to be widely dubbed the bush—was unfamiliar space. His aim was to cross and map it, his intention focused at a point beyond the present mission to the Overland Telegraph Line construction crews and the settlers who would soon follow them. Stuart's prospectorial eye needed to assess whether the settlers would be able to convert the space ahead of them into a place where Europeans might live and thrive. He brought much of his own food and carried as much water as he could, knowing he must find more during the journey, yet presuming his ability to do so would be limited. In doing this, Stuart managed a risk greatly magnified by his lack of local knowledge.

Stuart's was not a Romantic walking. The differences are evident in the physical effects and risk brought on by the privations of the journey and how these affected Stuart's perception of the unknown spaces he had to cross. Like some colonists, Stuart's walking was a form of work undertaken towards a goal. Moreover, it is the walking segments of Stuart's journey that are most significant in the nation's recollection of the achievement. Without Stuart's many difficult sojourns on foot, the obstacles he and his men encountered during the journey north may not have been overcome.

As well as defining the seminal moments of the journey, Stuart's walks are the means by which he gained the high ground, the vantage points he required to decide his next step. Remember also, that Stuart's journal serves to legitimise the right of Europeans to claim space and appropriate culture in what is essentially a story of dispossession. While the ramifications of this dispossession are still working themselves through today, none of this might be equated to a 'walk in the woods', nor does it negate the seriousness of the explorers' physical undertaking.[11]

As for the redoubtable Stuart, in spite of his rapidly deteriorating health he continues to climb a steep bluff or mountain in order to get his bearings and to scout the unknown country ahead. Such walking segments shape the journal's representation of the spaces Stuart must cross, for it is the image of the explorer on foot that clings most doggedly to the Australian psyche, perhaps because it is so frequently reinforced in nationalist mythologies. The walking milestones are remembered as the high points of a remarkable journey and later represented in art, poetry and literature, embedding them as cornerstones of a mythology of the man who conquered the Centre.

Despite two difficult days leaving the MacDonnell Ranges, Stuart is greatly impressed by them, writing in his journal of splendid feed, fresh native tracks, and on Sunday 15 April of 'as fine a pastoral hill-country as a man would wish to possess; grass to the top of the hills, and abundance of water through the whole of the ranges'.

From the summit of Brinkley's Bluff, Stuart had searched the horizon to the north-west where he spied a high peak he named Mount Hay after the South Australian Commissioner of Crown Lands. To the north-east, he saw another range he called the Strangeway Range, after the Attorney General. It was towards Mount Hay that he steered his party. But Stuart found little water in this direction and for two nights had to camp dry. At daybreak on 18 April Stuart sent Kekwick in search of water, then himself climbed a peak he named Mount Freeling after the Surveyor General. The climb was rewarded by sight of a small creek, and another glimpse of green in the direction Kekwick had taken. That night they camp near Kekwick's find.

The party has a tough few days traversing the country of the Anmatyere language group on an approach to the southern fringes of Kaytetye country, where Marlpwenge and Nalenale started their journey southwards an inestimable time earlier. Both language groups, their places, traditions and stories remained completely unknown to the newcomers.

On 22 April, and again reckoning his position by the sun in spite of failing eyesight, Stuart finds himself camped at what he estimates to be the Centre of Australia, some 200 kilometres north of the MacDonnell Ranges. Having reached the goal his mentor Charles Sturt had set for himself some fifteen years earlier but never attained, Stuart names the peak for his former leader.[12]

Next morning Stuart takes Kekwick and the British flag and climbs Mount Sturt, once again finding the going 'much higher and more difficult ... than I anticipated'. At the top he builds a large stone cairn, in the centre of which he places a pole with the flag nailed to it. Stuart records that he gave 'three hearty cheers for the flag, the emblem of civil and religious liberty, and may it be a sign to the natives that the dawn of liberty, civilization, and Christianity is about to break upon them' (23 April).

~

Situated in an 'age of discovery', Stuart's arrival in Central Australia marks the beginning of rapid infrastructure growth and dramatic change for Aboriginal people. Prior to his journeys, the interior was a blank canvas in the explorer's mind, the white void on the earliest map labelled simply 'unknown'. And yet, in another sense it was already filled with mystery and hopes as yet unrealised, a landscape ready for inscription, an object of desire. Some seventeenth-century exploration maps of the Australian continent, for instance, featured fanciful images of elephants roaming the vast interior. As the traveller Stuart made his journey, step by step, naming as he went, the landscape was recorded anew. Such a journey and record serves not only to realise the European settler dream, but also as historian Paul Carter has suggested, to 'bring the country into historical being'.[13] Fixing and refixing his position by the sun, Stuart renames the topography of Central Australia using a colonial nomenclature, effectively overwriting the Aboriginal home of Marlpwenge and others, a country known and named, a land of which Stuart is uniquely unaware.

While Stuart's climb is memorable, his words atop Mount Sturt are perhaps even more significant and certainly revealing of his motivations. Australia was colonised during a period in which Enlightenment values fostered a perception of Nature as a phenomenon to be studied in its own right. Emergent capitalism underscored widespread belief in progress, inciting themes such as economic development, growing the population and expanding from the south-east into the 'rest' of Australia. Such ideas drove the machinery of the frontier, that 'line of settlement that swept aside Aboriginal nations to allow the advance of the British'.[14]

But the frontier is at once a place and an idea, and the landscapes it invokes are both real and imagined. Frontier may describe a divide between worldviews, a collision of values and ideas of home. Explorers such as Sturt, Stuart, Giles, and Burke and Wills may all be seen as agents of an emergent science, and Nature something to be tamed and improved in the interests of human advancement. Exploration pushed forward the imagined line of the frontier and opened the dry interior to the productive gaze of capitalists. Inside this line was Culture, beyond it Nature. Nevertheless, others of a more Romantic leaning continued to revere the deserts as pathways to salvation and redemption, places far from civilisation and technology, where one found peace and solitude, and where God was close.

On Mount Sturt, Stuart prepares the way for a transfer of sovereignty and knowledge to the people. Such knowledge was power, and in keeping with an Enlightenment paradigm might allow the 'primitives' (who up until now Stuart has largely ignored) to 'better' themselves and perhaps (presumably) eventually to hold sway over Nature like the settlers. Enlightenment thought was considered 'progressive', a freeing of humanity from suspicion and fear. And yet such a conclusion clashes with Stuart's earlier representation of Aboriginal people as primitives and traditionalist, part of Nature. Were the natives to be considered primitives? Or were they a people capable of rising to Stuart's new dawn of liberty and Christianity?

The Australian Aboriginals had been considered part of Nature since the first encounter between whites and blacks at Sydney Cove in 1788.[15] In his 'Description of the Natives of New South Wales', Watkin Tench invites his reader to 'contemplate the simple, undistinguished workings of nature, in her most artless colouring'. In 1793, Tench introduced the concept of savagery as a stage in the early development of mankind, writing: 'If the Aboriginals be considered a nation, they certainly rank very low, even in the scale of savages'. And though the natives possessed 'considerable ... acumen, or sharpness of intellect' they also 'hate toil, and place happiness in inaction'. Tench's thoughts accord with the thinking of the Enlightenment era, under which progress required an 'application of labour'.[16]

Such ideas shape Stuart's walking as a form of work, a suffering in the interests of an end goal: the Top End certainly, but also his progression up the ladder of human evolution. Work set civilised man apart from the savages, his cultivating the soil a 'necessary badge of civilization'. Enlightenment ideas of progress were staged, and followed a 'natural' sequence, from savagery (hunting and gathering) to barbarism (nomadic pastoralism) to civilisation (agriculture and commerce). Tench was convinced of the superiority of European civilisation over the inferiority of Aboriginal savagery. Yet he perceived also a common humanity: Aboriginals were merely at a different point on the evolutionary scale, whereby 'untaught man is the same in Pall Mall, as in the wilderness of New South Wales'. His belief in progress brought hope that reason might bring 'knowledge, virtue, and happiness' to the deserts.[17]

Whatever acclaim Stuart might have received by traversing the Centre, it is conceivable there was another motive for his struggle: to modernise the 'primitives'. In this identity, Stuart shapes a further representation of himself as 'selfless' hero. But the conflict between his two representations of Aboriginal people is not resolvable, and merely denotes the ambiguities implicit in the journal. In a beautiful moment of irony, for example, Stuart observes from the summit of Mount Sturt that 'We can see no water from the top' (23 April). Recurrent in Stuart's entries now is the search for water. Yet the local Aboriginal people seem to have no trouble finding it themselves. Again, Stuart makes no comment about this. While this is what the reader has by now come to expect from the mission-focused Stuart, the lack of such comment highlights what is missing from the journal, and renders any imagined continuity of it an illusion.

In reality, many of the water sources Stuart found to the north of the MacDonnell Ranges were native wells, likely sites dug along songlines as part of Aboriginal people's efforts to develop a 'geography of survival'. The Europeans had to dig the same wells deeper in order to retrieve enough to drink. On the night of 4 May, for instance, they worked all night and got no sleep, bailing water in a small tin dish, all for 6 gallons (23 litres). It is very likely the well locates the expedition party on a songline.

Clearly, a precolonial political geography already ruled the landscape of the Centre. That this is not envisioned as part of Stuart's text is entirely expected from the outsider nineteenth-century explorer. Nevertheless, this lack of recognition contributes further to the imagined divide erected between the precolonial world and its re-placing under Stuart's journal. For although Stuart sights relatively few Aboriginals during the journey, his movements were, nevertheless, carefully followed. Tracking the party's movements were 'the keen eyes of proud, dark men and women, who were watching them with amazement, anxiety, and often with indignation'.[18]

Central Australia had remained free from the influence of the West until late in the colonial era. However, by the time of Stuart's arrival, it is likely news of Cook, Phillip's settlers and the early forays inland had already filtered through to the Centre by means of gossip and story exchange along the songlines that criss-crossed the continent. The use of messengers, or 'big speakers', was an Australia-wide practice, and enabled a communications net reaching all corners of the country. When the need arose, an Aboriginal messenger would transport an important message either verbally or on a stick with burned-in markings. Called a message stick or yabber stick, the messenger carried the item with them on the walk or, in an emergency, the run. From his 1897 volume *The Queensland Aborigines*, Walter Roth describes the stick as 'usually a piece of wood, gidyea, ti-tree or any other convenient, coloured perhaps black, red, or yellow, from two to four or more inches in length, but to various shapes from fat to round, and incised with various marks or patterns'.

In some areas, European letters—or paper yabbers—were tied to a yabber stick for delivery. In an emergency, some messengers would cover up to 130 kilometres on foot in twenty-four hours, or supplement the sometimes intermittent mail services. One messenger, called 'the note runner', carried letters tied to his head from Tennant Creek Telegraph Station, and is said to have run 450 kilometres in three days on more than one occasion. Charles Sturt in his journal writes how he sent a man named Camboli (usually called Jacky) down river with letters as he progressed up the Darling.[19] Stuart was on the Darling with Sturt, and would have been keenly aware of the practice.

Interestingly, on 28 April Stuart recorded seeing smoke from a nearby creek. As Aboriginals often used smoke as a way of communicating, it is possible that news of Stuart's presence was being sent on ahead. Much later, on 27 June Stuart writes, somewhat tellingly, that: 'This morning we see signal fires all around us'. The signal fires speak to a well-traversed Aboriginal homeland with strong and established networks of communication achieved by walking (or running). For Europeans clinging to settlements on the coast, however, one-third of the Australian continent remained unknown and was thought of as largely empty; Stuart's reported scarcity of Aboriginals only served to support this vision of a sparsely populated landscape.

The more likely reason Stuart saw so few Aboriginals was wariness on the part of the natives. Old northern Arrernte men who had been boys in 1860 and recalled Stuart's expedition told as much to T.G.H. Strehlow in 1933. According to Strehlow's informants, the Arrernte knew the footprint of all of the regular human residents of their country, as well as those of the animals and birds that frequented their homelands. Many Arrernte were startled and scared by the new tracks made by the strangers; one old man told Strehlow people were terrified by the new footprints.

'The boot tracks looked as though they had been made by human beings', the man told Strehlow, 'but what kind of creatures could men be who had broad, flat, toe-less feet, and a heel that was a hard lump, sharply edged from the main part of the foot?

'As for the horse tracks, we could tell that they must have been made by huge four-legged creatures, larger than any we had ever seen before.

'These creatures, too, had no toes, and their heavy feet had cut their way even into hard clay ground, and left their scars on the rock plates.

'Surely, we thought, both these kinds of creatures must be evil man-eating monsters!'[20]

In an Arrernte worldview shaped by walking and steeped in mysticism, not only were Stuart's men and horses cast as an unfamiliar Other, they were imagined to be man-eating monsters. Moreover, the mode of progress practised by the explorer party was one normally adopted in Aboriginal Australia only by roving bands of avengers when stealing across hostile country. While Stuart could not possibly have known that this was what he was doing, such an embodied signature may well have frightened the Arrernte.

All of the explorers failed in this same way to realise or acknowledge that the Aboriginals considered their territories home. The Arrernte had social protocols and courtesies to be observed when travelling in foreign lands or crossing borders between one language group and another. Conversely, and in keeping with ideas of the period, the explorers assumed that Aboriginals were nomadic primitives, and the closer to the Centre one came, the more primitive they were. For the European, such 'wandering' tribesmen had no need of a 'home', at least not in the European sense of the word.

~

Combined with Stuart's reluctance to seek help from the Aboriginals, his lack of knowledge brought difficulties later in the journey, especially to the north of Fisher in early May. Stuart had found few native tracks, which by then he was equating with a lack of water. As a result he retreated to Mount Denison. To this extent, Stuart was now reading the footprints of Aboriginal walkers to help guide his decisions. Meanwhile, Stuart's condition had worsened considerably and after a fall from his mount scurvy takes serious hold, his hands becoming a mass of sores that would not heal.

On 15 May Stuart writes: 'My mouth and gums are now so bad that I am obliged to eat flour and water boiled. The pains in my limbs and muscles are almost insufferable'. Again, had Stuart known, or if he had been able to communicate with Aboriginals, perhaps he would not have suffered so badly, as bush foods might have provided the vitamins he so badly needed. Next night, however, Stuart suffers worst of all, when 'Violent pains darted at intervals through my whole body'.

'My powers of endurance were so severely tested', Stuart writes, 'that, last night, I almost wished that death would come and relieve me from my fearful torture.

'I am so very weak that I must with patience abide my time, and trust in the Almighty.'

Stuart's passion in this passage reaches the heights of the sublime, where he is guided by God in his struggle. Alone in the desert, Stuart's situation evokes the plight of the pilgrim, who strives to obtain spiritual enlightenment by overcoming bodily pain and discomfort. Insofar as Stuart sees his mission as a 'fearful torture' and that only by resorting to 'trust in the Almighty' might he see it through, he envisions a similarly higher purpose to his journey.

Such a spiritual turn of events should not surprise. Ideas circulating during the Enlightenment were key to freeing Stuart from Nature's tyranny, exactly the opposite of the Romantic, who sought release in Nature's embrace. For Stuart, the Enlightenment prefigured an inevitable pact: God would end his suffering, his 'fearful torture', if only he could adhere to the plan and press on against all odds.

In part, here is the answer to Stuart's reluctance to accept guidance from Aboriginals. Persistent acts of courage are in concert with Enlightenment ideals. But for Stuart to have taken direction from the Aboriginals would have been to thwart this path to improvement for self and Empire. To accept help from 'primitives' would be to step across the frontier that Stuart's very being ascribes to the landscape and his experience of Aboriginal people.

Stuart's position invokes a binary between modern and traditional thinking, and emerges as 'the frontier' of Central Australia. This is a much less porous boundary than the intertribal borders between Aboriginal groups encountered during Marlwpenge's journey. Stuart's way of being was to invent the landscape afresh as an imperialist land of opportunity. Such a divide is erected not only across the land itself, but between the 'primitive' Australian Aboriginal and Stuart's road to Enlightenment. By virtue of his personal struggle and courage to determine his own personal identity, progress towards an enlightened society is also achieved at a political and institutional level. So the landscape becomes both an instrument with which to achieve political expediency, and a pathway to spiritual and material self-growth.

Aboriginal people are largely irrelevant to Stuart's project; they are considered neither civilised nor in any sense modern, and so are deemed primitive, traditional and part of Nature. Stuart's journal traces a first passage of this sort of thinking, and a much less permeable frontier, over precolonial Aboriginal space in Central Australia. The journey of Marlpwenge and Nalenale (and others like them) had established precolonial space as a storied geography of home. Stuart's act of flag planting on Mount Sturt attempts to erase this space and asserts over it an imperial geography, articulating in that moment the imposition of a colonial knowing over that of the Aboriginals. Despite this strong and clear contention, Stuart's representation of Aboriginal people is also inconsistent, and this is soon borne out.

Pressing on through Kaytetye country, the party reaches Bonney Creek and the Murchison Range in June, by which time Stuart's physical condition has deteriorated even further. His regular practice had been to scout ahead for water and a way forward before proceeding with the party. But after (re)naming and climbing Mount Strzelecki to build a cairn of stones on top only days before, on 3 June Stuart writes: 'I feel very unwell this morning, from the rough ride yesterday. It was my intention to have walked to the top of the range to-day, but I am not able to do so'. On 13 June the party encounters an Aboriginal group. Then on 23 June at Kekwick Ponds, two young natives bring gifts of food: 'four opossums and a number of small birds and parrots'.

The curiosity of the youngsters was intense, Stuart recording they 'wanted to steal everything they could lay their fingers on'. Eventually Stuart loses patience and orders them off. But around sundown, one of them returns with three others: an old man, perhaps the father, and two younger men, both tall and powerful. All were dressed seemingly for ceremony, whereby 'On their heads they had a neatly-fitting hat or helmet close to the brow, and rising straight up to a rounded peak, three or four inches above the head and gradually becoming narrower towards the back part'. Outside the helmet was net, the inside being of tight-packed feathers, an adornment Stuart surmises might have been for 'protection from the sun, or as armour for the battle-field'. Stuart notes also that 'One of them had a great many scars upon him, and seemed to be a leading man'.

In what may well be a simple case of imagination run wild, Stuart writes: 'After some time, and having conferred with his two sons, he turned round, and surprised me by giving me one of the Masonic signs'.

It is hard to imagine how Stuart might have been more gobsmacked. Stuart returns the sign, whereupon the old man pats him on the shoulder and strokes his beard. Once again, such incidents would seem to give pause perhaps to those critics who would have Stuart as obstinately uncommunicative.

On 26 June Stuart encounters a much larger native party and such friendly wariness on the part of the Aboriginals soon turns to violence. The gathering Stuart's party saw that day was, Strehlow believes, a corroboree or ceremonial gathering. Stuart writes initially of 'three tall powerful men, fully armed, having a number of boomerangs, waddies, and spears'. He wanted to pass them by, but then 'they continued to approach us, calling out, and making all sorts of gestures, apparently of defiance'.

'I then faced them making all sorts of signs of friendship I could think of,' Stuart records. 'They seemed to be in great fury, moving their boomerangs about their heads, and howling to the top of their voices, also performing some sort of dance.

'They were now joined by a number more, which in a few minutes increased to upwards of 30—every bush seemed to produce a man.'

Aboriginal culture of the time obeyed protocols and rules of behaviour of which Stuart was most certainly unaware. For example, a traditional way to deal with unannounced Aboriginal visitors to ceremony was to kill them. It is possible, therefore, that the locals had made allowance for the European visitors' unwitting stupidity; in other words, the explorers were fortunate to escape with their lives. Unfortunately, an ignorance of the appropriate rules of behaviour on both sides during instances of first contact led to misunderstandings. The natives showered Stuart's party with boomerangs and waddies and set fire to native grasses to drive them back, leading Stuart eventually to return fire, although not until the last possible moment.

The Aboriginal response to the incursion of the explorers could be interpreted as a defence of space, the sacred privacy of ceremony, and home. News of white explorers may have filtered north from South Australia along the songlines over the previous two decades. Perhaps Aboriginals feared the intentions of these 'invaders'. This defensive response would tend to collapse a representation of the Aboriginals as a 'doomed race' and imply instead a well-organised but patient resistance.[21]

Moreover, after ignoring Aboriginal people for much of the journey, and mistrusting signs of their presence (which might have led him to water), Stuart now shows a measured respect for their actions, writing the next morning in his journal that 'Their arrangements and manner of attack were as well conducted and planned as Europeans could do it'.

They observed us passing in the morning, examined our tracks to observe which way we had gone; knew we could get no water down the creek and must return to get it, so thus must have planned their attack.

Their charge was in double column, open order, and we had to take steady aim to make an impression.

With such as these for enemies, it would be destruction to all my party for me to attempt to go on … I think it would be madness and folly to attempt more [27 June].

Stuart's journal entry provides a momentary glimpse across the frontier, and demonstrates respect and restraint, waiting, as he did, until the very last moment to give the order to return fire. Here is a less politicised Stuart than others construct, a more nuanced man struggling to come to terms with a landscape very different from his own. As Strehlow observes, Stuart was 'infinitely more humane than many of his white contemporaries ever aspired to be'. Importantly, it is here we see clearly the Aboriginal's dominance and 'fit' in the landscape. The event also highlights the fragility of Stuart's construction of the frontier, leading to a similar conclusion as that which foils the doomed race representation: that the Aboriginals had been biding their time, and were in fact a force to be reckoned with. In the journal, however, Stuart remains philosophical, writing: 'it seems that I am destined to be disappointed; man proposes, but the Almighty disposes, and his will must be obeyed'.

Stuart retreated from the attack. But he was shaken by it, and so on, 27 June, citing the size and health of his party, failing water supply and 'hostile natives', he abandons the mission. Reluctantly, Stuart leads the party south towards Adelaide to begin planning his fifth expedition. They reach Hamilton Springs once again in August, remaining there until 1 September when the group proceeds to Chambers Creek. Here the journal ends.

~

Stuart's dedication to the imperial project ran deep, but the lengths to which colonial governments would go to control the inland perhaps ran deeper. After the success of Stuart's fourth expedition, subsequent Australian expeditions became a race to the Top End, against time and the better-equipped Burke and Wills project, which had left Melbourne on 20 August 1860, while Stuart was still retreating southwards from Attack Creek. Against this background, Stuart mounted an unsuccessful fifth bid to traverse the continent from south to north. Considerably better funded than Stuart, Burke and Wills reached the northern coast first, but both men perished on the return journey. Stuart, meanwhile, crossed and re-crossed the Centre three times in under three years before finally reaching the Top End on 24 July 1862, an extraordinary physical and mental achievement; and with no loss of life, a lasting testament to the man's leadership skills.

For the sixth, successful journey, Stuart had departed Adelaide on 23 October the previous year, only one month after returning from his fifth expedition. With little time to rest, the sixth journey exacted a terrible physical toll. A slightly built man of forty-six years, Stuart had to be carried on a litter slung between two horses for some 900 kilometres of the homeward leg, gripped by scurvy, unable to walk or ride. As a result, Stuart returned to England 'white-haired, exhausted and nearly blind', as the *Australian Dictionary of Biography* puts it, and died in London in 1866. His journey had, however, left a legacy to ignite the imaginations of generations of Australians, for whom he became one of several iconic figures of an emergent Australian bush mythology. Many consider Stuart entirely deserving of Strehlow's description of him as 'one of Australia's greatest explorers'.

Throughout his struggles, we see an adventurous, brave and persistent Stuart, whose dogged determination to see the mission through speaks most readily to constructions of an Australian identity, the daring and resourceful bushman refusing to give in. Such independence has arguably shaped a 'Central Australian legend', according with narratives of a national character such as Russel Ward's evocation of the 'typical Australian' in his *The Australian Legend* (1958). There is a paradox, nonetheless, between this independence and associated character, and the imperial purpose of Stuart's mission: to dispossess Aboriginal people.

Stuart's physical struggle can be seen as part of his Enlightenment mission in the desert. But while he traverses 'empty space' naming landforms and furthering the aims of Empire, the country also becomes his spiritual proving ground, a place in which to test his worth to God. Under this pact with the Almighty, Stuart's mission atop Mount Sturt is to liberate the primitives by bringing them the power of knowledge. And so an additional moral dimension frames his objective of converting space into place for people to live. In the context of Stuart's journal, Aboriginals are both primitives and part of Nature, but also capable of progress and therefore part of Culture. The respect and acknowledgement of Aboriginal people Stuart demonstrates at Attack Creek renders an already problematic frontier momentarily porous, and makes it difficult to see the text as a simple invocation of *terra nullius*.

But are these the only representations of Stuart and his journey that might emerge? Might other versions of his achievement, relationships, heroism and competence have been told? Few would know, for instance, of the walking Arrernte who remember Stuart's passing on his fourth expedition. Or of the fleet-footed Aboriginal message men who may have spread news of Stuart's party up and down the songlines. A more nuanced and inclusive version of identity for Stuart is certainly possible, celebrating his bravery and determination while at the same time acknowledging his weaknesses, his almost wilful blindness to the help that was, perhaps, so close at hand. For Stuart's walking is naive, insofar as his exposure to a new environment is too brief to have enabled him to make any real sense of it. And so the walking segments of Stuart's published journal represent the space of the Centre as harsh wilderness, unforgiving and difficult to traverse, a frontier to be conquered.

Nevertheless, Stuart had established a route north for the Overland Telegraph Line, and documented considerable pastoral resources. Largely as a result of the reports from Stuart's expedition, South Australia annexed the region now known as the Northern Territory in 1863. By 1870, a contract was let for surveyors and construction crews to string the Overland Telegraph Line northwards along the route Stuart had struck. The next time Europeans came into contact with the Kaytetye and other groups along Stuart's route, it was John Ross and four other men, who comprised the surveying team for the Overland Telegraph Line. By 1872, the first message was sent to Britain along the cable.

But the line's construction sparked a period of frontier conflict across the Centre in which as many as a thousand Aboriginals were shot and numerous whites speared. Intra-tribal and intertribal violence also continued.[22] Pastoralists took over land around permanent water supplies, culminating in the town of Stuart (renamed Alice Springs in 1933) being gazetted in 1888. The overwriting of Aboriginal home in the Red Centre had begun.

For Stuart and the settlers who followed him, home was far away in Britain. Central Australia held the prospect of future home, but, for the moment, remained an unforgiving wilderness to be conquered. Meanwhile, settler Australia had begun to describe the tangled beauty at its heart as a frontier, a divide between ancient and modern, black and white, primitive and civilised.

3

STREHLOW

Turning off the Larapinta Highway 125 kilometres west of Alice Springs for the Aboriginal community of Hermannsburg, you cannot miss the spectacular red escarpment that lies dead ahead. Keep bearing west across the Finke River and you would run bang into it, if not for the fact that the road finds its way through the hills and on to the tourist resort at Kings Canyon.

The escarpment is unexpected. By comparison, the broader sweep of country on approach to the remote town is rolling at best. But rise the escarpment does, like several giant bowls cut from the range and tipped on their sides. Everything in the landscape, from plain and slope to ridge and scarp, is covered in green courtesy of Christmas rains.

For a moment I am taken with the urge to keep driving, farther round the Mereenie Loop to the Canyon, to see exactly how green this red land has become. I would need a permit to cross Aboriginal country of course; one is readily available from Hermannsburg, but time is against me. The remote community, its church and surrounding buildings—setting for the linguist Theodor Strehlow's experiences there in 1922 recounted in his memoir *Journey to Horseshoe Bend*—will do for one morning.[1]

Named for a German village in Lower Saxony, Hermannsburg— the population of which is a somewhat variable 800—is an easy drive

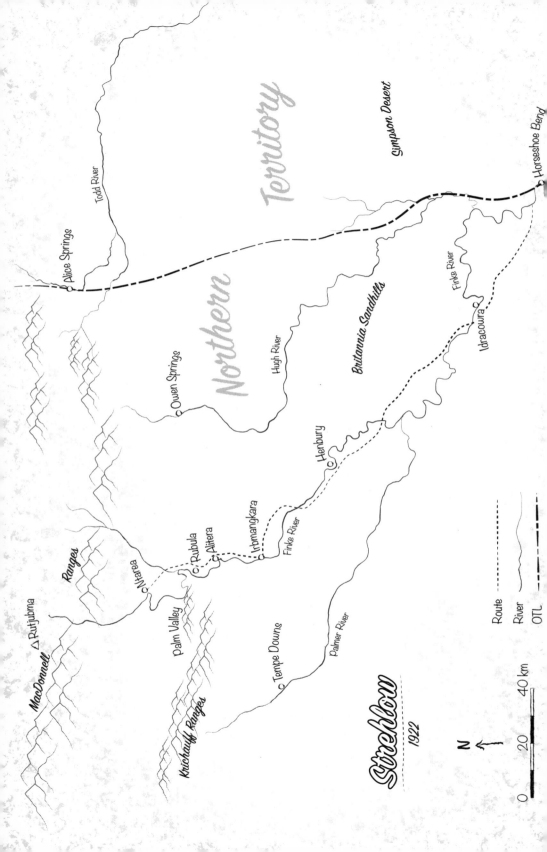

Strehlow
1922

N

MacDonnell
△ Rutjubma

Ranges

Krichauff Ranges

Palm Valley

Ntarea

Rubula
Alitera

Irbmangkara

Tempe Downs

Palmer River

Finke River

Owen Springs

Henbury

Hugh River

Britannia Sandhills

Finke River

Idracowra

Northern

Todd River

Alice Springs

Territory

Simpson Desert

Horseshoe Bend

0   20   40 km

Route ----
River —
OTL —·—·—

on the bitumen to where the settlement sits behind a slight rise under a grove of trees to the north of the highway. Its establishment is a barely credible tale. Some fifteen years after Stuart's arrival in the Centre, and only three years since the first message was sent to Britain on the Overland Telegraph Line in 1872, young Lutheran missionary trainees Hermann Kempe and Wilhelm Schwarz sailed from the German village of Hermannsburg to Australia on their first assignment. From Adelaide, they trekked northwards for a gruelling twenty months, arriving on 4 June 1877 to camp on the banks of the Finke River, where for the next thirteen years they would oversee the construction of a 'new' Hermannsburg.

At odds with its colonial history, a sign at the highway turnoff declares: 'Welcome to Ntaria', the name the local Arrernte call Hermannsburg. Below the welcome there is a sort of mission statement for the community—'Many voices, one dream, building a quality desert lifestyle'—while another sign declares the town to be the home of renowned watercolour artist Albert Namatjira. Both messages bely Hermannsburg's well-known propensity for violence.

For years on welfare day, women would hide friends, grandmothers and children as alcohol came into the community and husbands turned violent. Recently, many Aboriginal men have spoken out against such violence, including fifty-four-year-old Arrernte country singer and musician Warren H. Williams, himself a reformed drinker, a man well known and liked in the Centre.

I turn right into Ntaria, past recently built houses packed surprisingly close, a suburb in the desert, if one with little neighbouring development for hundreds of kilometres. The dwellings are the legacy of a $10 million government-funded construction and refurbishment program for the community set in motion from 2011.

A left turn at the supermarket and its ageing fuel bowser brings me abruptly to an older precinct. Rubbish lies ankle-deep in some yards, and upkeep of these older tin-roofed houses seems low down on the pecking order of domestic concerns. In one property, children run and play round and round a small pony, and what appears to be a rather scrawny llama.

I'm looking for the Finke River Mission general store, well equipped, open six days a week. It emerges to my right, and a sign out front informs me this is where the weekly men's group meets. My gaze traverses an adjacent graveyard fallen into disrepair, and to a nearby clutch of temporary offices or 'dongas', likely for government staff. Farther on, a new-looking Lutheran church distracts momentarily, but eventually I swing back to my goal, the heritage precinct.

From my last visit I've failed to remember a fence ringing the historic zone. The fence looks old, rusted; I'm stunned I don't recall it. For it is one of some severity, perhaps 1.8 metres high of up-pointed star pickets welded to pipes as cross-rails: a serious challenge to any would-be trespasser.

Inside is a dirt arena where twin gums shade a white rendered church, which at the peak of its gable end stands two storeys high. I lock the car, walk to one end of the building and step through an exposed-lintel doorway to an interior festooned with posters and information, all surprisingly well lit by two narrow windows on each long side of the oblong space. Built between 1896 and 1898, the old Lutheran church is the centrepiece of the Hermannsburg historic precinct.

A broader scattering of late nineteenth-century buildings encircles the church, the whole arrangement registered for national heritage. There are several houses, a school house, bakery, workers' accommodation and more, all low-set dwellings with similar exteriors, the original construction being lime-mortar slapped roughly over rubble stones. Naturally, as time wore on, the original thatched roofs of the buildings were replaced with corrugated iron, the inside walls plastered and the outsides lime washed.[2] Behind the church stands a small mortuary, stone walls enclosing a bare concrete slab that seems to stare mutely from the room's tiny window, where render falls away from the stone of the sill.

For a long while, this was the only European settlement to the west of Alice Springs, an evangelical bush mission that sheltered many Aboriginals and, as anthropologist Peter Sutton wrote recently, 'gave sanctuary against the murderous raids of pastoralists and troopers'. Some of those seeking refuge from frontier violence would become Aboriginal evangelists and work with even more remote groups. While the missions have been widely criticised for persuading an ancient culture to Christianity, many Arrernte would not have lived but for their efforts.

Dust now stains the church walls, which serves only to blend them even more closely with the rusted brown of the compound. I stroll the dirt from the deep shade of the church's spreading gum, past a relic steel-wheeled ox cart, to the middle of the wide space. It has the feel of a parade ground. Military. Reminds me of marching in a municipal brass band at Sydney's Easter Show Parade as a boy. An empty space, but one filled with voices that rise and fall like Souza's marches from my reading of Hermannsburg's fascinating history.

A dozen strides and I reach the house where the second of Hermannsburg's missionary line, Pastor Carl Strehlow, lived from October 1894. Squat under date palms and part-hidden behind a greying and frail fence of stripped saplings tied vertically, the Strehlow house now serves tea and scones, which I knew from my previous visits with Fiona were not to be missed. Called the Kata-Anga tearooms, I'm disappointed to discover the kitchen closed for summer.

Pastors Kempe and Schwarz had left Hermannsburg in 1891, and the mission fared rather poorly in the hands of lay workers until Strehlow's arrival. Pastor Carl seldom left the mission thereafter, but on one such occasion in 1895 he travelled briefly to marry a Bavarian orphan, Frieda Keysser, after a four-year courtship largely by mail. The ceremony was in Adelaide, from where Frieda accompanied Carl to Hermannsburg to live in the house with him.

Double doors hang in the entrance to the home under a wide and generously shaded veranda that sports tables for tearoom patrons of another season. Inside, I quickly become lost in the feel of the house, its antiquity and half-heard whispers, shouts, perhaps even arguments that my imagination tells me still inhabit its stone-walled halls and tiny rooms, all remarkably cool as the day outside climbs to 39°C.

When last I visited, the tearooms were run by Heidi Williams, at that time settler wife of Warren H. Williams. The marriage ended in 2013, and Heidi became a political apparatchik and eventually Northern Territory election hopeful for the then-ruling Country Liberal party. Of Swedish, German, Norwegian and Scottish ancestry,

Heidi came to the Centre in 2003, later telling a newspaper that bush communities like Hermannsburg had become known as 'widow cities'.

'The men are either incarcerated, they've moved on or they've passed on,' she said.

'We've got all these children who are being raised, sometimes by the mother, but a lot of times it's the grandmother, or the auntie, or whoever has her hands on deck to try and raise these children.'[3]

Despite their crimes, I feel for the men. And no less the women who so often suffer at their hands. On the Horn Scientific Expedition of 1894, anthropologist Baldwin Spencer judged the people of Hermannsburg as doomed to extinction. Their very being, men and women both, has been challenged and reshaped by frontier and mission, their laws torn up, power structures disrupted.

Where are the men's *tjurunga* now, the sacred objects of culture stolen from their caves and secret storehouses? How and for whom will these men rule? If children fail to meet Western expectations in school or under the law, who is to blame? The fathers? The grog some of them consume? Or modernity's assault on a social structure adapted to the desert, one unfamiliar with ideas of 'progress'. The people of the Finke River have weathered enormous change in little more than a century. Yet here they remain, driven and at the same time frozen by localism, standing at the eye of an ideological cyclone that arrived with Stuart and that seems fated only to accelerate and deepen.

I have no answers. But the questions haunt me as I stroll the Strehlows' house, its walls lined with photographs of the family. To the Arrernte, Pastor Carl Strehlow became *ingkata*, trusted leader and teacher. Trained in the seminary in Germany ahead of being called by the Lutheran Synod to Australia, Pastor Carl set about learning the local language, and by 1904 the New Testament had been translated into Arrernte. Frieda bore him six children, but in 1910–11 the couple visited Germany to leave their five elder children with relatives to complete their schooling. The youngest, Theodor George Henry, remained in Hermannsburg where he learned Arrernte along with German and English. Years later, T.G.H. Strehlow would continue his father's work, travelling extensively in the region.

Pastor Carl and Frieda Strehlow ran the mission at Hermannsburg for some twenty-eight years until Carl fell ill in 1922. With the tearoom closed, I drift back to the home's entrance and its heavy double doors. For it is there that Pastor Carl's final story of his family's desperate journey to reach medical help for his illness—recalled and retold through the eyes of his son Theodor—begins.

~

By sunrise on 10 October 1922, the mission at Hermannsburg was busy. The call of birds mingled with the sounds of men and women rushing about to ready everything for the *ingkata's* journey. Pastor Carl was gravely ill, and for nearly a fortnight, the 'big, heavily bearded' man, as his son describes him, had failed to emerge for church services. It had been decided the family would accompany him for the expected four-week journey south-east to the rail head at Oodnadatta, and on by rail to Adelaide where medical help was available. Oodnadatta was also the nearest location to which a doctor might readily travel. And so 'dark men' chopped wood, and 'dark milkmaids' milked bailed cows in a yard to the east of the station buildings. Meat was bagged or salted as freshly mustered buggy horses were driven from out bush and towards the mission. Few had slept. There was an air of excitement and urgency as every effort was made by the Arrernte to save their beloved Lutheran missionary.

Pastor Carl had become widely known as the 'grand old man' of Hermannsburg station, which by 1922 had, under his management, grown to be the largest settlement outside the administrative centre of Stuart. Indeed, the reverend's demeanour and courage is reported as staunch and even fiery on occasion. During his first months at Hermannsburg, for example, he encountered Mounted Constable Erwin Wurmbrand, offsider to the infamous Mounted Constable Willshire, who had been sent to Central Australia to pacify the Arrernte and render the area suitable for cattle.[4] As Theodor Strehlow tells it, both constables would ride out in the company of black trackers brought in from more southerly tribes, and shoot any Aboriginals found roaming those station properties where cattle-killing had been reported. This was a frontier land, he writes, where 'station owners, police officers, and most other white men were accustomed to act with the arrogance of feudal barons'.

On one occasion T.G.H. Strehlow reports that Wurmbrand happened across the campsite of a group of Aboriginal men, women and children, whereupon his party shot all those not swift enough to escape. Strehlow claims Wurmbrand later came to Hermannsburg with similar intent, prompting many Arrernte to run to Pastor Carl for help. According to Strehlow's version of events, Pastor Carl rushed to Wurmbrand's camp and in a rage demanded the officer release those he had taken prisoner. The Pastor's actions infuriated Wurmbrand, who nonetheless rode off and never returned.[5]

For many years Carl Strehlow met a demanding schedule of similarly robust pastoral work, as well as teaching and performing administrative duties. He tended the sick and ran the mission farm. Once when a ceremonial chief from the neighbouring Kukatja area had been shot by police—smashing one of his thigh bones and gashing part of his abdomen—Pastor Carl dressed the wounds and nursed him back to health. But in 1922, Pastor Carl himself fell desperately ill. The illness had begun with pleurisy, but long-neglected turned to dropsy, an oedema, or accumulation of fluid in the spaces below the skin with consequent swelling and inflammation. The condition, which may arise from a variety of causes, can cause a great deal of pain. Weak, and with his lower limbs so badly swollen his trousers had to be let out for him to wear them, Pastor Carl became increasingly short of breath. He was fifty years old. Sleep was only possible sitting up in a chair and courtesy of 'a full dose of laudanum'.

The dedication shown by the Arrernte to their pastor during his illness was remarkable. In one instance, a few weeks prior to Pastor Carl's impending journey, the urgent need arose to get a telegram to Alice Springs. There was no time to muster horses, for that would have delayed the matter by at least a day. One of the boys the reverend had saved from Wurmbrand years earlier had by then become a man, and was able to carry the message to Alice Springs on foot. He covered the 125 kilometres in 'the space of a day and a half'. Christened Hezekiel by an earlier missionary, the fleet-footed messenger waited in town for a reply then dutifully carried it back to Hermannsburg, completing the round trip of 250 kilometres in only three days.

It was not long after that the community was told of Pastor Carl's intention to seek medical help in Adelaide. Just fourteen years of age, Theodor spent the next fortnight packing up the Strehlow household, his mother busy tending her husband. The fruits of Theodor's labour, some twenty boxes of books, linen and other possessions, were stacked on the veranda of the house the morning of departure. In case of a heavy downpour, the piled boxes could be covered in a tarpaulin, lest the thinly constructed roof leak and ruin the collected possessions.

Meanwhile, inside the house Pastor Carl lay ill, battling 'desperately to preserve his trust in God'. The journey ahead to Oodnadatta would be rough, more than 600 kilometres over bush tracks, a trip he was unlikely to survive in such frail condition. And there was the added insult of the Lutheran bureaucracy having refused to send a car for its man, when none of the nearby stations owned a car or truck. When a fellow Lutheran offered one instead, the Strehlows decided to chance the journey downriver by buggy in order to meet the vehicle part way.

Outside the house, more than 170 Arrernte men, women and children waited for news. When finally Pastor Carl emerged, it was to their assembled voices, which rose and swelled into a great Lutheran chorale sung in their own language: 'Wake, awake! proclaim with power'. As camp dogs ran and howled, Pastor Carl and the crowd were reduced to tears.

Native stockmen helped the sick pastor to the buggy in which he and his wife would travel, the pastor's bloated body cushioned as best as could be arranged, in an upholstered chair strapped to the buggy floor. Four horses were hitched to the buggy. A van would trail behind carrying supplies and swags, and also, for at least some of the journey, young Theo. When the buggy finally moved away, the crowd turned sadly back to their camp, feeling 'an incredible sense of loss and bereavement'. And so, with Theo intermittently walking behind the van, which in turn trails his parents who travel in the buggy, the journey begins.[6]

It was not until 1966, however, following a serious bout of illness of his own, that Theodor Strehlow began to assemble his recollections of the family's journey begun that day, and of his father's untimely death at Horseshoe Bend. Strehlow kept a diary for much of his life, and so had begun the task of writing down the events many years earlier in a process biographer Barry Hill calls his 'dress rehearsal' as a writer. Indeed, Strehlow even kept a diary as a boy.[7] By 1964, however, Strehlow had given up any idea of making the journal a 'personal' record, writing to friends that his diary had become more public, akin to 'recording the sunset of an age'. His recounting of the events and journey of 1922 was finally published in 1969 as the memoir *Journey to Horseshoe Bend*.

By the time he wrote the book, Strehlow had studied the classics and literature, and pursued a distinguished but later controversial research career in linguistics and anthropology. Following his education in Adelaide, he returned to Central Australia in 1932 to study the Arrernte language, where, working with elders, earning their trust, he filled his journals with transcriptions of sacred verses and the maps of the totemic sites they shared with him. From Arrernte leaders he received many secret-sacred objects into his care, the owners rightfully afraid they might lose such important items in the chaos of dispossession.[8] Based out of Jay Creek west of Alice Springs from 1936, Strehlow served as a patrol officer and attended to the social, political and material needs of Aboriginal people.

Journey to Horseshoe Bend follows Theo—Strehlow's fourteen-year-old self—on the journey down the Finke River, a great deal of which he walked. Set largely in the Finke valley west of Alice Springs—not far west of Stuart's 1860 traversal—and sandhill country to its south, the narrative weaves Arrernte Dreamtime legends with descriptions of the landscape and encounters with pastoralists, thereby containing much reliable history of Central Australia.

Strehlow's story is a very different one to Stuart's 'crossing of the unknown'. For Stuart, home was far away in Britain, the Centre a brute wilderness to be conquered. But young Theo is perfectly at ease in the place where he grew up, among friends in familiar surroundings, his home. And so his story is enriched by a strongly personal 'place affect' and sewn with simple facts of the regional ecology, Aboriginal stories of the songlines, and the sometimes attractive bluster of the Centre's pastoral community, who help to evoke an emergent Australian 'bush' identity. Praise for the work has been sporadic, but uniformly enthusiastic. For historian Hart Cohen, for example, the text captures the 'interrelatedness of the Aboriginal people, their totems, culture and language, the landscape, white settlers and the Lutherans'. According to UN Academic Council Liaison Officer Michael Platzer, Strehlow is 'Australia's only fluent native interpreter', a man who 'never received the recognition he felt he deserved during his lifetime'. Cultural historian Paul Carter suggests, meanwhile, that the memoir articulates a more authentic poetics of the Australian environment.

Indeed, Strehlow's text might be thought of as fusing the two worlds produced separately by Thompson's totemic landscape of the precolonial Kaytetye, and that of the explorer Stuart and his 'conquered wilderness'. While no chapters divide Strehlow's memoir as such, identifiable segments each cover one day of the family's thirteen-day journey from Hermannsburg to their journey's tragic finish at Horseshoe Bend.

Unlike Stuart's explorer's tale, Strehlow's displays a great degree of exchange between Aboriginals and settlers, which serves to counterbalance ideas of a rigid frontier divide between the two groups, as is invoked by Stuart and others. The result is a more inclusive Australian writing of place than is to be found (generally speaking) elsewhere in the nation's literature. The hybridised setting engenders all the intimacy and reverence of home, while also embracing the postcolonial complexities of the Centre and directly confronting its representation as a divided frontier.

Even so, Strehlow's willingness to speak on behalf of his Other, the Arrernte, raises the question of who may rightfully and ethically write of their Other. As Aboriginal academic Anita Heiss has noted, many Aboriginal writers are 'tired of competing with white writers for the opportunity to write in the areas directly related to their lives'. Strehlow uses his father's story to argue he has roots and legitimacy in both settler and Aboriginal worlds. But to what degree is Strehlow influenced by his upbringing and Western education? What external factors shaped the memoir? Indeed, to what extent is an Arrernte person influenced by colonial discourse? Such questions inhabit the everyday lives of Central Australians, for whom some stories invoke the rigidity of Stuart's frontier, while others soften and blur the cultural divide—narratives like Strehlow's, which is quietly evocative of a hybridised settler home. Why it does this is multi-faceted.

While it is logical Central Australia would have become better known to settlers over time, a 'discovery' imperative (as in Stuart's journal) still pervaded many texts depicting the decades between World Wars I and II. The influence of anthropology was widespread and aimed at a popular audience. Newspapers, meanwhile, were busy giving national coverage to Aboriginal massacres. Walking and travel narratives were also abundant, though much Territory writing tended towards escapism, emphasising British 'pluck and courage'. The result, as historian Tom Griffiths notes, was that from the 1920s to the 1950s, interest in the Australian Outback surged.

Certainly a distinctive trace of 1960s Australia and its emerging identity politics colours Strehlow's rendering of a journey that happened in the 1920s. Nonetheless, Strehlow's childhood consciousness, combined with an intimacy with the landscape through repeated walking, underpins his narrative setting. Geographers call this a 'primal landscape', erected while young, a landscape of the mind that shapes subsequent understanding of the world. In this comfortable setting, Strehlow's remembered and reimagined walk of the Finke River captures several voices at once. However, any reading of place in *Horseshoe Bend* would be incomplete without accounting for the political expediency of Strehlow's self-aware construction of his own identity, one seemingly designed to address issues that would not arise until long after 1922 and his father's death.[9]

~

Before Theo leaves Purula-Kamara, the local area group of Ntaria, which was regarded as home to him and the other boys and girls, he takes a last stroll among his friends. Old Margaret, the mother of one of Theo's Arrernte playmates, gives some parting advice, telling Theo he is 'not just a white boy ... you are one of us'.

'You belong to the totem of the Twins of Ntarea,' she tells Theo. 'You are a true Aranda.'

She urges him to get a white education, but then to come back to the Arrernte, for they are his 'own people'.

From Margaret we are led to believe that Strehlow is of the Arrernte. And so even at this very early stage of events, a politics has emerged. For though our interest here is primarily with the world of 1922—that is, when the narrative's events unfold—the influence of the accumulated life experience of its author cannot be ignored. Considerable personal and related political pressures weighed heavily on Strehlow at the time he was writing.

By 1922, Arrernte peoples were attracting interest from academics internationally thanks to the earlier ethnography of Spencer and Gillen. Sigmund Freud's protégé Geza Roheim would later do field work near Hermannsburg in 1929. During the 1930s and 1940s, Strehlow amassed a wealth of material attesting to the rich fabric of Arrernte culture, some of which he published. By the early to late 1960s, however, Australia had entered an era of shifting politics when attitudes towards Aboriginal people broadened as the Land Rights era approached, and many eyes turned towards the Centre.

In 1959, Strehlow was called upon to defend Arrernte man Max Stuart in an appeal in the High Court. Stuart, who had little English, was charged with the rape and murder of a white girl in South Australia. He had been sentenced to death, but Strehlow argued that a typed confession could not have been made by a man who was semi-literate. During the case, Strehlow reportedly suffered a great deal of personal grief at the hands of the prosecutors, the commissioner and the press. As Strehlow's biographer Barry Hill notes in *Broken Song*, Stuart's defence was part of a wider battle waged by Strehlow against the failures of assimilation. And it was the beginning of a number of defensive strategies he would be forced to wage for the rest of his days.

The era saw mounting criticism of Strehlow's work, his apprehension of Arrernte culture and the start of a questioning of the legitimacy of his methods. Controversy over films of secret ceremonies and sacred objects Strehlow had collected during his years in Central Australia, and the later publication of pictures of secret materials in European journals, led to political backlash, Aboriginal resentment and adverse publicity during the 1970s. A cynicism sown during the Stuart appeals and Royal Commission of the 1960s infected factions within the Hermannsburg Aboriginal community, and assimilationists and others within the white community. In other words, Strehlow had plenty of motivation for setting the record straight with a memoir proving his identity as Arrernte.

Strehlow's memoir was written and later published amid this ideological maelstrom, arriving nonetheless at an opportune moment, as the successes and failures of the assimilation era were being more critically evaluated. Strehlow was certainly, and in no small way responsible for highlighting these policy flaws to the Australian public. His memoir took a new position in Australian literature, giving both a European view of landscape and an Aboriginal description of Country. But it also reflected the author's struggle for political identity and validation.

With Margaret's words still ringing on the morning air, the van loaded and his parents as comfortable as possible in the buggy, the barefoot Theo set out for Oodnadatta. The van follows half an hour behind the buggy with ten loose buggy horses trailing behind. Several Arrernte women walk with the van, accompanying the group to the edge of their local language group, as tradition demands. Soon enough the group crosses the boundary, which defines an Arrernte territory in similar terms to those of Marlpwenge, in Thompson's 'A Man from the Dreamtime'. To the east lay the territory of Pananka-Bangata, and the Ellery Creek people of the honey ant totem.

While the party trundles on, Theo walks to the nearby ruins of a burnt-out homestead, and looks across the plains to the blue of Rutjubma, Mount Sonder. He seems both nervous and excited as he gazes on the mountain, perhaps for the last time, and ponders his own crossing into new territory for the first time. Fresh country will open before him, and soon, at the end of a journey by road and rail, he will 'find himself in a country peopled wholly by white folk'.

Meantime, the wagon tracks the troupe had been following have disappeared and the party is forced to follow camel pads, on a settler trail that in places is barely a metre wide, and along which mail is brought to Hermannsburg from Horseshoe Bend. Occasionally a path has to be cut from ti-tree thickets, or, if a sandy stretch were reached, passengers would jump from the van to lighten the load, as the horses sweated and snorted their way across, to avoid becoming stuck in the heavy creek sand.

After about 20 kilometres of such heavy going they reach Rubula, a large waterhole where the Finke meets Ellery Creek, and camp on its gravel banks fringed with high bulrushes. Carl and Frieda retire to their tent and, with a cool breeze breaking the heat of the afternoon, Theo climbs into his swag beside the van. And 'under the spangle of a myriad of bright stars', to the sound of ducks on the waterhole, he falls asleep.

∿

Next day brings the party to Alitera, or Boggy Hole as it is known to Euro-Australians. Now a popular 4WD camping spot, the former police camp was abandoned in 1891 after Mounted Constable Willshire was taken south and committed to stand trial for the murder of Aboriginals. While Willshire was ultimately released, such frontier violence stands firm in the memory of those affected. In Strehlow's divergent narrative, however, such violence is juxtaposed with poetic descriptions of the Finke River that make use of Aboriginal and English names. And all the while the Strehlows' journey continued.

An advanced road party had been working up ahead to prepare the surface for Pastor Carl's buggy, but the flood-damaged terrain remains so rugged that the buggy must straddle many large rocks on its axles. The jolting was relentless: 'Every bump of his heavy swollen body against his upholstered chair had made him catch his breath and wince with pain'. It must have come as a great relief to run into white-bearded Old Jack Fountain and the camel-mail string from Horseshoe Bend. The party halted to receive the Hermannsburg mail and exchange news and pleasantries with Old Jack.

By noon they had reached Running Waters, another pool fringed by bullrushes but also populated by 'black-and-yellow butterflies flitting about gracefully among the blue flowers that grew along the damp bank of the quiet pool'. Around lunch-time, the party stopped to rest the horses and for Mrs Strehlow to read the mail to her husband by light of day. The Aboriginal name of the place is Irbmangkara, a game and wildfowl sanctuary, 'one of the cradles of mankind at the beginning of time', home to the duck Ancestors. Here was water, peace and a calm to offset the roughly corrugated track and the intensity of the journey's purpose. Yet even in this seeming Eden the effects of the frontier remained evident, for a 'rich store of myths and stories had gone down sadly in numbers since the advent of the whites'.

Moreover, at this otherwise utopian spot, an ancient rite and one man's transgression of Arrernte Law once contributed to a violent catastrophe. Irbmangkara is a ceremonial site well known to Arrernte of Western, Northern, Central and Upper Southern groups, as well as Matuntara folk. At a point in the manhood ritual, fully initiated young novices were given human blood from their elders to drink. The act was secret, and to give such blood to uninitiated boys considered a sacrilege punishable by death. Nonetheless, a ceremonial chief of Irbmangkara had once done exactly that, the equivalent of a priest having poured communion wine into the mugs of children at a party. Strehlow relates the history of the event and its consequences in some detail.

In response to the chief's transgression, avengers from another language group were organised, fifty or sixty warriors, enough to form a *tnengka*, a 'body of men who could overwhelm a whole camp of victims by means of an open attack'. And so, late one afternoon in 1875 the *tnengka* rushed into the camp of the Irbmangkara with spears and boomerangs flying. Within minutes the men of the chief's tribe lay dead, and the invaders turned their deadly attentions to the women and older children, spearing or clubbing them to their doom. As for infants, their limbs were broken and they were left to die 'natural deaths'. Strehlow estimates the dead numbered eighty to a hundred.

Unknown to the *tnengka*, one of the chief's wives had survived by shamming death, at the same time concealing her son's body beneath hers. And more trouble was afoot, for as the *tnengka* marched homeward, they met two hunters late home from a hunt. A fight ensued and one hunter escaped, Nameia, a man with relatives among those killed by the *tnengka*. Grief-stricken, Nameia swiftly spread the story of the massacre among kin.

Upon hearing Nameia's story, a revenge party was readied, comprising *leltja*, highly skilled warriors and guerrilla fighters empowered to move stealthily through hostile territory and kill targeted individuals.

But their revenge was a long time coming. Living off the land and wait-ing patiently between strikes, the revenge party executed the *tnengka* one by one over three years and across a broad territory. By the time the revenge party returned to the Finke River and Western Arrernte terri-tory it was 1878, and the white man had invaded their lands. Even so, no Arrernte had forgotten the reason for the *leltja* mission, and the men received a heroes' welcome.

For his part in this string of grisly events, Nameia was speared to death many years later by Aboriginals from the south as he lay by his camp fire on 9 January 1890. The death was recorded by Mounted Constable Willshire, who was stationed at Boggy Hole police camp at the time. Nameia had been marked for execution as part of a political deal struck between the warring tribes designed to end the feud. Ignoring the terms of the deal, the killers took liberties by killing Nameia while he was visiting his son at Alitera.

At first, Constable Willshire withheld judgement in the matter of a 'tribal execution' and took no immediate action. The constable likely had troubles enough of his own, as he was facing an inquiry into his treatment of the Aboriginals under his charge. Later, however, after being cleared by the inquiry, Willshire set out with four Aboriginal constables to Tempe Downs where he resolved once and for all the matter of Nameia's killing, by shooting two of three Aboriginal suspects who were found sleeping at a camp. A similar but later attack by Willshire on northern Aboriginals inspired him to write with undisguised relish of how his victims had 'scattered in all directions' during the raid.

'It's no use mincing matters', Willshire wrote. 'The Martini-Henry carbines at this critical moment were talking English in the silent majesty of these great eternal rocks.'

The remote west was not the only setting for such violence. In his walking classic *A Tramp Royal in Wild Australia*, Archer Russell relates an incident at Attack Gap around 1884 or 1885, about 15 kilometres south-west of the present-day location of Alice Springs. The story—as told to Russell by bushman Walter Smith[10]—is that Aboriginals alleg-edly attacked a supply wagon. In response, the largest party of whites ever assembled rode out. The men numbered about twenty: police, cattlemen, telegraph station staff. When the party found the alleged offenders, Russell reports they 'ran a cordon round the hill an' peppered 'em until there wasn't a "nig" showing'.

'Poor devils,' Smith tells Russell. 'There must have been 150 to 170 of 'em on that hill and I reckon that few of 'em got away ...

'But what could we do? We had to live up here. That was the trouble of it.'[11]

~

On the evening of the third day, the party camped on a gravel bank of the Finke River bed in the shelter of ti-tree bushes and gums. A red sandhill of steep grade, difficult for the buggy and van to negotiate, rose between their campsite and nearby Henbury station. A breeze had unfortunately failed to show, and so the night was still warm when two white men arrived, one of them Bob Buck from the nearby cattle station.

Buck was warm and generous to the old man, offering him fresh horses and donkeys to pull the van. The pastor was equally profuse in his thanks, but Buck made light of his generosity, telling the old man that 'tough bush people in these parts always had an unwritten law of mateship'.

'Every man must help everyone else in trouble,' says Buck, 'never mind whether the poor bugger's been his pal or his enemy. That's the only way us poor bastards up here've been able to survive at all in this tough country.'

In fact, had he known of Pastor Carl's plight, Buck, with 'just one month's notice', might have organised a car. After Carl's treatment at the hands of the Lutherans, Buck's pledge came as a welcome relief to the pastor, who struggled to 'control his emotions'. Next day Buck took the party under his care at Henbury and was particularly kindly to Theo, walking the buildings of the encampment with him.

Historically, Buck's generosity and kindness have to be considered side by side with the once commonplace attacks on Aboriginals by pastoralists, police and others. The situation is complex, and not amenable to the simplification offered by the term frontier, where clear lines are drawn between the two 'sides'. The result is a more nuanced and at times uneasy picture of the white settlers, where settler violence against Aboriginals is considered against a backdrop of intertribal and intra-tribal violence among the Aboriginals themselves.

By Saturday it is the family's fifth day on the trail, and Theo rises early. In the stillness before dawn he rolls up his swag while his three companions harness the donkeys. Barefoot once again he prepares to set out, and eventually, under the waning moon, the van moves 'away from the cheery blaze of the campfire into the moonlit sandhill silence', a liminal moment between sleep and the challenging heat of the day to come.

Theo's apparent knowledge of the history and biogeography of the landscape, as well as the Dreaming stories associated with the route, showcase Nature as a prominent feature of a Finke valley experience.[12] But perception of landscape always depends on the beholding eye. To the European settler, for example, a sandhill of the Finke Valley was 'a useless waste, almost devoid of life'. But to the Arrernte hunters, the middle Finke was 'a rich source of food'. The contrast is stark between Stuart's appraisal of this area as he struggled across the 'cruel' Central Australian desert and the veritable 'food bowl' described in *Journey to Horseshoe Bend*.

When the Strehlows reached dune country, the sandhills in winter were glowing and almost romantic with their rich colourings, dotted with 'flourishing' and 'magnificent' desert oaks. Their 'Straight, dark, ridge-barked trunks' rose up to 4 or 5 metres, and among them younger trees 'soared' thanks to a run of good seasons. Rather than the 'Dead Heart' of John Walter Gregory's description of 1901–02, here is a sandy desert bursting with life, 'rich in carpet snakes' as well as 'smaller marsupials'.[13] In tandem with food supplies from the flats, such highly prized edibles allowed the middle Finke dwellers to flourish and become numerous.

It is through the eyes of Theo (and of the older Strehlow) that the party's journey unfolds, and so we begin to encounter the waterholes as totemic sites, and the songlines soon become interwoven with the party's route downriver. The geography of the Dreaming meshes with the newer camel pads (trails) and other settler routes between Alice Springs and Hermannsburg. Again, Strehlow's strategic selection of secret narratives that intersect the journey path speaks to his insider knowledge of Arrernte culture, helping to construct a dual identity for himself as settler and Arrernte. From time to time, Dreaming stories are explained more at length. And with each step taken in Theo's journey the reader takes a step in a more ancient journey, one that intersects the routes of the Ancestors. Precolonial, colonial and postcolonial history overlap, and momentarily the frontier is porous.

As for Theo, he would become the hero of his father's final journey, overwhelmed by 'the silence and ... haunting loneliness that was brooding over these moonlit sandhills'. Theo imagines the walk is haunted by 'the iliaka njemba that had frightened him in his childhood, just as they had terrified the younger Western Aranda children at Hermmansburg'.[14] That Theo must overcome such emotional challenges helps the author Strehlow to render him all the braver for doing so, and that much closer to the Arrernte with whom he grew up. For all the while, underlying this land scaped as a frontier is the Arrernte cultural landscape, where 'The normal wagon road which kept to the Finke valley between Ekngata and Talpanama ... passed a long line of important Upper Southern Aranda ceremonial sites, each linked with a magnificent waterhole'.

Once again, the older Strehlow walks closely behind the younger, the years of accumulated knowledge filling gaps in the data that are revisited through the younger's eyes. Strehlow the elder arranges in order his own memories of place, purposefully sewing them with the politics he needs some forty years hence. The younger boy's memories of the colonial landscape are supplemented by the older author's intimate knowledge of Arrernte culture, where camel pads through sandhills trace the ancient route of a fish dreaming, and floods brought fresh fish downstream from Irbmangkara or from the deep gorge holes of the MacDonnells.

The stories tell of a landscape defying the longest of droughts, accentuating the geography of survival that such songlines sketch, and defying also widely held perceptions of a 'dead' Australian inland and its barren heart. Simultaneously, this is a frontier landscape, where 'pioneer settlers had ... built a stockyard at Ultjua'. Mustering and branding now dominate the middle Finke where once in Aboriginal story it was 'linked by myths with a number of other carpet snake sites'.

Strehlow sees the world of the Arrernte and the once unspoilt Finke valley as Australia's lost utopia, a landscape he alone remembers as he walks. Only he knows this utopian world the way it was, perhaps prompting his elegiac poetry as a rule by which to measure its loss. The world from which he writes—forty years hence in 1960s Australia— is only just waking to a sense of this loss. It is here Strehlow makes the most of his retrospective construction of an 'insider' status, but in doing so he yields a more nuanced view of the frontier. To the human suffering at the frontier, nonetheless, 'Nature is indifferent', implying perhaps that the Dreaming and its totemic political geography will long outlast the ructions of humankind.

Rather like the excursion narratives of the American philosopher Henry David Thoreau, *Journey to Horseshoe Bend* describes events that unfold across space, rather than solely in terms of time passing. The events that move this hybrid narrative forward are punctuated with extended moments of history, reverie, self-analysis—each divergent passage inspired and birthed by a moment in place, as well as time. This is an important consideration, for giving breathing room to space as well as time in this way is to run counter to literature's tendency, which, as constrained by the bequest of the Greek dramatists and historians, is to be temporal. As readers, we naturally desire a story to unfold over time. But as Thoreau surmised, walking allows a writer to become immersed in time and in place, thus unshackling the mind to play upon space and passage.[15]

Somewhere near halfway through Theo's journey, the destination of Oodnadatta starts to take on a hazy character. Adding to the poignancy of his father's plight, we are told that 'Gradually the dark eastern horizon became tinged with grey. The blurred and shapeless tree forms began to reveal their limbs with increasing clarity'. In the hazy milieu thus created, Theo turns from the aim of the journey to impressions of the landscape, reverie, the turn of mind of the walker. And so the path enables an inward journey of mind and spirit.

Once again there is, nonetheless, another layer to this complex tale of place, hidden beneath such existential roaming. *Journey to Horseshoe Bend* invites the reader to receive Strehlow's narrative as a simple retelling and arrangement of the Dreaming stories, an otherwise 'authentic'

representation of both the physical landscape traversed and the mythological landscape of the Arrernte Ancestors. In this interpretation, the
Dreaming stories remain intact, just as they came to Theo and were
later gathered by the older Strehlow, through Indigenous storytelling.
But is such a simple explanation sufficient?

To walk through a landscape is to acquire by perception some but
not all of the objects passed by or encounters made. Two factors are
crucial: the exact route taken, and which objects or events are chosen to
include in the retelling. Objects and encounters are gathered (or not)
according to whim or intent, interest, politics and psychology. In the
retelling of the walk, the meaning of the story is described by the arc
of the objects collected in memory, as well as any added imaginings or
other musings. Each path through the landscape may, quite logically,
produce an entirely different story. But what of the objects that remain
unseen or left out of the telling? The stories not told? Which stories of
a landscape are the most important? How might we measure the loss of
those not included?

With nearly 20 kilometres still to go to Idracowra Station, the mid-
morning heat becomes unbearable. Theo becomes conscious 'only of the
heat and the menace of the dune country'. He begins to imagine the
landscape as a 'merciless, intimidating waste', his greatest wish to 'get out
of this cruel red land'. In contrast with Strehlow's extensive knowledge
of the desert environment and his intimacy with it, here is a description
to rival the harshest explorer's appraisal. Indeed, it smacks of Sturt's 'hell'
and Gregory's 'Dead Heart', both outsiders in the way of John McDouall
Stuart. Theo's young body and its five senses find the searing desert heat
simply uncomfortable and the conditions make for difficult walking.
This is the flinch of bare skin on blistering hot sand, and so it is no
surprise that by ten o'clock 'the blazing heat of the sand', which had
begun to burn his toes, compels him to climb once more aboard the van.

Upon reaching Idracowra Station, Theo learns of his father's
'shocking day'. Bedridden, Pastor Carl had begun to doubt his own
faith, and by Sunday morning, 'hope itself seemed to have died'. Sadly,

as Theo wandered the station on his 'first Sunday without hymns, prayers or church services', his father's condition worsened, so that by the time Idracowra manager, Allan Breadon, arrived on Monday morning, he was shocked by the pastor's state.

For poor Carl, and in spite of the considerable comfort of having Frieda by his side, every jolt of the buggy along the tortuous route had been agony. Now at Idracowra, the heat and humid conditions conspired to bring him further suffering, from which he longed with all his might for an end. Breadon was convinced Pastor Carl should travel no further in the buggy, that a motor car would be best. With Lutheran Mr Wurst and his car due to have arrived at Oodnadatta on Friday night, Breadon despatches two stockmen as messengers to Horseshoe Bend, requesting Wurst to come straight on through to Idracowra.

Pastor Carl spent the night heavily drugged, and by Tuesday morning was turning over in his mind Christ's suffering at Gethsemane. Here, in the midst of Carl's own trial, Christ's was to take on new meaning; the words 'Thy will be done' coming to signify a prayer both simple sounding, but humanly almost impossible. And yet he found a peace, of sorts. And resolve: he would become more like Christ, praying for the strength to submit to the will of God. Between fitful snatches of sleep, Pastor Carl spent a difficult day contemplating his resolution.

The strain of his effort was finally broken at 6 pm with the arrival of Mrs Elliot of Horseshoe Bend Station. With her were the messengers Breadon had sent the day before, and there was more bad news: Wurst's car from Oodnadatta had broken down on Sunday morning. There was even some suspicion Wurst's driver, picked up in Oodnadatta, had been drunk. Mrs Elliot urges Pastor Carl to travel immediately with her to 'The Bend'.

'You'll be on the Overland Telegraph Line,' she says. 'There's a doctor in Oodnadatta at present, and you could get medical advice from him or from the Hostel by phone.'

The new chairman of the Hermannsburg Mission Board, Reverend Stolz, had, it transpired, been arranging with Mrs Elliot's husband, Gus Elliot, to ferry a doctor from Oodnadatta to Horseshoe Bend. With the promise of medical help so close, Mrs Elliot could only counsel their immediate departure, and even offered to lead the ride by lantern.

Pastor Carl was impressed. Here was a woman 'not only young and pretty, but strong, athletic, vital and courageous'. Her smile warm and sincere, and physique 'slim, tanned, and willowy', spurred him to a decision.

The narrator Strehlow imagines his father thinking, 'If she was prepared to stay in the saddle all night, then he too would, in God's name, nerve himself up for that last terrifying stage to Horseshoe Bend'.

And so, with Mrs Elliot leading the way and with six fresh horses courtesy of Gus Elliot, Pastor Carl and Frieda pressed on with the journey.

Theo and his companions rested overnight before continuing next day. But when a bend in the river brought Theo and companions to a place the Arrernte call the 'Land of Death', he became depressed, and decided to walk for a while. His last miles to Horseshoe Bend were covered 'chain by chain, yard by yard, step by step'. Theo's walking was mechanical, and he began to 'stumble like a sleepwalker', agonising at each step over whether 'the long expected station lights would ever come into view'.

Lantern lights swam into view around 10.30 pm: Horseshoe Bend, Gus Elliot's 'pride and joy', a home 'fit for occupation by his city-born wife who had come here as a bride from Melbourne'. Once the hotel had been considered Central Australia's most modern. But Horseshoe Bend was also described in the *Barossa News* as 'one of the minor Hells on God's earth' where 'all the sins against the Decalogue are committed … as no guardian of the law is near'.

The news of Theo's father was grim: he had been seized by an 'asphyxiating bout of asthmatic breathlessness'. To find the strength for 'the last few miles to the hotel', Pastor Carl had fixed on the idea of telephoning a doctor, perhaps even the comfort of the hotel as compared with the difficulty of riding in the buggy. But the hotel was noted for 'its cruel heat waves for as long as human memory went back'. In the Arrernte telling of the location, all the main totemic sites were associated with 'fire or with the scorching heat of the summer sun'. True to its reputation, by 10 am next morning the mercury had climbed to over 38°C. In his tin-lined room Carl Strehlow endured 'near bake-oven temperatures'.

Theo, however, daydreamed, of a journey on foot a decade earlier when the Strehlows were 'struggling to get back to Hermannsburg on the dry and desolate road leading north from Oodnadatta'. Theo and his mother had been forced to walk in front of the van and its horses, guiding the driver by storm lantern for some two hours. Theo remembered that walking was 'a more comfortable mode of progress than sitting on the springless van, whose bumps over the pebble-strewn gibber flats had threatened to dislocate all the vertebrae in the backbones of the travellers'. And so, as Carl Strehlow lay dying in the heat on Friday, Theo linked his own identity to walking, in the figure of a 'cheerful little freckle-faced boy who had ten years earlier walked many miles with his mother on the journey from Oodnadatta to Hermannsburg'. Since then, he reasoned, he had 'acquired the sturdy independent attitudes of a "bush kid" to a degree that his mother had not yet comprehended'.

Carl Strehlow, meanwhile, concerned himself with Lutheran elder Reverend Stolz, who had arrived from Oodnadatta. With his last reserves of strength, the dying pastor confronted the Lutheran with his accumulated bitterness and disappointment, railing at the religious bureaucracy.

When Pastor Carl's condition declined further, Mrs Strehlow was prompted to sing a hymn. But Strehlow merely begged her to stop, crying: 'God doesn't help!', and later 'My God, my God, why hast thou forsaken me?' Here in this harsh landscape, Strehlow seemed to be saying, even God is a figure to be doubted. It was a quarter to six in the evening by the time Carl Strehlow 'suddenly gave a gasp, followed by a deep sigh', and died.

~

In *The Lost Art of Walking*, Geoff Nicholson writes that 'words inscribe a text in the same way that a walk inscribes space'. From this we might conclude, somewhat obviously perhaps, that only those objects included in the telling comprise any story from the walk. As for any author, then, Strehlow included in his narrative only those events and Dreaming stories that suited his intention. To this extent, Strehlow's non-fiction journey narrative describes a fictional Central Australia, something partially true of any journey narrative. In the final telling of a walk, the objects and stories the author chooses from their environment to include in the tale *are* the tale.

This does not mean the world of *Journey to Horseshoe Bend* bears little relationship to reality, for Carl Strehlow's final journey was real; it takes place in a real landscape and is informed by real and tragic events: Pastor Carl dies at Horseshoe Bend. Yet the representation of the route and the events that occurred along it must be considered contrived, a mythical geography, as any identity of Strehlow must also be mythical. We might consider the Arrernte cultural landscape around the Finke River as a film negative onto which Strehlow's narrative develops a print of his identity, a representational and mythical self. Strehlow co-opts cross-cultural ideas linked to particular places and ties them to his political intent, thereby constructing a 'map' of his own identity, fusing them intimately onto that of the Arrernte.

But Strehlow's political purpose is not easily disengaged from the sense of place he achieves on this walk and in the retelling of events surrounding his father's death. For in retelling the stories of his choosing, the intimacy of Theo's experience of the landscape as a youth adds fresh authority to the accumulated knowing and wisdom of the elder Strehlow. The result is that the prose has a resonance of home. In the words of Barry Hill, Strehlow had 'walked over so much of the ground that [he felt] he had earned certain rights to it'. Perhaps. He certainly uses the Arrernte identity he constructed to step momentarily across the frontier divide in order to articulate the place he calls home from the other side of any notional frontier.

Political expediency is, nonetheless, clearly an element at the heart of Strehlow's intent. In the settler world, he becomes an authority on Arrernte life and culture, shoring up his reputation in the eyes of anthropologists. In the Aboriginal world of Hermannsburg, he legitimises his standing in the community where he grew up, and substantiates his translations and use of secret Arrernte materials. Such arguments feed a politics of identity, sparking questions of whether Strehlow has any right to speak for his Other, something that will emerge even more strongly several decades after his memoir is published. But cultures are seldom found in isolation, and are rarely dualistic. Nor do they describe a clear line dividing black from white after the fashion of the Australian frontier.

Politics and Strehlow's self-styled 'insider' identity momentarily aside, there is another conclusion to be drawn from the work: that it is undoubtedly the author's agency in both Arrernte and settler worlds that gives the text its hybridised traction. There is little doubting that *Journey to Horseshoe Bend* occupies a landmark position in Australian literature for its connecting of topography and Aboriginal Dreaming stories. For while Theo's journey traces one boy's search for identity, it also traces the older man's struggle to retain that which he has achieved, as well as a nationalist struggle to make sense of a violent past. In Theo is born a hybrid Australian identity. More than the lonely bushman of Russel Ward's conception, or the tough feminine determination of Mrs Elliot, Strehlow's identity is affixed to the resilient surface of Arrernte culture. We might say that Strehlow traces one rather complex white man's enactment of Country and its stories. In this way, Strehlow's journey is akin to the practices of the Arrernte, fulfilling his own place as a part of the landscape and its culture.

By walking the Country and places that are sacred to both Arrernte and the Strehlows, Theo welds the old tales with the new, in the process inscribing them afresh with his own story.[16] Beyond any political motivations for *Journey to Horseshoe Bend*, Theo's retold walk maps a way forward for settler depictions of Australian places, in a more nuanced appraisal of place than a crude binary of 'the frontier' can provide. It is Strehlow's evocation of a hybrid sense of home in a contested landscape that remains the work's lasting value to Australian literature, the 'promise of two cultures intermixing'.[17] For we are not separate from the world; rather, as the philosophers suggest, we interpenetrate it.

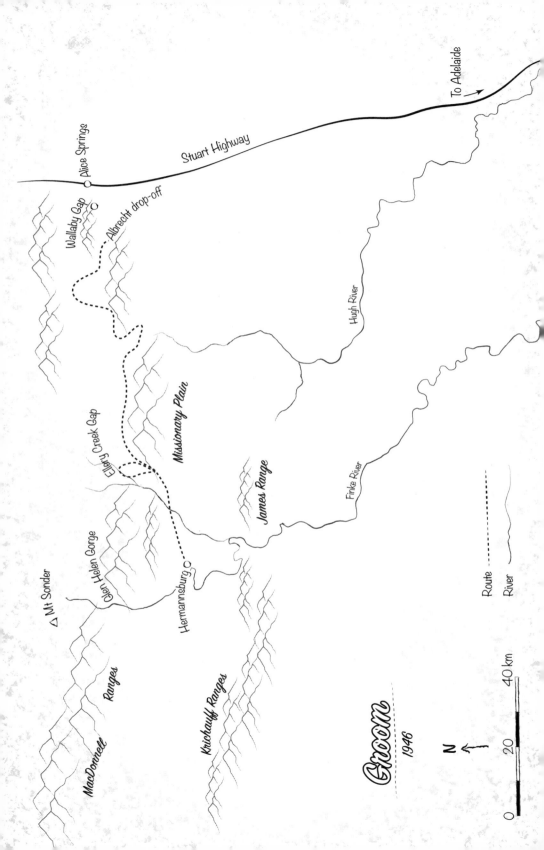

4

GROOM

I opened my eyes to four dingo pups carousing in the mulga 2 metres from my sleeping bag. The sun was yet to peek over Euro Ridge, yellow in the half-light of dawn and towering over our campsite at Wallaby Gap, on Section One of the Larapinta Trail at the start of the West MacDonnell Ranges. The moon still hung near-full to the west, clinging to the horizon after having traced a giant arc across the heavens during the night.

One of the pups flashed the creamy underside of its tail, which floated on the cold air like an up-curled feather duster. I tried to rouse Fiona, asleep on her mat next to mine. But only the merest wisp of her hair was visible from a puckered and tightly draw-strung hole at the top of her down sleeping bag. A quick check of my phone revealed the temperature overnight had plunged to −2°C. By the time Fiona stirred, the ochre-furred pups were gone and breakfast beckoned.

To the west, five hours of walking would bring us to Simpson's Gap by mid-afternoon. Were we to continue we would come, in perhaps ten more days, to our favourite waterhole, Ellery Creek. Yesterday we had walked from the east, and the topsy-turvy politics of Alice Springs. Watching the pups, the town and its troubles seemed very far away.

The 223-kilometre-long Larapinta Trail starts less than 2 kilometres from my front door, in Alice Springs' north. Call me lazy, but

I love an easy option, and starting the journey from my house had sounded like a plan. The reality is somewhat tougher, for at fifteen to twenty days a full-blown walk of the world's premier desert trek means carrying enough gear to down a small horse. Divided into twelve sections of varying difficulty, the trail ends at Mount Sonder, the Territory's fourth highest mountain at 1380 metres above sea level, 130 kilometres west of Alice Springs by road. Apparently, Section One is among the easiest.

Northern Territory Parks and Wildlife Service recommends carrying up to 6 litres of drinking water per day over those sections of the trail that are without supplied water. That makes a trek in West MacDonnell National Park a much more serious prospect than any saunter across more humid terrain with packed lunch and iPhone. Six litres of water equates to 6 extra kilograms—over two days, that's 12 kilos: a hefty load when you're dragging it all up some unforgiving slope of rock. I thought this advice madness until my first practice day on the trail, sucking fluids from my camel pack as if it were bottomless. It's surprising how much water is required to slake your thirst, especially in summer when daytime temperatures climb into the 40s. Mind you, no-one walks the trail then; that would be foolhardy. But many still take shorter walks, and even in winter the mercury often tips 30°C.

Thankfully, there were plenty of rewards for our efforts. The evening before the arrival of the pups, as sunset hurried us along Euro Ridge and I was sweating on how to traverse the final slope down to Wallaby Gap in the dark, Fiona waved for me to stop.

'Wedge-tail,' she whispered.

Near the high point of the ridge and in the middle of the shale and gravel path, silhouetted against the sun hovering centimetres from the horizon, was a wedge-tailed eagle, tall and regal, perhaps a metre high, wings drawn in. Silently, Fiona withdrew her camera and snapped.

Behind the bird, the sun was a great golden peach set in a haze of blue jelly. From the leaves of nearby acacias wet bulbs of late-afternoon light dripped like treacle. Behind us the valley snaked east to Alice Springs like an enormous stadium rather than the work of wind and water over the ages. And in the geology to the west was something of the Colosseum, God's amphitheatre.

The eagle lifted its wings, and there was time to see them fully spread—perhaps 2 metres tip to tip, but impossible to tell accurately—before it lurched from the rocky bluff into a layer of warm air billowing up from the valley. In the silence that followed came an aching stillness. In my mind the Centre became an ancient wilderness where Nature held sway and humans were nought but a passing fancy.

The bird rode the thermal without effort in steadily widening downward circles. Like many young boys, I spent my childhood wishing I could fly. The carefree way the eagle soared was magnificent, triggering my all-too-human yearnings for peace and freedom. Perhaps such things are possible in the wilderness, where 'man has not yet set foot'. But I gazed down at my limp arms, useless by comparison to the eagle's wings, attached to a body weighted down double by a heavier-than-reasonable backpack.

At least this is only a two-day practice run, I thought.

The eagle faded into the twilight and with the steep descent to Wallaby Gap campground now in sight I reviewed our progress. Counting a kilometre or two in wrong turns, and the fact of getting away late morning owing to a thousand last-minute matters that just had to be resolved, we'd walked about 15 kilometres, all of it lugging more than was strictly necessary so as to make the journey worthwhile as a training run. Not bad considering that when we first pulled on the packs at the Alice Springs Telegraph Station we wondered what on earth we had done. The packs seemed so heavy and the end so far, although since then we seemed to have found the rhythm of the walk and its demands.

Now as the light faded, the world and our start seemed less and less real. The reality was, however, that the Larapinta Highway was barely 2 kilometres south, obscured by scrub in the valley, but close enough to mock any idea of wilderness, nonetheless. The park is jointly managed by Northern Territory Parks and Wildlife along with the region's Aboriginal traditional owners.

The landscape's most recent history was pastoral; Bond Springs, still a working cattle station some 20 kilometres north, would have been a hive of activity at that time of day. And much older Dreaming tracks wound through these hills alongside the camel pads and cattle routes, paths where people once sought waterholes, food or ceremonial grounds.

I had thought the ranges a wilderness, but what exactly did that mean? By definition, the term would have me erase all such intimate human etchings from this magnificent and many-layered landscape. In and of itself, the label seemed to erect a frontier all its own. Either way I was becoming too tired to think. And any answer would have to wait.

I turned to Fiona and we picked our way down the stone steps of the trail to Wallaby Gap, where we found handy timber benches, a shelter and a modern gas barbecue. With only moments of twilight to go, we turned to each other without a word. Half-way. We'd be cooking in the darkness. Not bothering to remove our packs, we hugged like two turtles standing erect, almost overbalancing in the process.

～

It was the winter of 1946 when a journalist named Arthur Groom arrived in Central Australia, flying in from Brisbane via Adelaide, high over Lake Eyre, a feature of Australia's arid zone he would later find cause to describe as a 'cesspool of spent rivers'. Groom aimed to walk the country of the Centre in the hope of mounting a campaign to turn much of it into national park.

Earlier that year Groom had written to the Superintendent at the Hermannsburg Mission, setting out his intention to visit there and other sites including stations at Glen Helen, Tempe and Henbury, and Ernabella Mission. From such remote points he proposed to 'fan out systematically and mostly on foot in approximate 3 to 6 day excursions'.[1]

Mission Superintendent Pastor Friedrich Albrecht had been away at the time, but Pastor Sam Gross responded to Groom, suggesting his proposal to be a 'most unusual matter', and his plans 'rather strange', especially considering that 'to us you are a total stranger'. But he was not averse to helping Groom either, and even offered the visitor to ride aboard the mission supply trucks if and when convenient, so long as Pastor Albrecht approved the idea upon his return. In a return letter, Groom proposed he arrive by air in early June. At the time he was forty-one years old, married, and with three young boys.

At Alice Springs, Groom found a town in which everyone was 'a civic planner and a critic' pondering its future. He met Pastor Phillip Scherer, also from Hermannsburg Mission, and later managed to secure a permit to enter Aboriginal reserves, on condition he remained in the company of the Lutherans. There was much to distract him in the town, but Groom's eye soon roamed outwards, 'Straight out onto desert sand or rocky wilderness', where he intended to walk.

Groom's walking feats are legend, for he had an extraordinary ability to traverse great distances on foot and without support. In 1946, however, his proposed walk had purpose beyond the mere appreciation of landscape. In his letter to the Hermannsburg Mission, he explained he wanted to reserve in perpetuity 'outstanding examples of country of scenic or natural history value', so that the public might be taught of 'the importance of such reservations in a counter-balance to city life'. To do so, he needed to walk such a landscape, to see it first-hand. Groom 'clicks' with the young Pastor Scherer, relaxing enough to tell him of a further desire to help assure a future for the 'nomadic natives'.

Groom's romance with the Red Centre had begun some twenty-five years earlier as a jackaroo at Lake Nash cattle station, near the border between the Northern Territory and Queensland. Between January 1922 and June 1925, the young journalist's imaginings were filled for the first time with stories of a remote region 'cut off from the rest of the Northern Territory by eighty miles of spinifex desert'. Around campfires at night, stories were told and absorbed, Groom depicting his companions as 'men of the elusive West', a place that was 'always west of where the tales are told, at least one more day's travel beyond tomorrow'.

One day, while Groom and the group were mustering cattle, they spied a family with horses and a wagon droving a herd westwards: a man, woman and four children. The family was going to Central Australia: 'out to the Sandover River Country, east of the Overland Telegraph Line to take up land somewhere out there'. Though Groom described their mission as 'utter lunacy', the memory of the family and their audacious intent haunted him long after.

Groom left the Centre in 1926 to take up work in Brisbane as a journalist. But two unanswered questions left with him. Certainly he wanted to find the name of the man who, with family in tow, in

Groom's words, 'had taken faith and loyalty and crossed the desert'. Perhaps even more importantly, however, he wanted to 'find out what was being done to ease the passing of Australia's primitive man'.

To Groom's young eyes, the Centre was 'out there', east of the Overland Telegraph Line, a mythical outback. His rather glum future for 'Australia's primitive man' spoke to ideas still popular after World War II, that Aboriginals were doomed as a race. Actually, what came to be called Doomed Race Theory had pervaded the beliefs of Australian white society from the early nineteenth century. Studies by anthropologists had suggested that a race with genetic links to the 'Stone Age' could not survive the more advanced culture of the white race. Extinction was their expected destiny. The theory began to wither rapidly after the war, but it held sway in some quarters even so, throughout the Menzies era and beyond.

Groom returned to Central Australia in 1946 with an eye to tourism. He wanted to see 'if Central Australia's scenery was grand enough, the climatic conditions moderate enough, to warrant tourist development in any large degree'. But he had retained his concern to protect Aboriginal people and the wilderness areas they roamed, so as to 'preserve' both for future generations.

Though Pastor Gross initially thought Groom wrong-headed regarding his proposal to walk the Centre's deserts, the writer was in fact well prepared for the task. During World War II, he had 'lectured on survival in the jungle to the 50,000 Australian and American troops who passed through the Canungra jungle training centre'.[2] And he took a good photograph, with many of his evocative black and whites eventually illustrating his writings.

Groom's conservation credentials were just as solid. He had returned to Queensland from Lake Nash to work for *The Sunday Mail*, but in 1930 became the first honorary secretary of the National Parks Association of Queensland, having set up the group with Romeo Lahey. Later, the pair established Binna Burra Lodge in Lamington National Park, in the hinterland of what is now the Gold Coast. It was about 1930, also, when Groom walked across south-east Queensland by moonlight from O'Reilly's Guest House—also in Lamington National Park—to Mount Barney. Once there, as the *Australian Dictionary of Biography* describes it, he 'selected a camp-site, talked to landowners and returned, covering 70 miles (113 kilometres), midnight to midnight'.[3]

Such feats would hold Groom in good stead when he reached the Centre. Ideas of Central Australia as a broad expanse of undisturbed nature rose to popularity after World War II. And the vision proved quite durable, to the point where it now dominates a contemporary thinking of the Centre, an outcome that owes a great deal to Groom, whom some have called the father of Australian conservation.[4] During 1946 and 1947, Groom made dozens of lengthy and sometimes arduous journeys across the Centre, mostly on foot or with camels, occasionally by motor vehicle. Stories retold from twenty-three of those journeys make delightful reading in his non-fiction collection of walking vignettes, *I Saw a Strange Land*, first published in 1950.

I Saw a Strange Land proved popular to a public keen for insights into their mysterious inland. Its first run of 3000 copies sold out in eight months, prompting a second edition in 1952. Groom emphasised the very strangeness of the landscape that his readers were expecting, even incorporating it into his title. In an obituary marking Groom's death in 1953 at age forty-nine, the *Centralian Advocate* newspaper called the book 'one of the best-read books on Central Australia'.

The book is still mentioned occasionally in the Australian press; in 2013, for example, a journalist for *The Australian* newspaper, Nicolas Rothwell, wrote of how 'Groom loses himself in the landscape, a realm of depths, a space where the horizons lure the traveller on'. Robyn Davidson wrote the introduction to the 2015 Text Classics edition. The popularity of Groom's stories certainly makes the book influential, if not pivotal, in reconstructing the Centre as a wilderness for tourists. And despite their early reticence, the Lutherans at Hermannsburg would prove crucial to Groom's education regarding exactly what lay at Australia's heart.

$\sim$

It was a cold night in the desert about 30 kilometres from Alice Springs, when, with food for several days and 'water bottles that might last twenty-four hours', Arthur Groom headed west on foot into the MacDonnell Ranges. He was aiming for the Ellery River then on to

Hermannsburg, a distance of more than 100 kilometres.[5] Fresh and eager to go, Groom started out on this particular walk perhaps 15 kilometres or so west of Wallaby Gap, where Fiona and I would camp some seventy years later.

Pastor Friedrich Albrecht had been on his way to christen an Aboriginal baby at Henbury station, the drive ahead promising to be an all-nighter. But he still had sufficient time to drop off Arthur Groom for his walk, indeed, he was very likely glad of the company. Albrecht had replaced Carl Strehlow as Superintendent at Hermannsburg from 1926 and would not leave the outpost until 1952. Before driving off, Albrecht suggests Groom camp the night nearby, with some native stockmen.

Alone and unaware of the cold, Groom reflects on his admiration for 'men like Albrecht', for whom 'time and fatigue, disappointment and hardship meant little'. Their goals were selfless, 'far beyond the understanding of ordinary man'. In Groom's imagining, Albrecht was reminiscent of the bushmen of T.G.H. Strehlow's depiction, emboldened with the courage of the Christian missionary and not unlike Carl Strehlow. Pastor Carl had laid a foundation for Christianity, an achievement, it is implied, to rival the taming of the inland by pastoralists, as well as being a significant challenge, given the 'primitive' nature of his congregation.

The Aboriginal stockmen were camped 'about three miles' to the north and may well have happily received the stranger Groom into their midst late at night. Such hospitality speaks of a communal spirit flexible and welcoming. Indeed, many in the Aboriginal community had begun working on Outback cattle stations in greater numbers when the inland was still accessible only by horse and camel, proving themselves, Groom writes, 'good horseman and useful house servants'.

During one of Groom's later walks, Aboriginal stockmen came in to the settlement of Areyonga one Sunday night. After riding many miles they gathered round the fire to form a choir, Groom noting how 'the old favourites of civilization' were also 'favourites of these native men and women and their children'. Such simple anecdotes provide more than ample evidence of the Aboriginals fast adapting to the changes wrought by the arrival of white settlers.

Despite Albrecht's advice, Groom forgoes the comforts of the stockmen's campfire in order to head immediately 'through the brilliant golden night towards the Ellery River'. Within moments he had left the road to find himself among 'clay pans and stoney ridge country, with mulgas and ironwoods scattered thinly and shimmering like silver'.

Groom's botanically well-informed descriptions of Country rival those of Strehlow in *Journey to Horseshoe Bend* and give the same assuredness of the abilities and knowledge of the walking writer. Aboriginal stories of Country were simply told, of how a 'tremendous snake once slithered out of the west, heading towards the east, with long patterned body curved up and down along the ground'. Apparently the snake was 'ready to devour an unfortunate victim', when it was turned to stone.

Restricted to neither road nor camel pad and striking across the rough country any way he sees fit, Groom walks more than 60 kilometres by next evening. Most of the way he spends trekking beside a 'hot, sandy river bed, through and round unbelievable rock terraces, razorbacks'. He passes exposed strata that are 'piled up and down in mammoth switchback formation, hundreds of feet high and hundreds of feet down'. Even though it is winter, the temperature next day rises to 32°C, and, eyes narrowed to slits under a broad-brimmed hat, the 'sharp, abrasive rocks' split his heavy walking shoes.

By evening, however, conditions have cooled and Groom camps at his first milestone, Udapata, or Ellery Gap, where the Ellery River, a tributary of the Finke, has cut through the main range. The river had been named by explorer Ernest Giles for the English-Australian astronomer Robert Lewis Ellery, who was for some forty-two years from 1853 the Victorian Government astronomer. Now known as Ellery Creek Big Hole, the site has become a popular campground for walkers and swimmers in the West Macdonnell National Park, about 80 kilometres west of Alice Springs.

Given that he took the dip mid-winter, Groom finds Ellery to be an 'ice-cold pool', where to continue one had to 'swim its gloomy depths or climb high over steep cliff and massive rubble'. Here the river had cut 'down through millions of years of time and hundreds of feet of red rock'. In Groom's day Aboriginals still camped there, well back from the water, even though the waterhole had once been a meeting place and ceremonial ground for 'tribal wanderers'. In this landscape 'every gash and cave in the hills' carried a story from the Dreamtime.

Despite the native presence both present and past, Groom emphasises the scene's 'wild grandeur', the loneliness of echoes produced by any loud whisper or cough among 'the pines and ghost gums, and cycads and spinifex, and of the rocks and hills and valleys'. Of course, all of these elements can be experienced on many walks of Central Australia. As Robyn Davidson suggests, there is a 'tremendous freedom in setting off on foot ... The constraints of your life fall away, revealing a less cluttered self'. But the portrait also served Groom's ultimate purpose, which was to fashion the Centre as a wilderness.

~

Wilderness as an idea is used widely to represent Central Australia today. Eco- and adventure-tourism industries market remote places such as the Larapinta Trail and other routes to hikers, while others ferry tourists to climb or walk around Uluru and stroll Kata Tjuta's Valley of the Winds.[6] Other tourists follow four-wheel drive routes, retracing the steps of the explorers or old stock routes in their vehicle. The image of an Outback destination remains a major strategy of the NT Tourist Commission, with books, newspaper and magazine articles, painting, poetry, films and television all playing their part in shaping the Outback as a holiday destination. American tourists, for example, perceive the Outback as being at an earlier stage of development than the United States, a throwback to their own frontier no longer on show.

While already celebrated by Australian bushwalkers of the early twentieth century, the experience of a journey on foot into 'undisturbed nature' had started to enjoy a broader appeal by mid-century. Such walks were best done 'in nature', or better still, in 'wilderness', a term that had co-evolved with Henry David Thoreau's ideas on the benefits of 'wildness', from his proclamation that in 'wildness is the preservation of the world'.[7] Wilderness signified a place where nature was at its purest and the influence of people slight.

First to use the term to describe the Australian landscape was Alexander Sutherland, a Scottish emigrant who arrived in Melbourne in

1870, later establishing *The Melbourne Review*, a journal of philosophy, culture and politics. Between 1880 and 1882, Sutherland published a series of walking essays in which walking became a conceit to allow the contemplating of issues of the day. Walking was a time for 'intelligent discussion', to philosophise on the contemporary problems facing society. But Sutherland only felt comfortable with a bush cast as wilderness, a corollary to his work-a-day life in the city. He was happiest camped out in a forest somewhere (he always referred to it as the forest, not the bush) and in the company of cultured companions, where they might truly appreciate the beauty of the bush.

Sutherland's depiction of place as salve for the urban soul was a stark contrast to John McDouall Stuart's, for whom walking was a form of work, a necessary part of conquering and mapping Australia. It was different again from the sensuous writings of the Australian bush by poet John Le Gay Brereton, who, like Thoreau, found communing with nature a transcendental experience. For when he was in the bush, Brereton's self 'merged with the universe'.[8]

From the outset, therefore, wilderness was an urban imagining, hinged upon the difference between city and bush. By the 1920s, such notions had shaped the cultural activity called bushwalking, an activity in which a 'real' bushwalk meant a walk into the 'wilderness'. In inland Australia, on the other hand, food and water supplies had to be carried, often across great distances, making bushwalking a greater physical commitment than the polite saunter of the Romantic. Perhaps such hardships are what drove the Australian National Travel Association (ANTA) to encourage historians and educators to represent travelling to the Centre as a way of nation building.[9] After World War II, the ANTA encouraged 'nature-loving sportsmen' and 'artists of the wild' to wander into the 'heart' of the Australian 'wilderness', where they might 'contemplate man's place in natural creation'. By tying ideas of wilderness to the broader myth of the Australian Outback, the Red Centre's appeal as a tourist destination was thereby enhanced.

At the same time, however, Australian bushwalking was becoming more 'masculine', a testing of the human body against the elements, a challenge of survival in the tradition of the early explorers. In this case, Man's relationship with nature was adversarial, even though walking also embraced a coalescing of man with Nature for so many. Walking in the Centre combined the two, resulting in a powerful narrative force that shaped empathies towards a fast-emerging Australian identity.

The idea of Central Australia as a wilderness had become re-energised in the 1930s with the publication of *The Red Centre: Man and Beast in the Heart of Australia* (1935) by the mammologist Hedley Herbert Finlayson. Finlayson is perhaps best remembered for his remarkable 1933 walk of some 500 kilometres across the Rawlinson Ranges near the border with Western Australia. The region is considered one possible site for the location of a famed and mysterious gold reef, which Lewis Lasseter claimed to have discovered in 1929, and later perished trying to find again.

Finlayson's interest was not in gold but native fauna, his expeditions taking place prior to a massive wave of extinctions gripping the Centre in response to changing land use under pastoralism and the spread of foxes, cats and rabbits. Finlayson was the only scientist to have recorded ecological information for many mammal species now lost, such as the desert rat kangaroo and the lesser bilby. Unsurprisingly, Finlayson advocated for the conservation of large areas of the Centre.

Finlayson's journeys highlighted rising concerns that overdevelopment was destroying Australia's remaining 'unspoilt' wilderness. 'The old Australia is passing,' he wrote, and the environment that had supported the 'most remarkable fauna' in the world was changing, under siege by those bent on reshaping it in their own interest. Such themes already characterised a relationship between American literature and the American desert, a path blazed by Mark Twain in *Roughing It* (1872) and *The Innocents Abroad* (1869). Twain's unshakeable belief that 'domesticating the wild American Desert would be a fundamental loss to American culture'[10] parallels Australia's own struggles, Twain helping to illuminate the role wilderness played not only in America's emerging sense of itself, but also in Australia's. Nonetheless, as countless writers of the Australian inland would later do for the Aboriginals, Twain largely neglected Native Americans in his treatment of an American sense of place.

At its heart, Groom's 'wilderness' raises important questions about the meaning of Nature, always a complex matter. The Welsh critic Raymond Williams describes the term 'Nature' as 'perhaps the most complex word in the language'.[11] The word troubled ideas of the picturesque, popular in the literature of eighteenth- and nineteenth-century Europe and America. Mainly of interest to landscape painters, and meaning neither beautiful nor sublime but somewhere in between, the 'picturesque' described a landscape worthy of being included in a picture, something capable of being illustrated in a painting. In contrast to the landscaped garden, many picturesque scenes were of Nature in its 'untamed' state. Similar confusion now bedevils use of its etymological cousin 'wilderness', and intense debate arises as to how to manage wilderness areas and national parks.

But wilderness, like Nature, has several meanings, from 'the abode of beasts rather than humans: a place where civilized humans supposedly do not (yet) dwell', to an 'original innocence from which there has been a fall and a curse'.[12] When John McDouall Stuart arrived in the Centre, it was to a wilderness as a dangerous great unknown, the empty land of opportunity, a *terra nullius*.[13] In fact, for thousands of years Aboriginal people had established their own equivalent of wilderness areas, dedicated zones that were protected, not burnt, as ecological hotspots to be reserved and managed for valued plants, particular animals or other cultural reasons. This baseline knowledge of the Australian environment had spanned decades to millennia, embracing massive environmental upheavals from the last sea-level rise or volcanic eruption, to the recent invasion by Europeans.

During the Menzies era, however, wilderness came to be understood by Australians as a landscape in its primitive or original state, relatively undisturbed by humans and thereby 'closer to Nature'. A wilderness area was one of particular size and accessibility to those wanting a 'wilderness experience'. Such a landscape was attractive to city dwellers looking to escape from their everyday lives, a significant change from Gregory's earlier appraisal of the Centre as a Dead Heart.[14]

∽

After a swim at Ellery River, Groom makes camp and about midnight a 'whispering' comes across the hills. Here the ancient landscape helps to fuel Groom's imagining of a wilderness populated by primitive natives. For at first, the whisper is 'a complete sound in itself, distant and soft'. But gradually it becomes 'powerful and definite'. Indeed, soon it is 'part of the whole wilderness: part of the pines and ghost gums, and cycads and spinifex, and of the rocks and hills and valleys'. Surely this is 'the voice of an ancient people dreaming', Groom surmises, 'stirring once again in their ancient land, the ghosts of millions down the ages'.

As the wind increases in volume, Groom makes his link between Aboriginals and Nature even crisper, until he could 'sense acutely the first aborigines peering into the darkness and fearfully chanting the legends of mythology that are now in danger of being lost forever'. Such a romantic view of Aboriginal people works to support Groom's representation of the Centre as wilderness, where hymns are sung with 'the organ effect of the echoing hills', and there is 'a Sacrament and worship by primitive people in their own wilderness'.

Groom suggests elsewhere that songs had always been a part of the wilderness, an oblique reference perhaps to a performative dimension of the songlines through ritual, which include not only storytelling and song, but dance, performance and other rites. Yet the singing itself is offered as proof that 'the natives have fully accepted the white man's worship in song in place of some of their old and barbarous ceremonies'.

The very presence of Aboriginal people in the landscape should have worked to dismantle Groom's representation of wilderness. Instead, their presence renders them a part of his theatre of Nature. An actively modernising Indigenous person had no place on such a stage, their role far too weighty to fit the required costume of 'primitive', a museum piece reminiscent of Rousseau's noble savage.

Confusing matters further is that Groom's Centre was well populated by Aboriginal people. For example, early on he writes that he had 'believed the work of the Missions to be nothing more than a merciful delaying of the final death of the Aboriginal race'. Later he is moved to modify this articulation of Doomed Race Theory, when an unexpected contrast presents itself at Hermannsburg and he realises, 'This was no dying race—there were too many children'. Despite this more gracious depiction, it is Groom's representation of the Centre as wilderness that effectively condemned these same Aboriginals to remain part of a primitive Nature. Groom's argument becomes most plain when he welded the 'organ effect' of the singers' voices to the 'worship by primitive people in their own wilderness'.

Next day Groom climbs the 'high quartzite ridge west of the Ellery Creek gap, up through prickly spinifex and rocky outcrop, to the crest one thousand feet up'. There he is able to look out through 'winter's clear visibility over this strangely beautiful coloured land of parallel ranges both north and south, for I was in the middle of them all'. The calming effect of the ranges surrounds Groom, but the contradiction of the choir remains unresolved.

His walk back to Hermannsburg is 'cooler and more pleasant than the first hot day'. Having passed many 'stinking rock holes' from which he was unable to drink, Groom manages to find one good pool some 30 yards (27 metres) wide. Yet even such putrid holes are an oasis to hundreds of 'parrots, pigeons, finches, hawks, crows, apostle birds, butcher-birds, wrens and common chats' that gather near them.

By the time Groom reached Hermannsburg Mission, a Sunday night singsong was making ready in the yard beside the Superintendent's house. Groom sat beside Pastor Albrecht and the artist Rex Battarbee.[15] Soon, once again, a choir begins to sing, first in Arrernte then in English. Groom notes that 'by far the loveliest and deepest effect, which revealed the unforgettable harmony and ease of control and exhilaration in their voices, came from the rendition by these stone-age, primitive people of the hymns of Christianity translated by the early missionaries'. And yet Groom is also moved to imagine, quite tellingly, 'the patience of the teachers, and the bewilderment of the black man trying to judge and understand the strange new music of the voices brought by the white men'.

Once again, the scene contrasts starkly with earlier representations of the Centre. Of particular interest is *Australia Unlimited* (1918), in which Edwin Brady treats the Red Centre landscape as a *terra nullius* upon which great development might take place. His vision of a rosy future for Central Australia is based on the contemporaneous discovery of vast underground reserves of artesian water and a softening of perceptions of the inland as a waterless landscape, presaging the book as a powerful shaper of the Outback. Indeed, he proclaims that 'treasures of meat and wool' would one day pour from this 'mighty heart', feeding and clothing countless millions and flooding 'national life into the veins and arteries of the whole Commonwealth'.[16]

Brady's enthusiasm reflected the optimism of the early interwar era, the expectation of opportunities yet to be fulfilled. Groom's Menzies-era text portrayed a community in the throes of change, a settlement still on the frontier of colonialism and at the periphery of Brady's hopeful development. However, as Finlayson observed, the old Australia was passing, as culture and environment bent to religion and capitalism.

As for Groom, he cannot sleep, worried by this very fact. He is disturbed by the 'tragic passing of the native chants and ceremonies handed down with amazing accuracy and religious fervour by the patriarchal tribal elders'. Such tradition is now threatened with 'oblivion and forgetfulness', discouraged by the white man's laws. Slowly, through a 'period of bewilderment and transition', Aboriginal chants, myths and legends are being replaced by the hymns of the missionaries.

While there is no arguing with Groom's grim assessment, it is the Aboriginals' very agency that threatens his own desire to represent the Centre as a wilderness, which arguably has room only for a more romanticised and traditional Aboriginal. If the Centre is to become the destination Groom hopes it to be, something must change (other than the Aboriginals).

And Groom's embrace of Doomed Race Theory only serves to echo its popular reach. For example, early on Groom encounters a female tourist, who wanted to know all about the MacDonnell Ranges: 'Would they be able to walk through the ranges? Were the savages really wild? And had I a gun? Goodness! Why didn't I carry one? Were the missionaries exploiting the natives? And did Albert Namatjira do his own paintings or were they done for him? Could they get a pet kangaroo somewhere?' Perhaps best of all, suggests Groom, is her request as to where best to purchase weapons.

'My husband is most vitally interested in the aboriginal question,' the woman tells Groom. 'He already has several boomerangs and spears from the Nullarbor Plain, and is particularly anxious to get a big collection before these unfortunate people are allowed to die out.'

Groom's tourist articulates the frontier as a destination where a frontier experience might be had. Imagining the same country as a wilderness only serves to further deepen the conflict. Primitive Nature, with Aboriginals diecast as traditional or primitive hunter-gatherers, excludes the modernising Aboriginal, a circumstance Aboriginal academic Marcia Langton has rightly branded a 'travesty of justice'. In an article for *Australian Geographic*, she condemns the equally Romantic idea of the 'ecological Aborigine'. Such a native is both 'at one with' their primitive surroundings and in tune with modern political imperatives, a representation born of the Land Rights era and working equally feverishly against the interests of any 'modernising Aborigine'.[17]

Nevertheless, Groom captures well the difficult choices faced by Aboriginal people of the Menzies era, many of whom had never encountered whites. Noteworthy was a 'bleary eyed, dirty child' who had walked in from the desert with family to Hermannsburg. The boy is puzzled and frightened at his first contact with civilisation.

'Tomorrow he might be gone again with his parents into the wilderness,' writes Groom, 'or he might stay. The freedom of the nomad was his.'

One feels for the boy, unwittingly caught up in a world he is yet to understand. But his plight is, nonetheless, romanticised by Groom in the service of a conservation imperative. The lad finds 'the call of his primitive forefathers still strong and definite', but experiences only danger in the alien world of civilisation where 'the white man's foods were sweet and tempting'. There is no doubt the foods were tempting, and dietary change has since proven an intractable Indigenous health problem. But the image also serves Groom's own imperatives particularly well.

Later, while gathering a potted history of Hermannsburg from Pastor Albrecht, Groom observes that such a native was in dire need of 'vast space in his own domain, freedom, unlimited movement'. Aboriginals need 'time to gather [their] own bush food and water so necessary to provide a diet that was instinctive ... and as definite as the centuries'. Again, while this was almost certainly the case, the advance of the whites interfered at every step with 'known supplies of food and water', as the Australian frontier continued to spread across Groom's problematic wilderness.

～

From Hermannsburg next day, Groom travels 10 miles (16 kilometres) down the Finke River to a tributary called Palm Valley. The purpose of the day trip is for members of the Lutheran Mission Board to surprise Albert Namatjira, the watercolour artist, born at Hermannsburg in 1902. The area is a 'scenic reserve, but unpoliced'. As a result, visitors had been known to take young palms from the site in 'a vain attempt to grow them in city fern-houses'. While such trade was not yet great, Groom fears it might develop if left unchecked.

Groom frequently poses tourist vandalism as a danger to the wilderness. Central Australia was a landscape under threat, where the wilderness would be spoilt unless tourism and Nature were managed. But vandalism was not the only danger; perhaps more pressing was an adaptable Aboriginal, whom Groom addresses directly in his representation of Namatjira. For the artist's 'presence somewhere in the valley was known, but no smoke or track or sound betrayed his actual whereabouts'. Suggesting he might have been 'asleep somewhere beneath a tree', or 'away hunting for lizards', Groom rounds off a primitive portrait of Namatjira by describing him as 'an unspoilt man of nature'. In other words, the artist is a noble savage 'putting on record the colours of Central Australia', a situation that, Groom concludes, is a 'paradox almost unbelievable'.

Despite Groom's great love of walking and its situation at the very heart of his stories and their important observations, there is scant discussion of the Aboriginal 'walkabout' in *I Saw a Strange Land*. Yet Arrernte, Kaytetye, Pitjantjatjara and other groups all had their own walking traditions, which are still frequently maligned by the term today. A typical example occurred when a large group of Pitjantjatjara men arrives at Groom's locale, having walked some 'three hundred miles of rough desert from Ernabella', a remote community about 600 kilometres south-east of Uluru. Their purpose is to contact tribal members for an initiation ceremony. Groom tells us that they 'stayed a few hours, plotting and begging, and then vanished'.

Their vanishing does little to help understand why a group of men had travelled so far, and only deepens representations of Aboriginal people as mysterious and inscrutable to settler Australians. Similarly, while travelling with camels Groom deduces from smoke signals that 'natives were on a walkabout, heading south to Ernabella'. Earlier at the Old Woman's Cave at Uluru, Groom writes of the site as a 'Dreaming place'. And at another juncture, once a year, some Aboriginals would undertake a 'three-hundred mile walkabout to Hermannsburg or Areyonga for man-making ceremonies'.

The last is slightly more informative, though generally speaking Groom provides little to guide the reader to a deeper appreciation of the journeys or their possible meanings. At one point Groom does allude to a different way of travelling about Country, one that is a hallmark of travel on the Dreaming tracks, though he does not flag it as such. Following his guide Tiger through what the native referred to as 'My country ... only Tiger know 'em properly', Groom was forced to put 'all thought of travel by landmark or direction to one side'. And so he patiently follows Tiger through a veritable maze of passageways and crevices, 'between the giant domes, several miles toward the plateau's edge above Reedy Creek'.

With little information to go on, however, the reader remains unaware of the more sophisticated aspects of the Dreaming that may have underpinned Tiger's knowledge and methods, the pathways across the landscape later to be called songlines, the narrative mapping upon which Tiger's practice of wayfinding depended. As always, Groom defaults to the primitive.

One night camped at Ellery Creek after returning to the Centre for a second series of journeys in 1947, Groom once again hears the 'restless high wind'.

'It appeared to have no direction,' he writes, 'and it seemed as if the rocks and hills and trees were gasping in a frantic struggle for life.

'The calls of the birds in the gap ceased. No cattle moved in to water. This strange, whirling, unseen power of the heart of a continent is beyond understanding; it is awesome, bloodcurdling, yet inspiring.'

Groom's 'unseen power' has once again loaned a mystery to the Centre. And at the heart of such a mystery there is silence, where something momentous might have been learned in the lucid moments such silence brings: something 'awesome', yet 'bloodcurdling', and above all 'inspiring'. Groom's construction conflates two mythologies: wilderness, and the other notion of the Australian inland, the

Outback. However, the text brings the Dreaming geography to neither notion.

Groom's mood here is reminiscent of English walking philosopher
William Hazlitt, who believed that to journey was 'chiefly to be free of
all impediments and of all inconveniences; to leave ourselves behind,
much more to get rid of others'. Like Groom, who often walked alone,
Hazlitt preferred to walk without company. For Hazlitt, walking was
akin to shedding the cloak of the town, a place where one best shuns
companionship, which would only distract him from the 'undisturbed
silence of the heart, which alone is perfect eloquence'.

Such lone reverie is one of the great joys of walking in the desert,
where the opportunity for solace is ever present, imparting a peace
that permeates much writing of dry landscapes. As US poet Peter Wild
writes, some places are 'treasure troves of wonder and opportunities
for self-discovery'. More so in Europe than in America, poets, artists,
novelists and musicians have often found the deserts exotic. And indeed,
the greats of desert literature, such as French novelist Albert Camus
and American nature writer Edward Abbey, have heavily influenced
Western literature.

While Groom often leaned on a more journalistic style of 'objective
reportage', the same love of the wide-open spaces was everywhere in his
prose, and comparable to that of the art historian John Charles Van
Dyke. In his classic of American nature writing, *The Desert* (1901), Van
Dyke writes of how 'the desert has gone a-begging for a word of praise
these many years. It never had a sacred poet; it has in me only a lover'.[18]
Like Van Dyke, Groom is Nature's lover.

For like mountain landscapes, a strong 'place affect' is wrought in
the desert thanks to the sense of isolation and its sheer size compared
with humans. Once when camping alone near Glen Helen Gorge,
Groom finds ample time and leisure to think of many things as 'the
bowl of night turns slowly over'. Here under the stars the 'freedom of
thought and feeling is tremendous and lasting'. Then, as night descends,
the country 'vibrated and moved with life; mostly silent, mysterious,
pulsing, and tremendous beyond the knowledge of man'.

In these passages we find an unknowable Nature against which
Groom might have reflected upon his own life, that place of the mind

where humanity performs its difference.[19] However, a wilderness is 'pure only in the absence of human will, design and desire', and Central Australia was most certainly not this. The Centre is home to a great many Aboriginal groups whose culture, now threatened by colonialism, had once been hegemonic through a regimen of burning, hunting and ceremony. When historian Bill Gammage writes of Aboriginal Australia it is of a 'great estate', a highly managed nature. In her 2012 Boyer Lecture, Marcia Langton puts it most plainly, in that 'They are not wilderness areas. They are Aboriginal homelands, shaped over millennia by Aboriginal people'.[20]

In fact, traditional Aboriginal governance systems still exist over Aboriginal lands and beyond, constituting Law to many thousands of Aboriginal people. Yet even while such cultural Law remains, the long-term implications of somehow 'preserving' Aboriginals as primitive are insidious, and would prevent those who want to from adapting to change.

To a significant extent, Groom's vision was ultimately realised: the West MacDonnell Ranges and Uluru are now national parks. It is arguable that it was Groom's conservationist standpoint that encouraged wilderness to be fused with notions of Outback, forming not only an attractive destination for tourists, but helping to shape the next half century of government policy.

The shift to appraising the Centre as wilderness coincided broadly with a push for the Commonwealth to take a more national role in Indigenous affairs and to move to a more equal-rights approach. Such ructions eventually brought about the move away from assimilationist policies towards Aboriginal self-determination and later the homelands movement and Land Rights, all aimed at supposedly dismantling the frontier. The recent 'handback' to Aboriginal groups of the ownership and management of large tracts of Central Australia's national parks is, in part at least, testament to Groom's efforts. And it has done much to encourage a sense of dual ownership and use of these lands, while also remaining controversial in some quarters. Groom's Centre as wilderness nevertheless leaves a frontier legacy of its own: between itself and civilisation.

The problem for Groom's text becomes one of how such philosophical underpinnings might translate to policy and exactly how they might eventually become manifest in the political will. A Red Centre as wilderness, in which the world's most primitive natives dwell, invites two considerations. The first is that policies to encourage economic development of a race doomed to extinction might be considered wasteful. The second is that such investment might work against any intrinsic economic appeal of 'the natives' themselves, who, in their position as part of Nature, and in the setting of Groom's text with all its 'strangeness' and mystery, might be considered a lure for tourists from the coast to Australia's inland.

Both of these arguments are underscored by a political geography informed largely by the Lutheran Church and its pastors, who, in the main, are Groom's informants for his book. For example, Groom journeys to Haast's Bluff Aboriginal Reserve where mission policy backed by the federal government aimed to discourage the Aboriginal's tendency to seek the doubtful benefits of town life. The policy provided 'the basic tenets of a living in his own primitive wilderness', as Groom puts it, thereby encouraging 'a sense of comparative values'.

Such paternalism speaks to the era, during which there were already places of exclusion, and where there were 'many whites who defraud the full-blood native and half-caste at every opportunity'. The Lutheran missionaries provided a 'protecting barrier between such a parasite and the aboriginal hunting grounds so well placed geographically a hundred and more miles west of Alice Springs'. But even there, such hunting grounds ignored the precolonial hunting grounds that had existed already in the vicinity of Alice Springs, but which were now covered by the town.

The remote settlement of Haast's Bluff, taken over by the mission in order to rebuff the scourge of pastoralism, stranded the Lutherans between two sides of the normative frontier: whites and blacks. The resulting mixture of reserves and missions perhaps helped to trace a template for the homelands movement of the Land Rights era still to come, already sketched in by the mission movement. All of which comprised a new imperial geography overlain across a Dreamtime geography that had once been kin to that of Tommy Thompson's.

Brewed together with the wilderness ideal, the myth of the Outback remains solidly part of an Australian quest for authenticity.

Travelling to the Outback and the 'Journey to the Centre' were part of a search for something quintessentially Australian. As Australian historian and explorer John Béchervaise would write in 1949 for the popular magazine *Walkabout*, a first arrival in the Centre 'reconstituted the rite of standing atop the last sandhill to attain the first full view of Uluru [whereupon] waves of memories and emotions swept over the naturalist to produce an experience of deep cultural meaning and pride'. The fusion constituted another 'mythical' geography to overlay the existing landscape of the Red Centre, which, it must be said, was showing signs of becoming overburdened.

On such journeys as Béchervaise describes, there is less engagement with the complexities of the landscape's present, other than to reinforce ideas of a frontier. The casual visitor has insufficient time to develop a deeper appreciation of the place, and such contrived moments must suffice. The tourist gets what they have paid for: an experience according with a preconditioned appreciation of the destination.

Groom's slower appreciation of each location arguably provides, on the other hand, a richer appraisal. And from early on, Groom argues against the experience of Central Australia by car, where 'much of Central Australia's scenery is now panoramic, from a window' compared with 'the old camel pads that lead through deep mountain passes'. Even so, the idea of a safe and managed wilderness is sold to the tourist on the basis of the panoramic view. Similarly, Groom's Centre brings with it another set of problems.

During the Menzies era, the politics of Central Australia was muddied by entrenched beliefs and the adoption of fixed cultural and political positions. The Centre was becoming a patchwork of geographies of exclusion: white, black, old, new, ancient, modern. Sacred geographies that excluded whites had already emerged from the work of Spencer and Gillen and others. Pastoral geographies arrived with the drovers and settlers, tying Aboriginals to unpaid station work then later abandoning them to welfare. Urban geographies such as Alice Springs enacted laws to exclude blacks. This patchwork of different geographies, each with its own rules, became so intensely detailed and complex that it is a wonder the frontier was ever seen as a useful way to frame it.

Groom's walks cross many such boundaries and political frontiers. He provides readers with a more moral geography than the tourist experience ever could, a far more intimate 'being there'. When Groom camps around dusk in Glen Helen Valley after walking along the Finke River, for example, a large dingo walks in proud silhouette onto the highest crag. The dingo 'paused awhile, looking down at the sandy river below'.

Undoubtedly a stirring moment for Groom, the dingo makes for a 'magnificent tableau', then disappears into the silence. Groom sits on his swag 'still looking at the darkening slabs, and watched large night birds and bats flutter noiselessly out, one by one'. This open experience provides a rich sense of place, a sense that we are getting a glimpse of the 'real' of the landscape, rather than any deeper insight into the writerly imagination.

But in the very next paragraph Groom reaches for a sense of nationhood, whereby 'Daylight dwindled with all its life and colour, but Australia's wild heart beat on into the night'. The shift in point of view is sudden; in the preceding paragraph one is at Groom's shoulder watching bats wing their way out of the river canyon. In the second, there is a shift in perspective and one becomes lost, contemplating where such a wild heart might be hidden (if indeed, it exists at all).

It is the same for Groom's journey by truck a few pages later. Groom leaves Hermannsburg at midday, with Pastor Gross driving. Behind the cabin of the truck, Groom sits atop a 'large drum of water with Rex Battarbee on another. Pastor Simpfendorfer squatted before us with a shotgun. At every bump the iron roof beneath him boomed noisily'.

The reader is situated relative to the truck, rather than the landscape. All subsequent landscape description is from the truck, and comes with the embodied and uncomfortable feeling of every bump of the iron roof, immediately less personal and intimate than Groom's walking prose.

But even such prosaic and intimate prose as Groom's walking produces can be fraught and at times even misleading. While frequently acknowledging past Aboriginal traditions, they come to us largely without context and steeped in mystery. Such mystery is further muddied by Groom's insistence on a primitive role for Aboriginals in support of his main act: the Red Centre as wilderness. The nexus between wild place and a more moral national identity is never made plain and transparent to the reader, either through a sharing of self-doubt over the consequences of his plan to conserve the wilderness, or by articulating a future political geography he might already foresee, but fails to share.

～

As Robyn Davidson writes in her introduction to the latest edition of *I Saw a Strange Land*, you can't help but like Groom. His prose is simple and immediately engaging, delivered in a uniquely Australian voice and very much of its era. And there is no doubting his recounted walks of the Centre provide a sophisticated portrait of post-war Central Australia and an Aboriginal culture caught in a maelstrom of cultural change. His informed desert landscapes rival those of T.G.H. Strehlow, delivering a strong sense of place and a cultural landscape bathed in contradiction. Nevertheless, the book's constructed identity of wilderness—aimed at the traveller eager for an authentic Australia—raises serious questions.

Groom envisaged the Centre as a wilderness for bushwalking tourists, an area of some significance under threat and in need of preservation. In his earlier work, *One Mountain After Another*, Groom had already flagged the need for 'a great National Park for the Centre of Australia'. He pursued the goal throughout *I Saw a Strange Land* via his protagonist self—the archetypal walker-activist—to promote the conservation of the cultural and physical landscapes he describes.

As a promoter of conserving the physical landscape, Groom is an easy comparison with John Muir, the Scottish American nature writer and advocate of preserving areas of wilderness in the United States during the late nineteenth and early twentieth centuries. Articles by Muir in two 1890 editions of *The Century Magazine*, about threats to the Yosemite area and the Sierra, led to the region being declared America's first national park.

This type of walking, as protest or as an action characterised by political purpose, gained currency in the twentieth century. The walking activist in literature remains distinctive and familiar in Western culture, knitting ideas of pilgrimage with the military march and the labour strike or street protest. Firmly a part of this tradition, Groom and his walks provide as intimate a portrayal of the Centre's physical landscape as we are likely to read.

But the key to any deeper interpretation of *I Saw a Strange Land* lies in Groom's portrayal of Aboriginal people. A clever use of 'place affect' gives a nod to the physical grandeur of the Centre, and renders the landscape attractive to an emerging tourism industry. But it reinforces the Centre as a frontier, by rendering the landscape as wilderness, a place unknown to humans. Conversely, Groom's Centre is well populated by Aboriginals, a people who are, by all accounts, responding equally as well to the changes and challenges that confront them.

There remains this fundamental and perhaps unresolvable ambivalence in Groom's narrative, a paradox both supporting and challenging notions of Central Australia as a frontier. What remains is a Red Centre as exotic destination, a place where one might escape from home, into the wilderness, rather than a place to make one.

5

CHATWIN

By the time I crossed the dry Todd River to Olive Pink Botanical Garden in the heart of Alice Springs, the rain had disappeared and the heat was back with a fury. The unusual humidity was taking its toll. In a shady area called the Mulga Woodland I shrugged off my day pack and took a slug of water from my stainless-steel bottle. I ended up spilling half the fluids down my sweat-soaked top, and with the Beantree café now in sight, I poured the rest straight over my head.

Close by were two old ironwoods where botanical illustrator and anthropologist Olive Pink had set up a tent at age seventy-two and proceeded to live in it while she lobbied the Northern Territory Government to establish a flora reserve around her. I can't imagine the hardships she must have endured in that tent, while still managing to serve cake and tea to her many visitors. The woodland and gardens are Ms Pink's determined legacy—finally gazetted in 1956—and one of my favourite spots in the town to aimlessly saunter, to sit and to think.

But I'd come to write, to explain to myself how this town had come to live in me, as indeed, I live in it. Because Alice is as much a town of my imagining as it is a town of bricks and mortar. The seventeenth-century French mathematician Blaise Pascal believed all our grief as humans stems from the inability to live at peace in a room. I would have to agree. But for the writer trying to describe such a room, being

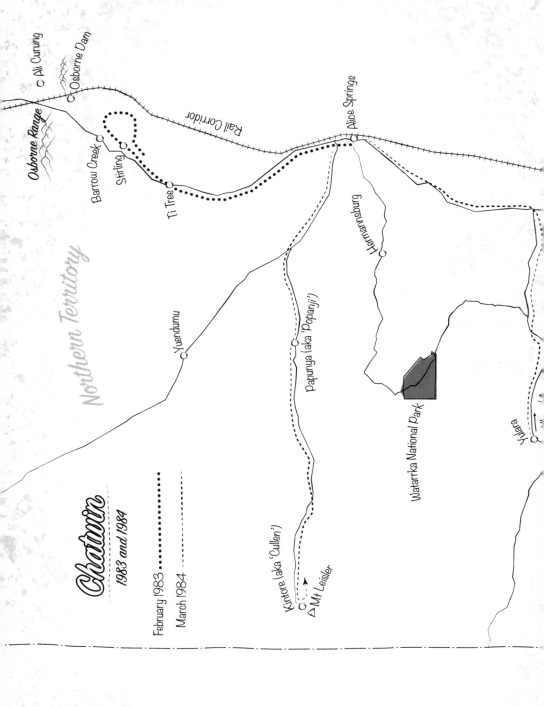

inside only amplifies the choice it represents: to leave or to stay? For there is so much beyond the room to include in the telling, not least our lives outside and the experiences we arrived with. Most troubling are the senses, a portal to the world, yet the information they collect must be filtered through the imagination. We are, in the end, both cause and effect: the describer and the described.

I wandered to the edge of the carpark where a ranger had once pointed out a bower bird's nest, an elaborate thatching of dry grass and twigs under a witchetty bush. The nest was still there, and for the umpteenth time I watched as the bird hovered nervously nearby, afraid I might have arrived to undo his pretty handiwork.

Rather than rely on good looks and plumage, the male bower bird builds an elaborate home to attract a mate. He decorates it with objects he collects, often brightly coloured, though he has a penchant for blue. Here bits and pieces of plastic, silver and white, and there, at one end, a blue juice lid.

Dry grass, carefully teased up from the mat of grasses and twigs underneath the nest, formed a free-standing U-shaped affair, a tunnel-like entrance to the inviting space between vertical arms of the U. All without tools or hands with opposing thumbs. Apparently the females compare bowers from among their suitors' efforts to decide on a mate. No wonder he is nervous, I thought, and quietly congratulated the bird on his gallant carpentry.

Later, walking back to town, the rain came down briefly and in big heavy drops. I drained the last of a take-away coffee from Olive Pink, crumpled the cup and tossed it in a dot-painted council bin. An Aboriginal family sharing cigarettes at a phone booth looked up at the sky and back again. I called hello to the man, who was dressed in pink shorts and a baseball cap. He smiled a big smile, took a deep drag on a freshly lit fag then coughed, and we both laughed.

Again it tried to rain, and the cool drops hit the super-heated road and steam rose, as if Central Australia's wide red landscape were a hot plate doused under a garden hose. But once again the relief was short lived. Worse, the brief spit only fuelled the humidity, which swirled in a low-level fog; I opened my fingers and waggled them, letting the smoky tendrils run through. Men rolled up shirt sleeves, young women in sweat-ringed singlets, tongues poking out, turned their backpacker hands palm-up to catch more of the big drops. It was like Darwin in the build-up before the monsoon. Only the air was ten degrees hotter.

Near the town centre I paused where local historian Dick Kimber had walked by with British travel writer Bruce Chatwin on a similarly grey day in the early 1980s. There had been a signing at a nearby book-shop. Being the only one to turn up, Kimber had asked Chatwin to sign his copy of *In Patagonia*, the award-winning meditation on nomad-ism set in South America. According to Chatwin's biographer Nicholas Shakespeare, Kimber reckoned Chatwin a 'sad, lonely, lost man', a shame considering his breakaway book about the Centre published some five years later.

At a Todd Mall café nearby, an Aboriginal woman was hawking her paintings to diners and had sat herself down at one of the outdoor tables. A tourist reached nervously for her handbag and beckoned for a waiter, while her boy squirmed in his seat whining for the drink that hadn't arrived. You can simply wake up in a bad mood in this sort of weather.

Then the rain came down properly, steady and persistent. And what a relief. The mother grabbed her boy and joined other diners making for the shelter of the café's indoors. She lingered ever so briefly at the entrance, long enough to lift her face to the sky and feel the rain on her cheeks, pleasure written sweet on her lips.

The Aboriginal woman half-proffered her sodden wares as she passed me on her way to try her luck elsewhere. I stood in the open and silently prayed for the rain to stay. A few minutes at least, longer if there really was a God. For with it some invisible hand had taken everything down a notch. As if the town had drawn a deeper, more satisfying breath.

~

A decidedly more pleasant introduction than his grey day in Alice Springs with Kimber, were the blue skies and glorious summer days that greeted Bruce Chatwin on his arrival to Australia in December 1982. Into his suitcase Chatwin had packed the biggest of his big ideas: nomadism as the cure for an ailing West. The ideas were crammed into notebooks and a card index left over from a fifteen-year-old unpublished work entitled *The Nomadic Alternative*. Flying first into Sydney, he aimed eventually to 'hole up somewhere in the desert, away from libraries and other men's work and take a fresh look at what they contained'.[1]

Born in Sheffield in 1940, Chatwin had begun his career as a porter at the art auction-house Sothebys. Within eight years he had risen to become one of their youngest directors, but left to pursue travel interests, and between 1972 and 1975 wrote for the *Sunday Times*. Much of Chatwin's writing took him to South America, but he had wanted to come to Australia for some time. He had a cousin who worked in Broken Hill, maintained a friendship with *Tracks* author Robyn Davidson, and through the work of T.G.H. Strehlow had developed a fondness for the Australian Aboriginals, whom he suspected might be just the peg on which to hang his nomadic themes.

As early as 1970, Chatwin sought advice from Australian historian John Mulvaney on the Aboriginal 'walkabout'. Mulvaney had no recollection of the meeting, but Chatwin claims the conversation steered him towards T.G.H. Strehlow. From his reading of Strehlow, Chatwin formed a dislike of the term Aboriginal 'Dreaming tracks', but later he would write of the tracks' complexity as so 'staggeringly complex, and on such a colossal scale, intellectually, that they make the Pyramids seem like sand castles'. Nevertheless, he pondered how to write about them, 'without spending 20 years there'.

Of his search for nomads, Chatwin had once scribbled in his notebook that it was 'a quest for God'. It's hardly surprising, then, that upon his departure from Britain for the Antipodes his mother wrote she was 'glad he's finally gone ... he's had a fixation about it for years'. The beginning of Chatwin's Australian sojourn was, however, spent staying with Penelope Tree, the former sixties British fashion model, reading, windsurfing, socialising and going to the gym. It wasn't until February that Chatwin left Sydney on a somewhat brief but 'extremely expensive zigzag' from Adelaide to Alice Springs then Broome, the Kimberleys, Perth and back to Sydney. His rather brief time in Alice Springs helped him shape his ideas for an 'Australia' book.

'Alice is a hornets nest,' Chatwin later wrote to friend and ITV researcher David Thomas, a town of 'Pommie-bashers, earnest Lutheran missionaries, and apocalyptically-minded do-gooders'. And summer conditions in the desert were even less appealing. In a letter to Diana Melly he noted that 'You fry in the Centre of Australia: but I can't complain. I never once FELL for the country, except perhaps in the most abstract way with the landscape'.

In fact, Chatwin had celebrated the country and its climate in his early letters. But by April he had left Australia altogether, feeling 'flat, dried out and alienated'. He was having trouble writing about a place 'intractable to the pen' where there was 'none of the rich vein of fantasy you can tap by simply landing in S. America'. Then in March he would write again to Melly, this time announcing he had found what he was looking for: 'the Australia peg on which to hang my nomadic material'. By the middle of that year, what's more, he had also found a 'better' name for the Aboriginal Dreaming tracks, from then on referring to them as the 'songlines'.

But his 'Australia' book remained unwritten, and Chatwin longed to return to the Centre. So in January 1984 he wrote to anthropologist Petronella Vaarzon-Morel about a possible trip to the remote Aboriginal community of Kintore, roughly 530 kilometres west of Alice Springs. He even had an excuse for coming: an invitation to the Adelaide Writers' Festival. He would travel with friend and fellow writer Salman Rushdie, who had also been invited and asked if he might travel to the Centre with Chatwin. In early March that year the pair flew to Alice Springs, which Rushdie described as an incredibly moving landscape, like 'the moon with atmosphere'. At the Adelaide festival Chatwin had been lucky enough to meet Rob Novak, who ran the store at Kintore, and so he had his in.

The end result of Chatwin's fresh look at nomadism would be a seminal work, *The Songlines*, first published in 1987. *The Songlines* arrived near the end of the Land Rights era (1970s and 1980s), when there was a marked reappraisal of attitudes towards Aboriginal Australians and their land rights. Successive governments since 1972 had fostered challenges to European perspectives of history and identity.

Official Aboriginal policy carried a new emphasis on decolonisation and was keen to give due consideration to Aboriginal voices in planning.

A controversial crossover of travel writing, autobiography and novel set in Central Australia, *The Songlines* highlighted many of the political challenges Australia was facing at the time. It also had critics stumped over whether it was fact or fiction. That did not stop readers from heartily embracing the book, which on publication went straight to number one on the *Sunday Times* bestseller list and stayed in the top ten for nine months.

And a quarter century of strident criticism since then has done nothing whatsoever to dampen popular enthusiasm for the book. When publishers Random House launched a twenty-fifth anniversary edition in 2012, Dick Kimber—who remains fiercely critical of the work—nevertheless conceded it was 'one of the best-selling books about Aboriginal culture that has ever been'. A new foreword to the edition by British conservative politician and author Rory Stewart claims *The Songlines* transformed travel writing.

By my own reading of his text and life, Chatwin came to Alice Springs looking for a way to die, for a 'right death' in the way that Jean-Paul Sartre had sought an 'authentic' way to live. Increasingly ill while researching the book, Chatwin discovered he had AIDS during its editing, and passed away in 1989, aged forty-eight.[2]

A dedicated walker, Chatwin nominates walker-writers such as William Wordsworth, Matsuo Basho and others as literary mentors, once writing in his notebooks that 'there is nothing worse than walking with those who can't keep up'.[3] He talked incessantly as he walked, a constant flow of ideas and new projects. When Chatwin was dying, his editor, Susannah Clapp, writes that he was afraid of an unidentified woman, who, he said, was trying to kill him. He appealed to the composer Kevin Volans at his bedside, 'They think I'm mad: you must get me out. I'm not mad at all, I'm just thinking too fast for them. They can't keep up'.[4]

It is unlikely the two thoughts were connected. But taken together like this—however fanciful such a joining might be—they speak boldly of a man who believed his stride to be the language in which he best expressed his own existence, his understanding of the world around him, indeed, the architecture of its form, as much as any geographic measure of its undulations.[5]

Both *The Songlines* and Chatwin himself have been widely studied, reviewed and critiqued. Yet English writer Jonathan Michael Chatwin notes that most critical interpretation of *The Songlines* focused somewhat exclusively on its political implications and genre bending.[6] Deepening such debate was concern over the 'truth' or otherwise of Chatwin's narrative, based closely as it is on historic events and living persons, many of whom were upset by his 'fictional' presentation of them in the book and critical of the author's ethics. The result was that most readers regard the text as 'Bruce's own adventures in the Australian outback'. As to the accuracy of it translation of cultural traditions, anthropologist Howard Morphy describes the text as 'wont to oversimplification and overgeneralisation, but not seriously misleading'.[7]

Even so, Chatwin never rested in the truth, neither of his sexuality, nor his illness once it fully gripped him, and even when he lay dying of AIDS. From all accounts he seemed a terribly anxious man. In *The Songlines*, such restlessness betrays its opposite: a longing for home, for which perhaps he found some answers in Central Australia. Considering the book's notoriety and Chatwin's celebrity, it is unlikely to disappear from view anytime soon. Critic Ruth Brown goes so far as to suggest that when Australia 'fades from the forefront of European consciousness, Chatwin's Australia may be a dominant surviving image'.[8]

In broad terms, *The Songlines* describes an encounter between a British travel writer and an unfamiliar and exotic Aboriginal culture, and in doing so represents the place where their encounter occurs. Unlike most travel writing, however, and as critic Thomas Smith puts it, '*The Songlines* has a thesis—that all humans are by nature migrators or nomads'. More concerned with a philosophy of walking than with actual traversal, *The Songlines* is not a walking narrative in the conventional sense of, say, Robyn Davidson's *Tracks* or Tony Kevin's *Walking the Camino*. In fact, as fellow travel writer Paul Theroux related in a 2015 radio interview, Chatwin rarely gets out of his four-wheel drive during the book.[9] Central to Chatwin's thesis are the songlines themselves, which the text describes as 'a labyrinth of invisible pathways which meander all over Australia and are known to Europeans as Dreaming-tracks'. The story traces the education of Bruce—Chatwin's fictional self—in Aboriginal ways and culture, as all the while he hunts for a nomadic psyche of humankind.

Yet Chatwin is also concerned with Aboriginality as a sort of thematic scaffold for his quest. In the text's humanist comparison of Aboriginal and settler, it retraces paths to a hybrid Australian identity seen earlier in Strehlow's journey of the Finke River in 1922. Comparable also are the controversial efforts of the Jindyworobaks, a literary movement of mostly white poets of the 1930s and 1940s, who wanted to integrate Aboriginal mythology into the writing of Australian places.

The narrative divides readily into four 'acts', which capture not only the structure of Chatwin's text and thinking, but also the course of his field research. The first act takes place over two days in Alice Springs; the second concerns a trip 'out bush' to the north and west of the town based on separate actual trips taken by Chatwin in 1983 and 1984. The third act is the controversial 'Notebooks' section, a somewhat disjointed tracing of the peripatetic and other themes and metaphors across the history of literature and Chatwin's real-life travels. The fourth is an epilogue: journey's end and a death scene that brings together many of Chatwin's divergent themes.

~

The Songlines is told through 'Bruce', a character based closely on the author, while emphasising his best possible face to the world. Walking and nomadism feature largely in Bruce's childhood, courtesy of Chatwin's/Bruce's grandfather, a 'great walker', and a wanderer father who was 'away at sea, fighting the Germans'. Even the surname Chatwin, originally the Anglo-Saxon 'Chettenwynde', means winding path; thus 'poetry, my own name and the road, were, all three, mysteriously connected'.

Bruce even recalls childhood impressions of Australia, in 'the fumes of the eucalyptus inhaler and an incessant red country dominated by sheep'. His favourite bedtime story is of a coyote pup that bolts for the wild, which he somewhat naively connects to the Australian slang term 'walkabout'. Bruce explains his understanding of the term as 'those tame blackfellows who, one day, would be working happily on a cattle station: the next, without a word of warning and *for no good reason*, would up sticks and vanish into the blue'. The italics are Chatwin's, implying Bruce has since come to a special understanding of walkabout that may soon become clear to the reader. The point is that the parallels between Bruce's life and Chatwin's actual life are so close they mark the book clearly as autobiographical.

Walking credentials aside, Bruce needs an insider for his quest, a guide into the wilderness of the Red Centre. And so, in an Alice Springs café we meet Arkady, an exiled Russian who maps Aboriginal sacred sites for a railway company. Arkady is restless, a nomad himself, and agrees to help Bruce decipher the meaning of the songlines. The thinly disguised 'character' is based on real-life anthropologist Toly Sawenko, who helped Chatwin while he was in Central Australia.

Arkady becomes Bruce's insider. He might even be considered Chatwin's Strehlow, a European with traits borrowed from the Aboriginals, but nonetheless different from Strehlow's hybrid identity of *Journey to Horseshoe Bend*. Strehlow had constructed himself as being 'of the Arrernte', a more cogent strategic position than Chatwin's status as a newcomer, and one who relies far too heavily on the figure of Arkady.

In the café, Arkady tells Bruce of witnessing secret Aboriginal ceremonies before abandoning Central Australia for Europe. Once there, however, among 'the monuments of western civilisation' in a Europe of mindless materialism, he longs for the old Aboriginal men of Central Australia, who seem 'wiser and more thoughtful than ever'.[10] The Aboriginals believe the world was sung into existence by the Ancestors, poets in the original sense of *poesis*, meaning 'creation'. Such a world existed first in the mind before it was sung, and all living things were 'made in secret beneath the earth's crust'.

A worldly man himself, Arkady once 'sat with sadhus on the ghats of Benares', a sadhu in Hinduism being a wandering ascetic monk who has renounced all material and sexual attachment. He had 'few possessions apart from a harpsichord and shelf of books', the implication being that 'nomadic' Arkady is a kindred spirit of Bruce, who has found a like mind.

Arkady 'invents' his own job, interpreting 'tribal law' into the 'Law of the Crown'. A quick intellect honed in the rugged conditions of the frontier, Arkady is a non-conformist, unsuited to the 'hugger-mugger' of the Adelaide suburbs or a 'conventional job'. Hair thick, straight and the colour of straw, his lips cracked but not drawn-in, Arkady rolled his r's in a very Russian way. He played Bach on the harpsichord after a hard day in the Outback ('their orderly progressions ... conformed to the contours of the ... landscape').

Like many clues Chatwin leaves scattered throughout the text, even the name Arkady is significant. Namesake of a Russian saint, Arkady means 'an unspoiled paradise', having roots in 'Arcadia', a mountainous area of ancient Greece known for the pastoral peace of its people. In his novel *The Raw Youth*, Fyodor Dostoyevsky introduces narrator and hero Arkady Dolgoruky, a 'living symbol of the spiritual crisis of our times'. Dostoyevsky's fictional crisis between father and son speaks to a larger crisis of Russian society around the mid-nineteenth century. Chatwin situates Arkady at the geographic and spiritual heart of a similarly dire twentieth-century Australian crisis, between a postcolonial struggle for identity and an Aboriginal one to survive.

Arkady had found solitude in Alice Springs and an escape from his former wife. Indeed, Arkady is crucial to Chatwin's construction of a more pluralist Australian identity than historian Russel Ward's outback bushman, that 'rough and ready' Anglo-Saxon who was disparaging of affectation and blind to the existence of Aboriginals. In Alice Springs, immigrants of all types find a place, and, like Arkady, in one way or another challenge the well-worn Aussie stereotype they are so often said to emulate.[11]

Equal parts free-wheeling bush intellectual and Aboriginal-as-noble savage, Arkady seems likely to go 'walkabout' at any moment. His character suggests the first hint of Chatwin's appropriation of Aboriginality towards a settler identity. Not unlike Arthur Groom's self-protagonist of *I Saw a Strange Land*, Arkady thought nothing of 'setting out, with a water flask and a few bites of food, for a hundred mile walk along the ranges'. Like Groom, a carefree embracing of the 'wilderness' through grand feats of walking and its conflation with the finest cultural habits speaks to the sort of character who thrives in this romanticised Central Australian landscape.

Walking provides the lens through which such alternative standpoints are viewed, for always in *The Songlines* such themes are channelled back through ambulating. Attachment to land, for example, is that which is covered by known human feet. Aboriginal people, says Arkady, 'trod lightly over the earth', in such a way that 'The world, if it has a future, has an ascetic future'. All events point to 'the centrality of travel, especially walking travel, in human life'.

Later, Bruce reinforces such notions, invoking Blaise Pascal for whom: 'Our nature lies in movement, complete calm is death', alongside the Buddha's last words to his followers: 'Walk on'. While critical understanding of Bruce's quest focuses largely on Chatwin's relentless pursuit of the theme of nomadism, it seems remarkable there has never been a dedicated reading of *The Songlines* for walking, perhaps its single clearest attribute.[12]

~

In Alice Springs, Bruce swiftly begins to gain an appreciation of the ways of Aboriginal people, of the complexity and beauty of the ideas and philosophies behind their culture as well as the challenges they face. His ideas are heavily mediated through conversations conducted almost entirely with whites. And though Bruce's sources have often lived in the Centre for many years, Bruce aims to learn everything in a matter of days, which does not endear him to his hosts. Nonetheless, again and again, through Arkady and his vast network, Bruce meets someone to bolster his belief in nomads as 'the crank handle of history', each time acknowledging more and more of a role for walking.

At a party he meets Father Flynn, a character modelled on former director of the Central Land Council, Pat Dodson, the first Indigenous Australian Roman Catholic Priest and once in charge of a mission in the Kimberleys. A lengthy conversation with Flynn continues Bruce's education about the Dreaming, the songlines and culture; and we find ourselves in the hands of an author steadily building his case. Through Flynn, Bruce gains special insights regarding a system of land tenure prevailing before the European settlers arrived, when 'no one in Australia was landless, since everyone inherited, as his or her private property, a stretch of the Ancestor's song and the stretch of country over which the song passed. A man's verses were his title deeds to territory'. Such title deeds could be loaned to others, one could even borrow a verse or two, but the verses couldn't be sold or handed off.

Bruce's education is continued through the memory of old acquaintances, such as Father Terence, who liked to compare walking in the footsteps of one's Ancestors with Christ's saying 'I am the Way'. But it is in Chatwin's concise and unadorned descriptions of his encounters that we learn most. At Arkady's office, Bruce met an Aboriginal girl. A secretary, she 'came in with a stack of papers ... a pliant brown girl in a brown knitted dress. She smiled and said: "Hi Ark!" but her smile fell away at the sight of a stranger'. Here was a young woman in every way unremarkable, perhaps shy with newcomers, preferring to keep to herself.

Compare the young office girl to Chatwin's encounter in Katherine at a lunch-time rendezvous when 'a black whore pressed her nipples against my shirt and said, "You want me darling?"' Both characters confound Aboriginal stereotypes. Indeed, rather than romanticising Aboriginal people—which critics roundly accused Chatwin of doing— *The Songlines* presents a continuum of Aboriginal humanity, a potpourri of traditional and modern, according well with a lived experience of the town and other 'contact zones'.

As a result, and out of such confusion, it was possible for the Romantic appeal of the Dreaming to emerge without dominating the narrative. For instance, when Bruce visited the bookshop (where Chatwin gave a signing and met with Kimber), an American tourist viewed a painting, and 'liked to think of the honey-ants dreaming their way across the desert with the bright sun shining on their honey sacks'.

Bruce spent the day after the party with a bottle of Burgundy reading Strehlow's *Songs of Central Australia*. By evening he had turned to brandy and settles in to write his own Aboriginal Dreaming story, as a hybridised reimagining of Genesis. Chatwin's 'dreaming' takes up as the Ancestors rise from their slumber beneath the earth's crust. The Ancestors cry out: 'I AM!' 'I am—Snake ... Cockatoo ... Honey

Ant … Honeysuckle'. For Bruce, this is the very first 'I am!', a 'primordial act of naming' later to be held as 'the most secret and sacred couplet of the Ancestor's song'. Each of Bruce's Ancestors then puts his 'left foot forward and called out a second name. He put his right foot forward and called out a third name'. The Ancestors named the features of the topography, bringing it into existence: 'a waterhole, the reedbeds, the gum trees—calling to right and left, calling all things into being and weaving their names into verses'.

Here Bruce has stepped boldly across the Australian frontier, the cultural divide between settler and Aboriginal, and at what is perhaps its most sensitive location, the appropriating of an Aboriginal Dreaming story. In a world called into being through walking but traversed in a dream, Bruce has linked place to its creation, through walking, naming and dwelling. Everywhere he travels in *The Songlines*, Bruce traverses the interface between such worlds, from the nipples of a Katherine whore to the beauty of Aboriginal Creation, and all rendered amid social circumstances at once revelatory and confused.

Rather than a frontier, this was more of a disruption of being, a transition zone where a sense of place fluctuates and is dynamic, varying markedly with location, time and social demographic. Even Bruce's own producing of textual space in the book compares with that of the Ancestors, where with each step 'calling to right and left, calling all things into being and weaving their names into verses', they usher the world into being through storytelling.

～

Before heading north with Arkady to Middle Bore, Bruce goes for a morning run in Alice Springs. Some Aboriginal families have 'parked themselves on the municipal lawns' and are 'freshening up under the lawn sprayer'. The family sits close enough to the sprayer to get wet but 'not too close to kill their cigarettes'. Meanwhile, snot-nosed children 'tumble about … glistening wet all over'.

Bruce says hello to the family and their reply causes everyone to laugh. The scene lends a street-wise humour to the Aboriginal family and their appreciation of their own position in the community. Again, such characters emerge crisp and understated, and substantially human, reducing the apparent 'strangeness' of Aboriginal people in the town.

With the day already heating up, Bruce walks back to his motel to shower and pack for Middle Bore. He brings the notebooks from the 'Nomad book', a manuscript he claims to have burned. Here any semblance of fiction is once again lost as Chatwin the autobiographer speaks, rather than the fictional protagonist Bruce. The text is inconsistent in this way, moving from fact to fiction without warning.

In fact, the trip to Middle Bore draws closely on a real journey with Toly Sawenko on 8, 9 and 10 February in 1983, when the pair drove through northern Arrernte country and beyond to Kayetye lands, visiting the communities of Ti-Tree, Stirling and Osborne Bore. While the actual journey is disguised in the text, the 'Notebooks' he brings with him brazenly form part of Bruce's later literary and historical trawl of walking performed in the Notebooks section, Act III of *The Songlines*. Here Bruce holes up in a caravan at the remote community of Cullen for a 'couple of weeks' to read them. To this extent, the author Chatwin steps periodically outside the narrative to acknowledge his own textual production of space, an important and innovative feature of the book, but one which, again, led to widespread confusion over its genre.

Much of *The Nomadic Alternative* re-emerges in *The Songlines*, which critic Jonathan Michael Chatwin calls the 'foster child' of the discarded first attempt. When Chatwin arrived in Central Australia, he presented the as-yet-unnamed 'songlines project' to his sources as a similarly serious work of non-fiction. Later, however, after significant reworking and an argument with original publishers Jonathan Cape, Chatwin's new manuscript *The Songlines* was released as a novel, and widely touted as fiction by the author.[13] My own reading of *The Songlines* is foretold in Chatwin's admitted 'preoccupation with roots': that it juggles the momentous tension between two divergent human imperatives, a desire to discover new experience through journey, and a yearning to belong, for a sense of home.

Arkady collects Bruce in a Toyota Land Cruiser for the drive to Middle Bore. His purpose is railway business, to ensure that the voice of an important Aboriginal elder, Alan, is accounted for in planning the rail route. The day before they set out, however, Arkady learns he is also required in Cullen (Kintore), near the border with Western Australia. As a result he decides they will drive on to Cullen via Popanji (Papunya) after they complete the work at Middle Bore, once again a journey drawing heavily on Chatwin's real travels of early 1984.[14]

Before leaving town, Arkady stops to buy a copy of *Metamorphoses*, by the Roman poet Ovid—'reading matter for the trip'—and tosses it to Bruce: 'a present for you'. There are numerous references to *Metamorphoses* throughout *The Songlines*, each signposting a theme to be highlighted in events that follow. The choice of text is interesting. Published around 8 AD, Ovid's collection was gathered from a range of sources, and at times Ovid is the only written source of an otherwise oral narrative. The similarities to Aboriginal storytelling are clear and, taken with all of Chatwin's other pointers in the text, we might conclude this is code for Chatwin's own construction of *The Songlines*.

Each story Ovid gathered was embellished and re-embellished throughout European literature. Citing Ovid speaks therefore not only to the form of Chatwin's text, but to the effect of his own journey, which produced its own unique space. Ovid influenced Chaucer, and both Chaucer's and Ovid's methods resemble the storytelling practices of the Aboriginal songlines. Chaucer's *Canterbury Tales* is based on a pilgrimage during which the characters tell stories at significant points along the way. In similar fashion, Aboriginal walkers of the songlines gather periodically for ceremony, dance and storytelling. Ovid's story is concerned with creation of the world and construction of civilisation, inviting a further parallel to Aboriginal Creation mythology.

Through Bruce's reading of Ovid, then, Chatwin signals his own journey as a quasi-Creation story, not just *analogous* to the journeys along the songlines of Aboriginal mythology, but also one that *produces space* in its own right. And such a space tells a sometimes harsh reality. During the drive, Bruce and Arkady pass pastoral leases, which Arkady says have been 'bought up by foreigners', highlighting the confrontation of values dogging land ownership in Central Australia. Arkady also describes a cattleman who once drove up while he was working, and, 'waving a shotgun, hollered: "Get off my land! Get them coons off my land.""

After passing the pub at Glen Armond, Bruce and Arkady turn off the highway to visit an old bushman, the loner Jim Hanlon, a drinker in his seventies. Of a similar disposition to the pastoralist with the shotgun, Hanlon is sceptical of Land Rights.

'Sacred bloody baloney,' he says.

Hanlon's house is unkempt and uncivilised, a frontier dwelling. Though Bruce and Arkady are only a short distance from Alice Springs, they have arrived in a world far from Western norms. Earlier, Bruce and Arkady had discussed the British H-bomb tests at Maralinga to the south. Out here, where a hydrogen bomb could be dropped and 'all the best pastoral leases had been bought up by foreigners', anything might happen.

Even time was different: 'Late? What's late and what's early?' asks Hanlon, affecting a more Aboriginal chronology. Nevertheless, he divulges the story of the Maralinga tests and its cloud, which 'instead of sailing out to sea to contaminate the fishes, sailed inland to contaminate us ... lost the bugger over Queensland ... Vaporized a few Abos on the way!' In Hanlon is seen the white man's isolation in the bush, fobbing off the uncaring attitudes of the British—proven in their act of negligence at Maralinga—which Jim likes to conceal with bravado and a show of intellectual rigour through his reading of Marx. Yet as Arkady and Bruce prepare to leave, Jim becomes ill, and suddenly is laid bare the very human frailty of Hanlon and his remote circumstances.

Further north at Skull Creek Camp are more signifiers of the frontier, including an entry sign threatening a $2000 fine for bringing in liquor. Prohibition is widespread across Central Australia, sometimes enacted by government and other times voted in by the elders of an Aboriginal settlement. Skull Creek is a 'sleepy camp where nothing much seems to be happening', and it is here that Arkady will pick up Kaytetye elder Timmy, who knows the old stories of Middle Bore.

Arkady parks under 'a pair of ghost gums, alongside a small white-washed house'. Songbirds chatter in the branches while 'Two full-bosomed women, one in a loose green smock, lay asleep on the porch'. Surrounding the expanse of red dirt are about twenty humpies, 'half-cylinders of corrugated sheet, open ended like pig-shelters, with people lying or squatting in the shade'. Timmy stands in the doorway to his house, an 'impish-looking man with a wispy beard and one eye clouded with trachoma'.

Chatwin's description of Timmy is vivid, his 'brown felt hat at an angle and a red handkerchief knotted at his neck', a man so skinny as to have to 'keep hitching up his pants'. But while there is a strong sense of place, there is also a discomfiting lack of fit between worlds, a disjuncture across the frontier between black and white, the half-cylinders of corrugated sheets and the whitewashed house.

For all that, the portrayal speaks not of primitives or even victims, but of human beings caught in trying circumstances. Later at Popanji, Bruce discovers that local Aboriginals have managed to lose a large piece of earthmoving equipment, a grader, demonstrating their reduced social capacity in the settler world. At the school, furthermore, the pupils have been known to 'shit on desks'. Compared with the explorer J.M. Stuart, for whom the Australian landscape was an object of desire, for Aboriginals the space of the desert is home. Neverthless, that home had been disrupted and old ways cast adrift on the new. Before leaving Skull Creek Camp, several others join the expedition, so that 'We were a party of six now and the smell inside the Land Cruiser was rich and strange'.

~

At Burnt Flat Arkady stops the car for 'gasoline', only to find a policeman taking affidavits regarding a white man in his twenties found dead on the road. The policeman apologises for having to ask questions: 'Run over a coon in Alice Springs and no one'd give it a thought', he says, 'But a white man!' The incident echoes Alice Springs of today, where a local driver colliding with an Aboriginal pedestrian might not stop to help for fear of a violent confrontation with relatives (often fuelled by alcohol).[15]

Tensions mount further inside the roadhouse, where the proprietor (also named Bruce) had made his money selling fortified wine to Aboriginals until a change in licensing laws. He tells a drinker at the bar of his relief in having bought 'a place in Queensland where you could still call a Boong a Boong'.

In contrast, Arkady indicates he likes Aboriginals, even learned a couple of their languages and came away 'astonished by their intellectual vigour, their feats of memory and their capacity and will to survive'. 'They were not,' he insists, 'a dying race.' Even so, he also admits to mixed feelings about the Aboriginals in his work, often having to 'defend [them] from people who dismissed them as drunken and incompetent savages', and that there were times in 'the flyblown squalor of a Walbiri camp, when he suspected they might be right'.

Arkady then recounts an anecdote about Mike, owner Bruce's former barman. On the spirits shelf at the roadhouse had been 'an old bottle with yellow liquid and labelled: "Authentic NT Gin Piss".'[16] In Arkady's story, four Pintupi boys had stopped to get fuel and a drink, when one of them became offended by the 'Gin Piss' bottle. The lad said something abusive, was refused service, and violence ensued. The boy aimed a beer glass at the offending bottle and missed, but Mike retrieved owner Bruce's .22 calibre rifle from under the bar and fired above the boy's heads.

'That, at any rate,' said Arkady, 'is what Mike said at the trial.' The reality was 'the first shot hit the kid through the base of the skull. The second shot hit the wall ... a third ... went into the ceiling'.

To raise funds for Mike's defence, locals had staged a 'gala with a topless show from Adelaide'. The verdict was self-defence; for cultural reasons no Aboriginal witnesses had testified. Prefacing this extraordinary exchange, however, an engineer at the bar had expressed his distaste when his half-caste mate was refused service. Here again was a frontier not linear, but sporadic and confused. Indeed, Chatwin's cultural divide seems to manifest when least expected, perhaps in the comment of a fellow drinker: 'know the best thing to do with a sacred site? ... dynamite!'

Then, without warning, Chatwin once again cleaves to Romanticism, describing that from what he knew of the songlines 'the whole of Classical mythology might represent ... a gigantic song-map: ... the to-ing and fro-ing of gods and goddesses, the caves and sacred springs ... could be interpreted [as] totemic geography'. Later, when an Aboriginal man named Joshua traced a songline in the sand, however, Bruce has trouble understanding. Until he realises: 'this was a Qantas Dreaming. Joshua had once flown into London'.

The frontier is a confusing place, Chatwin seems to say, where misunderstandings are clearly evident, but it is also more of a transition zone, a crucible of change, than any clear-cut cultural divide.

Later, around a campfire and having finally reached Middle Bore, the group hear more stories of the frontier. Bruce and Arkady find Alan, a 'kaititj' elder who once watched his father and brothers gunned down by police. But Alan knows the story of the Lizard Ancestor, a Dreaming story of the site that is remarkably similar to Tommy Thompson's 'A Man from the Dreamtime'. Once again, in Alan's story there emerges the 'geography of survival', when 'the lizard and his lovely young wife ... walked from northern Australia to the Southern Sea, and of how a southerner ... seduced his wife and sent him home with a substitute'. In summary form like this, the Kaytetye story closely mirrors Thompson's, and contains much Aboriginal culture, even though, as Arkady later tells Bruce, it is a 'false front, or sketch performed for strangers'.

'The real song would have named each waterhole the Lizard Man drank from, each tree he cut a spear from, each cave he slept in, covering the whole long distance of the way.'

Nonetheless, the frontier remains close, for Arkady worries the railway might destroy 'the eternal resting place of a Lizard Ancestor'.

Importantly for his quest, Bruce witnesses Alan's animated performance of the story, gleaning that 'certain phrases, certain combinations of musical notes are thought to describe the action of the ancestor's feet'.

'So a musical phrase', [Bruce] said, 'is a map reference?'

'Music,' said Arkady, 'is a memory bank for finding one's way around the world.'

Following this epiphany, Bruce recalls an interview with Austrian zoologist, Nobel Prize winner and prominent Nazi sympathiser Konrad Lorenz, in which he and Chatwin discussed Lorenz's theory of aggression as a natural trait. During the fictionalised discussion, Bruce is given to understand particular geographies as being the 'home' of Aboriginals. His conclusion is clear: that white men are seriously mistaken to assume that 'because the aboriginals were Wanderers, they could have no system of land tenure'. Bruce has already learned this from Father Flynn back in Alice Springs, that 'Aboriginals … could not imagine territory as a block of land hemmed in by frontiers: but rather as an interlocking network of "lines" or "ways through"'.

For all the criticism of *The Songlines* for its apparent Romanticism, its depiction of Aboriginal walking is not the idyllic wandering or reverie of Thoreau, Chatwin, nor any other Romantic writer or walker. Rather, order, structure and observance of Law are core to the Aboriginals' socially binding endeavour, as depicted in Thompson's Dreaming narrative (and Alan's). At the heart of such storytelling is survival in an arid environment. Also, as Bruce learned in an earlier conversation, the trade route is the songline: 'Because songs, not things, are the principal medium of exchange. Trading in "things" is the secondary consequence of trading in song'.

Western translation of Aboriginal walking business as 'walkabout' suggests a random, inexplicable act, incomprehensible to Westerners. From *The Songlines*, however, the reader gleans a more serious business afoot, of attending to ritual and observance of an underpinning Law that relates self to land and movement across it at specified intervals.

At the party in Alice Springs, Father Flynn had explained how the elders of a carpet snake clan might sing their song cycle from beginning to end. Messages would be sent up and down the track, summoning owners to assemble at a 'Big Place'. One after the other, each 'owner' would sing his stretch of the Ancestor's footprints, always in correct sequence.

> 'To sing a verse out of order,' Flynn said sombrely, 'was a crime. Usually meant the death penalty.'
> 'I can see that,' [Bruce] said. 'You'd be the musical equivalent of an earthquake.'
> 'Worse,' he scowled. 'It would be to un-create the Creation.'

In other words, the Law and the land and the ceremonial act of walking the songlines are intimately bound up in a sophisticated culture of placemaking. But the pillar of Chatwin's grand theory of walking—a role for language—remains still out of reach. In fact it is not clarified until near the end of the book, when at Cullen Bruce remarks of the ethnobotanist, Wendy, that 'she was beginning to wonder whether language itself might not relate to the distribution of a different species over the land'. Later Bruce asks Wendy: 'You're saying that man "makes" his territory by naming the "things" in it?' To which Wendy replies: 'Yes, I am.'

For Arkady and Bruce, meanwhile, word arrives that Jim Hanlon is ill. The pair return to Glen Armond, then press on to Popanji police station and the remote community of Cullen.

~

At Cullen it begins to rain. All the roads to Alice Springs are closed, but a plane is able to set down in the muddy conditions to pick up Arkady. He will be away for ten days on rail business, leaving Bruce to explore his moleskin notebooks. Here, finally, is the controversial Notebooks section, about which editor Susannah Clapp was concerned: 'the narrative of the book comes apart and is never put back together again in an entirely satisfactory way'.[17] But eventually the narrative does pick up once more, as Bruce goes first hunting, and then for a walk up nearby Mount Liebler.

With two extra bottles of water foisted on him by host Rolf (Rob Novak), Bruce walks towards the mountain, 'over a plateau of sandhills and crumbly red rock, broken by gulches that were difficult to cross'. As he walks, Bruce notices 'the bushes had been burnt for game drives', and 'bright green shoots were sprouting from the stumps'. The reference is to the Aboriginal practice of patch burning, which drives small game on the hunt and spurs new growth for bush tucker. Farther on he looks down at the plain: 'I understood why Aboriginals choose to paint their land in "pointillist" dots. The land was dotted'. And in a nod to the pioneers: 'I understood too, better than ever, what Lawrence meant by the "peculiar, lost weary aloofness of Australia".'[18]

On the far side of a chasm, Bruce finds old Alex 'naked, his spears along the ground and his velvet coat wrapped in a bundle'. They both nod, and Bruce asks Alex what brought him here. 'Footwalking all the time all over the world,' the old man replies.

Soon after, resting spreadeagled under a tree trunk, Bruce swigs greedily from his water bottle, deciding it would be 'madness to go on' in the hot conditions. He turns to go back, 'sweat pouring over his eyelids so that everything seemed blurred', but is stopped by a 'seven feet long' monitor lizard, 'the lord of the mountain, Perenty himself'. Chatwin uses the moment to explore the role of beasts in Aboriginal lore, the megafauna of long past, finally turning briefly to a role for violence in Aboriginal culture. Then crossing a stream he encounters a king-brown snake, whereupon 'I put my legs in reverse and drew back, very slowly'.

Climbing another slope, and after having clambered up an escarpment, Chatwin emerges onto 'a knife edge of rock'.

'It really did look like the perenty lizard's tail', he writes, referencing the Lizard Dreaming that embraces the hill.

When Bruce finally does alight from his four-wheel drive in *The Songlines*, the effects of walking are pronounced, and in just the way that French philosopher Michel de Certeau suggests: that steps in a walk are akin to lines on a page. Ways of seeing a landscape are culturally constructed. But while everyone sees a landscape differently, Chatwin renders the hill's totemic significance for Aboriginals momentarily visible.

The walk has become an entertaining deconstruction of a 'desert palimpsest', where walking and the words resulting from the walk are closely linked, the walk fusing the prose and the place into 'a unified tale of belonging'. And punctuation helps the story's oral delivery, showing the narrator where to pause for breath, every step a sounded word, or silent inhalation, perhaps even betraying the roots of punctuation itself.

Chatwin's descriptions of walking and his encounters with others get past the disorder and squalor of Aboriginal camps to focus on people and their lives. Here is a 'moral geography' through which one might 'see through to the real', to 'variety and complexity' rather than the simple binary of difference, of black and white, the frontier.[19]

And so, through walking itself, Bruce finally reaches the end of his quest and is able to assemble the three legs of his theory: landscape, language and walking. He describes 'a vision of the Songlines stretching right across the continents and ages'. Wherever humans have trod this path, Bruce surmises, they leave a 'trail of song' reaching back 'to an isolated pocket of the African savannah, where the First Man opening his mouth in defiance of the terrors that surrounded him, shouted the opening stanza of the World Song, "I AM!"'

In Bruce's appraisal, Man conquers his fear of space through language and makes place through being, movement and naming, the act of dwelling. Echoing his earlier reimagining of the Genesis story, Bruce turns to Adam and Eve, so that Adam 'puts a left foot forward and names a flower. He puts a right foot forward and names a stone'. It is clear now that in Bruce's restless childhood self the answer was apparent all along, there just as clearly in the Anglo-Saxon roots of his surname and an identity wherein poetry, his name and the road were all connected.

To walk is to possess the key to unlocking Chatwin's own restlessness. Bruce relates walking to language only to discover that 'The verb carries him to the next stanza of the song'. By such a measure, humanity is doomed to restlessness, forward motion being the only means by which one may come to know a place. Any existence caught somewhere between restlessness and home is, however, not for Bruce, who navigates by triangulation using his holy trinity of language, walking and landscape. And so, through the tripartite of grammar: subject–object–verb, he saves humanity from the void in a poignant final scene that completes the circle.

At Palm Valley Bruce walks towards three Aboriginal men in the bush. Each man is lying outdoors on a hospital bed with no mattress, content with impending death. In a letter to British travel writer Patrick Leigh Fermor and his wife Joan, Chatwin once wrote that 'Aborigines, when they feel death close, will make a kind of pilgrimage (sometimes a distance of thousands of miles) back to their conception site; their centre, the place where they belong'. These men have followed the same specific rules of Aboriginal Australia, to return to their conception place, to where their 'tjurunga is stored'. The three men are almost skeletons, their beards and hair gone. But they were all right, Bruce muses, finally understanding: 'They knew where they were going, smiling at death in the shade of a ghost gum'.[20]

~

As he himself lay dying, Chatwin asked friend and documentary film-maker Werner Herzog to carry his pack for him. Chatwin, clearly, was obsessed with walking as metaphor, and his request speaks pointedly to the death scene of *The Songlines*. In the final scene Bruce comes full circle from restlessness through journey to a witnessing of home. His longing for home is resolved in the search for a right place and a right death. Once a way of being-towards-death is found, the cycle can be complete.

Chatwin's humanist portrayal of Central Australia and its people softens the frontier, a representation that had hardened considerably during the Menzies era in texts such as Groom's *I Saw a Strange Land*. Part of the fabric of a precolonial home for Aboriginals in Central Australia and elsewhere, the Dreaming tracks had been studied by anthropologists and retraced by the young Theo Strehlow and others. But the songlines had, nonetheless, disappeared from public view for settler Australians, hidden under changing perceptions of Nature, the wilderness of Arthur Groom's imagining, and amid the widespread confusion generated by the term 'walkabout'.

In *The Songlines*, we are reminded that Australia is a living cultural landscape, where in Aboriginal belief 'an unsung land is a dead land'. Here, if the songs are forgotten 'the land itself will die'. In an arid landscape where rainfall is patchy, movement is vital, and it is perhaps a truism of the Australian landscape, then, to say that 'to stay in one place [is] suicide', while to feel at home in such a country depends also on being able to leave it. With help from Chatwin's text, the songlines resurfaced in the public sphere during the Land Rights era, and the Aboriginal Dreaming tracks emerged as a symbol of the relationship between journeying and placemaking, a populist echo of the free-wheeling travel habits of the hippy generation. Perceptions of Central Australia thereby shifted from the adventure playground of Groom to make way for the political battleground the region has become.

Throughout Bruce's quest, walking helps envision a crossroads between European journeys and the Aboriginal songlines, both of which are tracings of a human existence. This is the central significance of Chatwin's text, a humanist comparison between Aboriginal and settler Australians. The right way to live is with eyes firmly fixed on death, a guide for the journey common to both groups. Only in death may be found a belonging properly oriented towards the ultimate destination: home.

6

HOGAN

It was a Saturday afternoon, summer 2007, when Fiona called for a lift from the Alice Springs pool. For a small town in the desert, the pool is well equipped. Sited in the Gap district just south of the CBD, it's also handy and we do laps there most days. When I arrived, however, something was amiss. Outside the pool entry gate, Fiona sat on the footpath with a middle-aged Aboriginal woman, both of them cross-legged.

'She wants to be taken to hospital,' Fiona said.

A glance at my watch told me we'd have to be quick; it wasn't long until I had to pick up my daughter. I asked the woman her name.

'Rosie,' she said, gazing at the concrete. I told her everything would be OK, and knelt next to her: 'What's wrong Rosie?'

'Sick,' Rosie said. She looked up then, nodding at her left side. 'Bastard stab me.'

'Who?' I asked.

'Husband.'

'Your husband?'

'Daughter's. Wouldn't give money for grog.'

I placed my hand gently to her shoulder: 'Where did he stab you?'

With her right hand Rosie lifted her T-shirt, and with the other cupped and lifted her left breast. There, marking the expanse of brown skin over her ribs, were two neat slits. Each was at least 2 centimetres

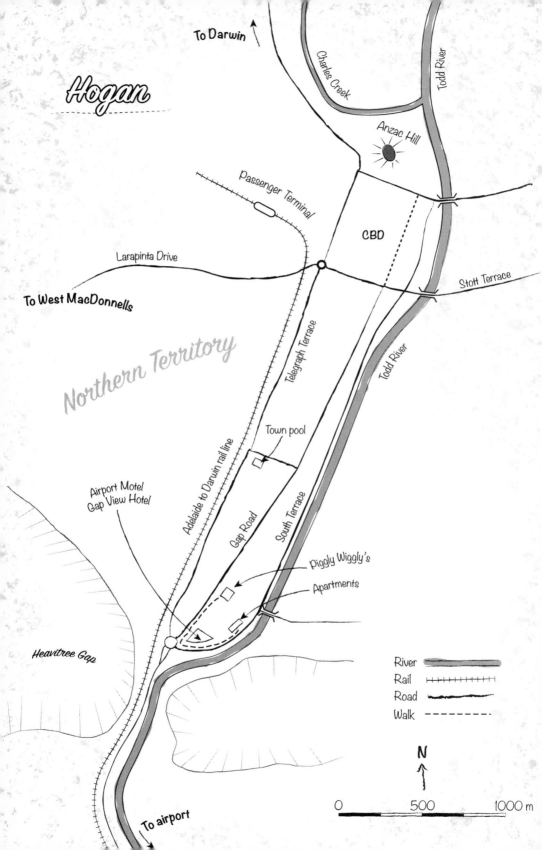

long. Blood stained Rosie's stomach, but thankfully the wounds had stopped bleeding. I phoned triple-0 to tell them a woman had been stabbed.

'It could be a while love,' came the answer. 'There's a bit on just now; is she still bleeding?'

I looked at Rosie then at my wife. To be honest, I was a bit thrown by the response. Surely a stab wound was important? Admittedly, Rosie was breathing fine. And no, she wasn't bleeding. But still.

I told the woman on the phone Rosie seemed OK, for now. And that she actually seemed relatively comfortable where she was. Rather than risk disturbing the wound by taking her to hospital—only two blocks away—Fiona and I decided we would wait with her for the ambulance. When they arrived about twenty minutes later, the paramedics couldn't have been kinder.[1]

It was around the same time that the chief surgeon at the Alice Springs Hospital, Dr Jacob Jacobs, published statistics for the number of stab wounds treated by medicos there. Between 1998 and 2005 the hospital logged 1500 admissions for stab wounds, 605 of them Aboriginals, and sixteen of those dead on arrival. Published in the *ANZ Journal of Surgery*, mainstream media soon picked up on the findings.

In July 2007, the ABC's *Lateline* revealed 'disturbing stabbing figures' had surfaced in Alice Springs. In March the following year, the Brisbane *Courier Mail* cited the same figures, adding that almost 40 per cent of the stabbings were thigh injuries, 'most likely meted out by Aboriginal elders as traditional punishment'. Headlines dubbed Alice Springs the 'world's stabbing capital'.

The tag stuck. By December of 2008, Natasha Robinson for *The Australian* was reporting that T-shirts were being sold in the town 'that are no joke: Alice Springs—Stabbing Capital of the World'.

The problem with Robinson's report and others like it was that they told an incomplete story: back in April 2008, Dr Jacobs had reported to the ABC that stabbings treated at Alice Springs hospital had halved since his previous report. In the same interview, Dr John Boffa of the Alice Springs People's Alcohol Action Coalition pointed to alcohol restrictions and a 10 per cent reduction in the consumption of pure alcohol as being responsible for the improvement. Nevertheless, to the rest of Australia and international observers, Alice Springs remained 'the stabbing capital'.

The label came hard on the heels of Alice Springs Crown Prosecutor Nanette Rogers' horrific revelations of widespread sexual abuse and violence against Aboriginal children and babies, broadcast—again on *Lateline*—on 15 May 2006. Many would later conclude that Rogers' interview was what sparked the momentous government actions that came next. It was certainly a catalyst. But while her report came as a shock to the rest of Australia, it was old news to Territorians. News outlets had reported on such matters for years, but rarely did their reports gain traction in national or interstate media.

Nonetheless, prompted by the ABC report, on 8 August 2006, Clare Martin, Chief Minister of the Northern Territory, commissioned an investigation by the Northern Territory Board of Inquiry into the Protection of Aboriginal Children from Sexual Abuse. The inquiry was headed by Rex Wild QC, the recently retired Northern Territory Director of Public Prosecutions, and the prominent Aboriginal leader Pat Anderson. A year earlier, Wild had presided over the conviction of Broome diesel mechanic Bradley John Murdoch for the murder of British backpacker Peter Falconio.

The inquiry took eight months, the board finally making public its report entitled *Ampe Akelyernemane Meke Mekarle*: 'Little Children are Sacred' on 15 June 2007. Amid some intense politics between federal and territory tiers of government, the Martin Labor Government was accused of sitting on the report, which it had received some six weeks earlier on 30 April 2007.

With a tough federal election battle looming for the conservatives, it was in Prime Minister John Howard's interests to act politically, and so he decided it was time to step in.[2] Less than a week after the report's release, on 21 June 2007, the federal government launched a 'national emergency response to protect Aboriginal children in the Northern Territory from sexual abuse and family violence'.

The plan had bipartisan support for a range of measures under a five-year timeframe to be applied mainly to remote communities in the Northern Territory. These measures included more police and military personnel, restrictions on alcohol and pornography, compulsory health checks for children, new housing construction, and welfare income management.

A week later, troops from the Australian Army moved into Alice Springs, from where they fanned out to several remote settlements. A six-month ban on alcohol was immediately enforced, even though public drinking had already been banned in Alice Springs the previous month. Doctors and other health workers with no experience of the region or its challenges were flown in. Locals already working in the field protested the move, pleading that existing programs were working but needed more consistent funding, and that change would take time. The day the army arrived, however, Mal Brough, the Minister for Indigenous Affairs, told the Melbourne *Herald Sun*—with sound-bite precision—that 'a 20-year plan is not going to cut the mustard for the children that are going to get hurt tonight'.[3]

From the start, confusion reigned on remote communities and in the Alice Springs town camps. For example, Conrad Wiseman, the chairman of Ilparpa Town Camp south of the Heavitree Gap, told me: 'We haven't heard anything about [the plan]. That's [only] for the bush communities'. It wasn't. As it turned out, Intervention legislation was amended early in 2008 to include them.

Wiseman was equally unaware of plans to halve all Centrelink payments to guarantee the money was used for essential supplies such as food. When income management and the Centrelink Basics card were introduced to inhibit the sale of alcohol, tobacco and pornography, many shops—and particularly bush stores on remote communities—were unable to use the system. The result was an outpouring of Aboriginal people from remote settlements and into Alice Springs, where they could use their Basics card at Woolworths or Coles. Very few people, including Aboriginals themselves and those already working in Indigenous welfare and support, had any idea of exactly what might happen next. As Australian Army trucks dragged clouds of red dust towards remote communities, some Aboriginal women hid their children, for fear they might be 'stolen'.

Four years earlier, Melbourne writer Eleanor Hogan arrived in Alice Springs to work as an Indigenous policy specialist. As she flew over an 'ocean of burnt earth' towards her destination, she felt a sense of exhilaration and was swiftly 'seduced by the landscape'. Previously Hogan had worked in what she called the 'Aboriginal industry' on the east coast, and it was partly her research there that led her to the Red Centre for more information about 'issues such as petrol sniffing, family violence and income management in remote areas'. Soon enough, however, she found herself involved in the life of the town, joined the cycling club and became intrigued by the many 'conundrums and paradoxes' the region displayed. In a later interview she would call the town a 'meeting place of battlers, blackfellas and do-gooder urban types such as myself'.

'If you're an urban professional', says Hogan, 'you often have a better quality of life than you would in your home town, but find yourself slap bang up against indigenous disenfranchisement, the schism the nation is built on'.[4]

By 2010, however, Hogan had left for Melbourne, weary after 'being confronted regularly by basic human need' in a town of 'too much extremity'. In this respect, there is little to separate Hogan from the town's traditionally transient population, where people stay for several years then move on—statistics register roughly a 30 per cent annual churn.

Even so, it wasn't long before Hogan published a memoir of her time in the Centre, *Alice Springs* (2012). The book tries to take the town's measure for the publisher's *Cities* series, which commissioned prominent authors to write about their homes. Launched while the Intervention was still in effect (though it was already morphing into various other policy platforms), the book blends political geography and memoir to narrate the town using a variety of methods, including a walk.

The book opens at Hogan's office in the town's CBD 'in a small, subdivided house, a converted butcher's shopfront near the Gap', not all that far from the town pool. Here Hogan worked as a policy officer for an Aboriginal Health Service in a location she compares with New York's Bronx or Sydney's Redfern.

Outside on the streets there are 'splashes of broken glass' and 'trails of blood', which for Hogan serve to trace out a history of Indigenous dispossession. 'Disembowelled tawny port casks' scud about, as a 'stubby holder from the local escort service' tumbles across the street along with used condoms. Even a disposable nappy sees its way clear to begin 'wrapping itself around my ankle like a giant kelp' one morning as she walks to work.

Soon a group of Aboriginal girls troops into Hogan's office, 'all gorgeous'. The girls have 'huge brown eyes, wide smiles and long, slender limbs', and although they are dressed in 'grubby sportswear topped off with rough-edged, home-styled haircuts', they possess a 'lanky, model-like quality'. Hogan wonders what will happen to the girls, when 'so many teenagers end up pregnant out here, or worse, infertile from sexually transmitted diseases by their mid-twenties, or the victims of family violence'.

Tragically bearing out Hogan's concern, within three months one of the girls was dead. As journalist Kieran Finnane had reported for *Alice Springs News*, this was 'J. Ryan, who died in January 2006, having been assaulted and raped by other young Aboriginal people and left for dead by the side of Grevillea Drive', in front of a local high school.[5] These introductory passages of the book are gripping, and announce Hogan as an eloquent storyteller.

But as Finnane observes in a review of the book, while the girl's death was terrible, Hogan's anecdote prompts no analysis other than to highlight how 'white middle-class residents [have] become inured to Aboriginal violence'.[6] Indeed, the scene signifies the beginning of a frontier thematic that pervades the remainder of the book, during which Hogan remains similarly at arm's length from her subject. The result is a telling and succinct account of the town's challenges from drinking and Aboriginal violence. But it lacks important context. The book's dust jacket declares 'this is where the real world ends', and in *Alice Springs* we find just that: a line in the sand marking the end of the real world and the start of a mythical one, the Australian Outback. But the Outback is also a myth-maker and an important shaper of national identity. And so *Alice Springs* marks a return to the frontier.

It is difficult to separate Hogan's book from the political moment in which it was born. The Intervention had a profound impact on life in Central Australia during the period Hogan spent living there, with changes widely documented in the Australian and international press. And Intervention policies and actions would later provide much impetus and material for her writing. Media reporting of the federal Intervention tended, however, to polarise remote Indigenous issues, and, as Hogan herself says elsewhere, proffered 'only simplistic solutions for a situation not amenable to simple solutions'.

Alice Springs reveals at least two levels at which people's lives are being conducted in the town, and relies heavily on frontier representations to do so. Implied, but largely unexplored, are many more imagined spaces in a more complex political geography than the term frontier can adequately explain. Periodically throughout the book, Hogan takes to the streets where she notes ideas, observations and encounters, emulating the *flâneur*, who, according to the *Oxford Dictionary*, is one who 'saunters around observing society'.

In the second chapter of *Alice Springs*, entitled 'The Gap', for example, Hogan ventures from her CBD apartment on a shopping errand and encounters Aboriginal people along the way. Two types of journey are performed: one a rambling stroll spent in conversation with people she meets or writing down her thoughts and observations, around which Hogan hangs a second journey, a first-person traversal of a political geography of 'grog'.

With the conceit for her walk established, memoir is mixed with journalism for an ongoing discussion of the hotly contested politics of alcohol in the Centre, as well as a historic and cultural positioning of the town of Alice Springs.[7] In this respect her walking might be compared with the rambling of lawyer Raja Shehadeh in the hills around his home in *Palestinian Walks*, in which he uses 'each meandering walk to amble no less circuitously around received ideas about the region'. Another is *Street Haunting* by Virginia Woolf, where on the pretext of buying a pencil the author steps from her house on a fine evening for a walk of London's streets. In the act of leaving home, Woolf sheds her known self, the character her friends know her as and 'the shell-like covering which our souls have excreted to house themselves'. With such a cloak stripped back and broken, nought remains but 'a central oyster of perceptiveness, an enormous eye'.

~

Curious to know 'why so many Aboriginal people are in the Gap Area this weekend', Hogan sets out one Sunday to walk to Piggly Wiggly's, an independent grocery store catering to a largely Aboriginal clientele. During her time in Alice Springs, Hogan lived in a secure apartment complex near the CBD, not far from the Todd riverbed, where groups of Aboriginal people would commonly drink.

Like the Ancestors Marlpwenge and Nalenale in 'A Man from the Dreamtime' (but with significantly different motivations), upon leaving home Hogan notes encounters and objects of place she passes on her walk. As she does so, she introduces elements of a popular political discourse: that a cyclone security fence surrounds her home, which some call 'the compound'; that there are troubling statistics for the number of murders in her area; and that much of this reported violence is 'black-on-black'.

Hogan's construction nervously queries her safety, serving not only to recount the town and its mood, but also to lend a degree of bravado to her self-protagonist. While she has heard of residents waking to find an Aboriginal man standing over their bed, luckily, she has only experienced 'one petty break-in' herself. Hogan uses her relative safety to characterise the difference between the lives of black and white populations of the town.

Aboriginal people are Hogan's focus on this walk and throughout the book. Few white people appear in her rendering of the suburb known as the Gap or elsewhere, though whites form 79 per cent of the town's population. Like other walking writers, Hogan mentally collects the objects she sees and arranges them in order on the walk, using them as portals through which to view issues or interesting anecdotes, jumping-off points to expand, discuss and analyse her point of view.

It is not a long walk from Hogan's house to Piggly Wiggly's, but she takes the long way round via Heavitree Gap, the southernmost entrance to the town and its most central suburbs. On the way to the Gap, Hogan

spies a police troop carrier as it 'grinds around' in the sand among the
gums of the riverbed. The driver parks the vehicle and 'a couple of cops
jump out', who just as swiftly disappear into 'the shrubbery'. Hogan
suggests the cops 'might be checking on people or looking for stashes of
grog or other signs of illicit drinking'.

Sighting the police vehicle in the river allows Hogan to turn her
attention to the broader intent for the walk, the politics of alcohol in a
frontier town. In the chapter called 'The Gap', there is little discussion
of walking itself and, in contrast to Shehadeh, Woolf and other walking writers, Hogan's 'self' rarely makes an appearance. Hogan is not the
Romantic solitary walker of Hazlitt, or even Rousseau whose 'senses are
possessed by a deep and delightful reverie'. Indeed, she may have abandoned such notions for pragmatic reasons: the price of any Romantic
sojourns being a weaker connection with matters political.

In the walking segments of *Alice Springs*, Hogan's role is urban
detective in the manner of the *flâneur*, poised for social encounter.
Though the concept of the *flâneur* dates to the sixteenth or seventeenth
century, Edgar Allan Poe's *The Man of the Crowd*, published in 1840,
marks the first literary appearance of the detached observer, a solitary
walker who observes and records the emergence and evolution of the
modern city.

Poe's story begins in a London coffee-house, where his protagonist
catches sight of a 'decrepit old man, some sixty-five or seventy years of
age', causing him to rise, and, 'seizing hat and cane', make his way to the
street, where he 'pushed through the crowd in the direction which I had
seen him take'. So begins a narrative chase, which weaves its way across
the city in pursuit of the old man. Poe's character ultimately catches his
quarry but fails to 'read' the face into which he stares. A metaphor for the
city he has just walked, it is a face that '*lasst sich nicht lesen*', or does not
permit itself to be read, reflecting the increasingly unfathomable nature
of the modern city with its crowds of strangers and heightened throng.

The *flâneur* of Charles Baudelaire was similarly a 'passionate spec-
tator' of his environment, but was also by turns a 'popular journalist,
urban reporter, caricaturist and story teller'. The *flâneur* would 'read'
the city as one would read a text, an idea implied by Poe, but most com-
pellingly described much later by Michel de Certeau, who suggested

the act of walking was to a network of city streets as speech is to the language spoken.

But the tale of the *flâneur*—and the clue to Hogan's literary construction—does not finish there, for one of the great scholars of walking and cities, Walter Benjamin, added a political dimension to ideas of wandering the urban environment, elements of which are clearly evident in Hogan's walks. Adopting a more 'subversive' stance, Benjamin's *flâneur* uses a street position to protest the pace of the city and the impact of modernity. Benjamin referred to such strolling as 'botanising on the asphalt', encouraging any would-be *flâneur* to become lost in the city where progress, he suggests, should be slowed to the pace of a turtle being walked in the Parisian arcades, which, apparently, was briefly fashionable around 1840.

Hogan's walks are similarly polemical, and so her choice as to which objects and encounters to include in the recounted walk remains paramount. For Hogan's gaze, the intent she brings to the walk, determines the nature of the story being told. Again, by way of example, contemporary British walking writer Iain Sinclair—who, incidentally, describes himself as a 'born-again' *flâneur*, interested in 'noticing everything'—argues that what he passes on the path is not as important as what he chooses to record. For it is only what Sinclair records that we see in his prose.

In the first of nine walks of London recounted in *Lights Out for the Territory* (1991), Sinclair traverses the streets and back alleys of his route in a bid to record its graffiti, the resulting narrative being 'serial composition: the city is the subject, a fiction that anyone can lay claim to'. For Sinclair, the graffiti of the city emerges as a reliable alternative to reading the newspapers; reading tags, he says, is akin to reading one layer of the urban environment.

The resulting prose is overtly political, lying as it does at the intersection of Sinclair's self and the path he walks. His tracing is a locus of points describing the arc of the places where his mind and memory meet the environment. The narrative becomes the sum of his interests and background multiplied by the objects he sees, the answer writ large on the blackboard of his politics. The effect might be compared, in fact, to the intent of an early Australian explorer, for whom the country so often emerged as the offspring of his intention.

The same applies to Hogan. Like Sinclair reading the tags, Hogan traces one layer of Alice Springs, and in doing so traces the psychology of her self-narrator against the background of the town, a factor central to any understanding of the narrative as non-fiction. So while Hogan suggests early in the book that she hoped to 'move past the polarities of political debate and media perceptions of Alice Springs', instead she frequently focuses on them directly. Hogan compares Alice Springs with the east coast, thereby infusing the text with a strangeness that serves only to deepen its frontier representation.

As Hogan continues on towards Heavitree Gap, she notes 'dark figures' in the river bed drifting between the trees towards a picnic area. Though there is little to indicate it today, for Arrernte the area is sacred, where only men were allowed to go. Traditionally, Hogan tells us, 'women made a detour 30 kilometres west down through Honeymoon Gap, another deep orange slit in the ranges, because of the presence of men's sacred objects at Heavitree Gap'.

Were a woman to pass through the Gap, it would be in the footsteps of the men. The woman's head would be bowed, eyes fixed on her feet. Indeed, as Hogan tells us, some women who walk this way still 'avert their gaze out of respect in the area'. While we are transported momentarily to precolonial times, this experience fails to illuminate satisfactorily. Unlike Bruce Chatwin or T.G.H. Strehlow, who might have explored an open version of a Dreaming narrative or consulted an elder or anthropologist, Hogan does not. As readers, we remain uninformed as to the context for this cultural belief.

In fact, such sacred objects are *tjurunga*, and were once held in a *tjurunga* cave, or *mukka mukka*, at nearby Heavitree Gap, where secret-sacred objects were stored and guarded. Such objects and their associated knowledge are intrinsic to Aboriginal culture in a very pragmatic way, playing their part in traditional story and representing Law and authority to those instructed in their use. The objects were suitable to be seen only by initiated members of a tribe and, normally, carefully hidden from women and the uninitiated.

Unfortunately, many such objects were either stolen by thieves or collected by anthropologists early in the twentieth century for exhibit in museums. Some caves were destroyed, for example in the widening of Heavitree Gap to accommodate a railway line and roadway. Other secret-sacred objects have been retrieved, some were entrusted to whites for safekeeping, such as to T.G.H. Strehlow, who was given secret-sacred materials now stored securely at the Strehlow Research Centre in Alice Springs. Others are still to be unearthed and repatriated to the centre from private collections and museums across the globe. Many others are lost.

The importance of these items to Aboriginal people, the knowledge and Law associated with them, and their safekeeping in Central Australia, cannot be overstated. For it is the knowledge and authority they represent, more than the actual objects themselves, that is so important. Arrernte man Shaun Angeles, repatriation officer at the Strehlow Research Centre, told me in 2016: 'All these special treasures that left this place; that's the reason why Aboriginal men are struggling now'.[8]

Hogan's skirting of Aboriginal cultural matters leaves us none the wiser on this important issue and others. In an interview at Melbourne's Wheeler Centre, Hogan explains: 'I felt it would be inappropriate for me to cover'. The decision reflects and highlights a divisive argument over the right of settler authors to speak on behalf of or even about Aboriginal culture. It also raises a broader question of how anyone might adequately write postcolonial places if they are to follow the argument to its logical conclusion.

Cultural researcher Christine Morris argues non-Indigenous writers should refrain from 'anything that comes under customary law or depicts our basic worldview and values'.[9] One such example could be giving any 'deeper' explanation of conditions at Heavitree Gap. Morris rules as admissible, however, any 'issues involving interactions between blacks and whites', which is, generally speaking, the path taken in *Alice Springs*. Her view seems predicated on a belief that Aboriginal culture is completely separate from non-Aboriginal culture and that the non-Aboriginal writer can therefore write only about where the two supposedly separate cultures intersect.

Imagining the cultures as completely separate—given, of course, that this was once the case—has advantages, including fostering the emergence of Aboriginal writers and the promotion of Aboriginal role models in the field. But it nevertheless reproduces a frontier. And the fraught result, if one culture is forbidden to write about the beliefs of another, is to leave both settler and Aboriginal writers ill-equipped to articulate what is an increasingly interwoven sense of place in Central Australia and elsewhere.

For Hogan, the decision results in a hollowing absence of traditional relationships to place, relationships that persist today in the day-to-day lives of the Centre's Aboriginal population. If such ideas had been included, they might have provided a balance to the various challenges that are highlighted, such as the inequality wrought by colonial expansionism, local profiteering from alcohol, its over-consumption in some quarters and the violence that results. Ironically, by concentrating so directly on the problems and not giving context, *Alice Springs* offers several competing representations of Aboriginal people all of its own.[10]

~

At Heavitree Gap, Hogan counts off the layers of modern infrastructure that now top-dress the precolonial world: the Ghan railway line, a five-way roundabout and highway, a dry riverbed where once flowed a 'spring', and finally The Gap View Hotel. The effect is to juxtapose momentarily the past with the present, emphasising the significant impact of colonisation on Aboriginal lives.

Hogan aligns herself with the political underdog, the dispossessed; she is on their territory. Earlier, however, she had described Aboriginal people making their way down the Todd Mall as 'shoals of disconsolate fish'. Later, when she sits to chat with some Aboriginal people, it is in the shade of a 'dyspeptic palm'. Her conversations with Aboriginal people can be awkward, yet she clearly takes their part in her political dissection of their predicament. All of which betrays a curious imagining of self, which may well speak more broadly to the confused state of an Australian identity.

Some forty years earlier, newspaper columnist Charmian Clift assumed the role of the *flâneur* in her short travel piece *The Centre*, expressing similar uneasiness upon arriving at Alice Springs, that 'landscape of saints, mystics and madmen'. In her descriptions of Aboriginal people in the town's shopping mall, Clift observes how modernity has affected them; she protests injustice and anticipates being haunted by 'that daily frieze impasted on banks and tourist agencies and galleries and gem shops and rock shops. Patient. Waiting'. The people she sees move 'if at all, from one side of the street to the other. The women and girls squatting in ripply black silk circles around groomed trees in a groomed park. Looking on'.

Like Hogan's 'disconsolate fish', Clift's Aboriginal pedestrians are hapless outsiders, at odds with the space they inhabit, 'looking on' to the white man's world of 'groomed trees in groomed parks', modernity, and an alien world in which they seem to have little agency. 'What are the Dreaming people dreaming now?' Clift wonders.

As in Tommy Thompson's story of Marlpwenge—except that now a whitefella is the narrator—Hogan strolls the impact zone of black and white, and chronicles an Aboriginal culture grappling with modernity. But at the same time the story relates a more personal search, like Clift's, for an explanation of colonial dispossession. And while Hogan's walk reveals a culture concealed and forgotten, it fails to explain what has been lost, how Aboriginal people related to place prior to dispossession, or that many of them still do.

Meanwhile, Hogan herself slowly becomes inured to the more challenging aspects of the town, filtering out 'the sprays of glass, the trails of blood, the figure lying on the road—in an attempt to maintain some personal equilibrium'. Hogan as outsider and *flâneur* constructs Aboriginals as dysfunctional and problematic, whitefellas as racist, and the town largely by its difference from an east-coast 'normal', with Sydney and Melbourne offered up as the gold standards of civilisation. Hogan's portrait resuscitates the old differences between city and country, smoothing over any complexity of feelings and relationships in the town.[11]

Hogan's Alice Springs thereby emerges in sometimes trite terms, as if the subject of offhand observation, such as 'the place where you change your name, your hair and your sexuality', referring obliquely to the 15 per cent of the town's women who are lesbian. Here Hogan's interviews help; the source of the figure is historian Megg Kelham, who suggests Alice is a 'refuge from the constraints of corsets, stilettoes and the good-girl manners of city living'. For Kelham this contributes to the town's broad appeal, to which she adds: 'It's not a yobbo, male-dominated town. There's a cultural sophistication that doesn't happen in other inland towns'. Such moments are welcome but all too rare in *Alice Springs*, for if the purpose of the book was to take the measure of the town—the purpose of the *Cities* series being to provide the last word on Australia's cities and major settlements—it fails to reach beyond a tight focus on the more troubled quarters of the town's Aboriginal community.

A sense of home and belonging is more clearly manifest in other contemporaneous memoirs. Local artist and writer Rod Moss's *The Hard Light of Day* (2010), for instance, depicts life for Aboriginal people in the town through his personal relationships over several decades. A violent 'frontier' environment is still apparent from the text; nonetheless, Moss finds reasons to feel at home. Nowhere is this as evident as in his love for his daughter Ronja, and her acceptance by Moss's Aboriginal friends, especially the elder man Arranye.

'He regarded most of the Arrernte kids as his grandchildren', Moss writes. 'They were all little grubs living under the power of the Emily Gap Dreaming. And he related to Ronja in this way too.'

From his essay *Two Cultures Can Hold Each Other*, local writer Michael Giacometti explains Moss's achievement as the product of respect and relationships that 'develop over many years; for some it takes most of a life'. The memoir would not have revealed 'the great depth of understanding or empathy if Rod Moss had only been in Alice Springs for a year or two'.[12]

At the Heavitree Gap roundabout, Hogan peers into the rear of the Gap View Hotel, sometimes frequented by whites and where she notes 'couples and families lounge by the pool'. The impression is of a resort, but a short stroll further on she reaches a very different environment, a 'dusty tongue of dirt' where the 'familiar surf of bottle tops, VB cans, casks and silver foil bladders' ebb at her feet. Littered with beer cans and bottle tops, the place is represented as an Aboriginal world, where, under large XXXX signs, Aboriginal women linger in the driveway of the bottle-o, waiting for 'cheap take-away grog' from the shop—'small and dingy, with grimy fly strips'—where staff are 'surly and patronising towards Aboriginal people'. Here is a common enough Australian representation of the 'drunken Aborigine', indeed, a familiar sight on the streets of Alice Springs.

In a 2013 article, 'The "Right to Drink" in Alice Springs', Hogan makes a rigorous examination of the economic and health effects of excessive alcohol consumption in the Northern Territory.[13] She notes that '60 per cent of all assaults and 67 per cent of all domestic violence incidents involve alcohol, costing our community an estimated $642 million a year'. International research has shown that such intra-racial violence derives from a complex set of factors, and is widespread in Indigenous communities worldwide, not restricted only to Aboriginals and Torres Strait Islanders.

In Central Australia, anthropologist Diane Austin-Broos attributes such violence to the loss of 'a way of being' through dispossession of land and culture. Bess Price, pro-interventionist, former Territory MLA and Warlpiri woman, herself a victim of violence, speaks of a widespread confusion over the system of governing laws, and believes the only answers lie with Aboriginal people themselves. There is no doubt the violence is abhorrent. Playwright and novelist Louis Nowra visited Territory communities in 2007 and was 'sickened by the violence I saw against aboriginal women'.

'The violence, much of it fuelled by alcohol, was public and astonishingly brutal', Nowra writes in his essay *Bad Dreaming*.[14]

'Some of the women's faces ended up looking as though an incompetent butcher had conducted plastic surgery with a hammer and saw.

'The fear in the women's eyes reminded me of dogs whipped into cringing submission.'

Understandably, perhaps, and in light of such horrific violence, Hogan in the Wheeler Centre interview reflected on her time in Alice Springs to conclude 'there was a lopsided emphasis among urban elites on media representations and symbolic issues at the expense of a focus on basic need, especially in relation to social justice and difference'.

Representations are, nonetheless, often the reason why remote residents remain so ill-served by government, and are manifest, according to recent research, in their 'frequently shocking political and social circumstance and in often destructive debates that surround them'.[15] It was somewhat surprising to learn, though, that Hogan identifies herself with a growing number of critics who encourage 'a more sophisticated view [of Aboriginals] than the archetypal one of the native as perpetual victim with no hope'. Surprising because wherever the reader ventures in Alice Springs they find Aboriginal suffering, the narrative concerned largely with disadvantage.[16]

In *Alice Springs*, Australia's 'drunken Aborigine' is equated with a violent one. Yes, alcohol has been responsible for a monumental transformation of the Central Australian landscape. And the contrast between Marlpwenge, a traditional walker of the songlines, and the problem drinker waiting for a fix at the hands of profiteering publicans could not be more starkly wrought. But an unfortunate pattern emerges in *Alice Springs*, nevertheless, which foregrounds the drunk, demonises whites on their behalf and portrays blacks as victims. The result is to deepen predominant media representations of Alice Springs as a frontier.

In contrast, Land Rights and Native Title provisions have had a profoundly positive effect on the town and its people, at least by Western standards. There is, as Keiran and Mark Finnane note, the 'rise of an Aboriginal middle class ... black business and the accumulation of black capital'; such economic developments 'accompany and are frequently in tension with the main focus of Australian (Federal) Government investment in the town', which provides welfare to a large and mobile population.[17]

$$\sim$$

Further up the road Hogan meets an Aboriginal man in a red-checked flannelette shirt and a ten-gallon hat, an Alice-born stockman named Henry working from time to time on stations near the border with Western Australia. The pair is soon joined by two Aboriginal women waiting for a lift, Geraldine and Lynette. The man asks where Hogan is from, which she notes is a typical opening line for Aboriginal people.

Change for the Arrernte, from Thompson's Dreaming landscape and the world Stuart encountered on the Finke River in 1860, to the one Hogan describes, came abruptly. The passage of the Arrernte from one state to another created a great deal of tension over time between two value systems of unequal power.

Social environments as well as individuals were affected by this shift; embedded identity, the very meaning of what it is to 'be'—a 'being-ness' if you like—was twisted and redefined. Nothing demonstrates this more clearly perhaps than commonplace practices of conversation. In *Arrernte Present, Arrernte Past*, anthropologist Diane Austin-Broos compares the life of a hunter-gatherer with life in a market society: the former kin-based and emplaced, the latter characterised by the bureaucratic state, cash and commodities. Specifically, Austin-Broos compares an Arrernte person asking: 'To whom are you related?', to a non-Aboriginal person asking: 'What do you do [for a living]?'

In Hogan's rendering, however, the question remains unexplored in any meaningful way as to the differences between a place- and kinship-based culture and a profit-based one. In fact, the conversation with Henry and the two women is at times quite awkward, and at one point Hogan tells the reader as an aside: 'I don't want to deluge him with questions whitefella-style'. But here I must wonder: isn't that why she is there? Ultimately, Hogan warns the trio of the alcohol laws:

'You know you can get in trouble with the police for drinking in a public place?,' I say.

Geraldine nods.

'Does it bother you?'

She shrugs.

'I saw the police driving up and down the riverbed a little while ago.'

None of them seem fussed.

Like Marlpengwe and Nalenale in 'A Man from the Dreamtime', and the women with heads bowed as they walk through Heavitree Gap, perhaps these Aboriginal people abide by different laws of space, defined by tradition, where the old (but not necessarily fixed) ways still hold sway. For them, contemporary Australia has been superimposed over the top of these old ways. Yet the fusion of both spaces is now confused by alcohol.

None of this takes away from Hogan's highlighting of a very serious problem in Alice Springs: alcohol is pervasive in both black and white communities, and the nearby Gap View Hotel itself remains a problematic fixture in the landscape. Hogan interviews Darryl Pearce, CEO of Lhere Artepe Aboriginal corporation, a representative body for Alice Springs Native Title Holders, who elaborates further on the breadth of the alcohol problem. Specifically, he notes the difficulty the Gap View Hotel has promoting itself as a sophisticated establishment, when: 'At two o'clock closing … all the blackfellas are leaving and we're loading them into the minibus and getting the minibus to circle back through the bottle-o'.

'The hypocrisy of the town is the issue', says Pearce.

But there are problems on both sides, given that in 2010 Lhere Artepe Enterprises Pty Ltd—LAE, a company linked to native title organisation Lhere Artepe—purchased three IGA supermarkets in the town, each of which holds a liquor licence and hosts a take-away liquor outlet. The purchase was made using funds provided from the Aboriginal Benefit Account (comprising royalties earned from mining on Aboriginal lands in the Territory) and Centrecorp, an Aboriginal business advisory service that owns significant shares in local shopping centres, and other businesses in the Centre. In defending the purchase, LAE argued they would be in a better position to combat excess liquor consumption by having control of the outlets.[18]

Writer Anna Krien describes the Gap View Hotel in some detail in the essay 'Booze Territory', as one of Alice Springs' three so-called 'animal bars', a place dedicated to hard drinking by Aboriginals. Another is the Todd Tavern's 'Riverside' bar, 'complete with blackened windows creating a kind of false night for its drinkers, who chuck their empties into wheelie bins dotted around the room'.

Territorians spend between 50 and 100 per cent more per capita on alcohol than the rest of Australia. Alcohol has long been a signifier of the frontier in representations of Alice Springs, and Hogan notes a raft of laws as relevant since 1928, when a law prohibited Aboriginal people from entering 'within a two mile radius of the Governor's residency in the town's centre'.

Previously a mark of masculinity on the frontier, drinking, Hogan argues, has been rebadged as an 'Aboriginal problem'. The 1928 law was overturned in 1964, enabling Aboriginal people to purchase alcohol.

As a result, Hogan points out, local elements have exploited the situation by 'delivering liquor to town camps when its sale to Aboriginal people was first legislated and later engaging in practices such as selling high-content alcohol products at cheap prices to attract low-income heavy drinkers'.

Hogan's coverage of the region's alcohol-related woes is concise and extremely troubling. Bans on the public consumption of alcohol as well as restrictions on its sale have been variously trialled since 1984. Yet, Hogan counts seventy liquor outlets across the town, nineteen of which sell take-away grog, often alongside healthy food options like fruit and vegetables, or even in tandem with petrol at service stations. By 2005–06, Hogan notes, alcohol consumption across the whole of the Alice Springs community 'averaged 20 litres of pure alcohol per person—twice the national average and four times the planet's average'.

On her brief return to the Centre around the same time, Robyn Davidson remarks similarly that she was disillusioned at how little the town had changed over the years for Aboriginal people.

'I watched the drunks down the creek, identical to the drunks of three decades before,' she writes.[19]

Alcohol in the Centre is a problem for both settler and Aboriginal communities, yet, as Hogan rightly observes, heavy drinking in Alice Springs is represented as predominantly an Aboriginal problem. This is partly owing to its higher visibility: some Aboriginal people drink in public, in the riverbed or on pathways and in parks. Less visible are the drinking camps set up on the fringes of town, on or behind hill slopes, tucked out of sight. As Hogan argues, however, a high percentage of Aboriginal people are teetotal, particularly those who have seen first-hand the trouble alcohol can cause.

This contrast between evidence and its representation suggests that, like the settler interpretation of walkabout, the problem of 'grog' and Aboriginal drinking is at least partly a cultural construction serving to alienate Aboriginals from a European 'norm', thereby deepening the frontier. Still, as Anna Krien notes: 'No claims of high visibility can explain away certain facts'. Begging for money to buy alcohol is all too frequent, prompting Alice Springs' CBD security guards and police to encourage Aboriginal pedestrians to 'keep moving on'.

The important conclusion to draw from this complex array of highly politicised spaces is that the Aboriginal people Hogan interviews are largely ignorant of or deliberately ignoring legislated means of controlling the flow of alcohol. Perhaps this is a form of silent revolt, and maybe to be expected in a town where regulations create white space that excludes blacks—for example, where in the past dress codes prevented Aboriginals entering some clubs, certain café owners discouraged blacks from al fresco tables, and security guards patrolled shopping malls to police unruly, drunken or loud behaviour. Some of these behaviours continue.

But black spaces also prevail. Photographing or trespassing on sacred sites, for example, is forbidden by law. Visitors to town camps require a reason and permission from Tangentyere Council, the responsible managing body. Crossing some regions of Central Australia or visiting certain remote communities requires a permit issued by the Central Land Council.

When Hogan finally reaches the Gap Road Smart Mart, or Piggly Wiggly's, the footpath is full of people. They are 'sitting in clusters, facing the road. Mothers breast-feed their children. An entire family, including a baby in a stroller and a child on a pink scooter, watch the traffic come in and out of the Gap View'.

One of them, a 'granny with matted, yellowing white hair', calls out to Hogan: 'Hey, do I know you from somewhere? You got twenty dollars?'

Finding more nuanced understandings of Aboriginal people is challenging. Robyn Davidson reminds us that 'People come to the Centre hungry to learn—the town floats on the tourist dollar—but how are they to penetrate something so inherently secretive and complex?'

'How can they see past the drunks and the misery', she asks, '… to the sophistication and beauty of Aboriginal ideas?'

In *Alice Springs* we see little of Davidson's 'beauty of ideas', and much more of the 'drunks and the misery', the tragedy of dispossession and violence now so heavily researched and widely blamed on alcohol. Hogan represents an important aspect—but only one aspect—of the town's multi-stranded narrative. The tight focus contributes to a deepening of the frontier, and a distraction from representations of home or belonging.

In the contested spaces of Australia, belonging can be problematic. For instance, Australian writer Paul Newbury agonises over his own reaching for a sense of belonging 'because I do not want to be forever an immigrant in Aboriginal land'. Newbury desires what might be called a 'moral sense of belonging', one acknowledging what has gone before, the layers of the palimpsest.

And who can blame him? To put down roots, is, in the words of philosopher Simone Weil, 'perhaps the most important and least recognized need of the human soul'. The question is central to deciding exactly what might constitute an inclusive idea of home in the Centre, as opposed to the frontier of popular conception.

Some long-term Centre pastoral families, predominantly whites, feel their own strong sense of place. Ross Stanes and Jo Kesby, for example, left the city to return to Lyndavale Station, a cattle property 260 kilometres south of Alice Springs. Ross is fourth generation on Lyndavale, which the Stanes have owned since the 1920s. Ross's father, John, who runs Lyndavale, told me the family 'Obviously ... have a love for the land'.

'We try to look after country as much as possible', says John, 'low stocking rates, fairly intensive management systems ... It's something we've learned from being here a long time'.

Important to the Stanes are the journeys of their ancestors, remembered through story. This pastoral memory produces its own pastoral landscapes, which map circles of identity: personal, group and national, all yielding experience, meaning and belonging. The Stanes' sentiment is not so dissimilar to an Aboriginal sentiment for land, borne through intimate knowledge of land and family connections. In addition to a long-term practice of pastoralism, the Stanes and others share with the Centre's Indigenous people a tradition of placemaking through storytelling and journey, of droving and settlement, a tradition that is core to constructions of Australian identity.

Nonetheless, many still question the rights of settler Australians to feelings of emplacement, wondering, indeed, whether—as anthropologist David Trigger suggests—any sense of belonging they might acquire 'would be morally inferior', stuck fast in questions of 'nativeness'.[20] This line of reasoning has underpinned the call for settler authors to leave

Aboriginal culture alone, to which Hogan has duly responded. But like Bill Stanner's 'Whitefella [who] got no Dreaming'—indicating, roughly speaking, that settler Australians lack a cultural narrative with which to articulate their landscape—Hogan and her readers are left homeless.

~

At the close of her book, Hogan observes Aboriginals at work on a car in the CBD: 'I'm not exactly sure what they are doing: changing a fan belt perhaps'. This leads to a comment on Aboriginal ingenuity: 'They are *ninti*: ingenious, adaptable survivalists'. By this point Hogan has invested a great deal in representing Aboriginal people as victims, lost in the maelstrom of modernity, and the town as a divided frontier. Her more sophisticated construction of an adaptable Aboriginal comes too late.

Considered alone, and in the absence of other life-worlds of Alice Springs to temper the picture, Hogan's *Alice Springs* constructs a frontier populated by a larger-than-life contingent of Australia's drunken Aboriginals.[21] Equally misled, however, would be any reader who digests only the 'strong-in-culture' Aboriginal of 'A Man from the Dreamtime' as representative of a smoothly continuing tradition. Such an approach risks substituting one stereotype for another: the 'romanticised' Aboriginal or 'noble savage' for the 'violent drunk'. A more insightful representation might embrace both of these and many more shades of grey in between. Ignored in both of these representations, for instance, is an emerging Aboriginal middle class, conducting lives as best they can in a culturally diverse town that exists somewhere between polar extremes, where Indigenous and non-Indigenous are, as Bruce Kapferer writes, 'enmeshed in interpenetrating social worlds'.[22] In such a town, for better or worse, both cultural groups are being reshaped together in what is arguably a process of social evolution.

Perhaps most importantly, a clear sense of home is absent from Hogan's *Alice Springs*. A precolonial sense of home, established along the songline of Thompson's Dreaming story, erased by Stuart's frontier conquering of the wilderness, reappeared as a blending of cultures in Strehlow's memoir. Home was lost again under Groom's tourist wilderness, a Menzies era frontier all its own, but resurfaced in Chatwin's *The Songlines* of the Land Rights era. Hogan's most recent depiction of the Centre has returned us to the earlier frontier and a region divided.

Hogan's decision to eschew matters of Aboriginal culture constrains her ability to reflect the complex relationships and dependencies that characterise the Centre. Rising popular interest in the songlines apparent during the era of which Hogan writes is also absent, further detracting from any deeper sense of place it might otherwise have achieved. Interestingly, a role for place affect is less significant in *Alice Springs* than in other texts of the Centre such as Arthur Groom's (1950) humanist articulation of place. But while Groom's text largely fails to account for a politics of space, Hogan's produced the reverse: an effective political geography of alcohol that lacks a hybrid, or even inclusive, sense of place. As a result, *Alice Springs* speaks mainly to the enduring power and appeal of the frontier metaphor, while also undercutting its credibility as a way to represent the life-worlds of Central Australia.

Hogan's wariness to speak about Aboriginal culture is certainly understandable, especially in the midst of what is becoming an increasingly divisive debate and identity politics. In the interview for the Wheeler Centre, Hogan says she 'avoided including commentary on areas where books had already been published'. She cites Indigenous publisher IAD, which had 'published several books where traditional Arrernte talk about their culture and spirituality, an area where I would have been entirely out of my depth'. Unfortunately, excluding matters of Aboriginal culture has proven to be a serious handicap for writing a place where the two cultures co-exist.

There can be no doubt, however, that the issues of alcohol and violence raised in *Alice Springs* are vitally important. Many Aboriginal people spend an impossible proportion of their lives attending funerals, undertaking sorry business. Rod Moss writes in his memoir: 'In my twenty-five years in Alice Springs I've been to over sixty funerals of my Aboriginal family. Only three or four were over fifty'. Lives are too often lost, too early. A generation of young Aboriginal people is growing up confused and, aimless. But there are other questions we must ask before we might hope to address such problems, for if a predominantly white bureaucracy is to help black communities at all, cross-cultural understanding must precede policy.

In Alice Springs, Arrernte fiercely defend their bond to Country. It is their home, their lifeblood. Country calls to them, they say. It sustains them, feeds and nurtures them, and provides them with the strength to weather the challenges they face under colonisation. And yet throughout colonial history they have shown a ready willingness to be accommodating, and to share their space. Australian discourse is, however, framed by one culture dominating the other, whereby Indigenous people are encouraged to 'put the past behind them and move on'. How might this be possible on their home turf? What of the killings of countrymen, which many remember all too vividly? And where might they move on to? Rather than have another conversation aimed at a clear winner, perhaps we might query first how to better understand each other? What knowledge of this land can we give to each other? Is sharing this space also fostering a shared culture? What might that look like? How might we address any possible sharing of such spaces without losing our individual identities?

An ethical framework in which one cultural group is prohibited from writing of or about another precludes such questions, and serves only to deepen a frontier divide between them. It is worth remembering once again the question posed by Robyn Davidson: how might the outsider penetrate something so secretive and complex? This might flow two ways: whites understanding blacks as well as the reverse. Many suppose the time has come for whites to stop writing about Aboriginal people, history and culture altogether, to 'vacate the field'. Yet, unravelling the complex dimensions of place in the contact zone would seem key to fostering an Australian literature that embraces and promotes cross-cultural understanding. We need the voice of both groups, alone and together. Otherwise, Aboriginal people and culture remain inscrutable in any settler story of place, as they do in Hogan's *Alice Springs*, trapped on the other side of a frontier divide, which is no place to call home.

EPILOGUE

At the top of the rise I slow my breathing and stretch each calf against a low stone wall. The first hint of sunlight bleeds across nearby Mount Gillen, suffusing the peak warmly in red, which fades to pink as my eyes follow the ragged spine of the MacDonnell Ranges from the high point west and into the desert.[1]

From the summit of Anzac Hill is visible the entire central business district of Alice Springs and its southern entrance at Heavitree Gap. A concerted sprint up the last of the slope has brought me here in time for dawn. But my legs are paying the price. By the time my gaze falls fully west, the sky is a deep blue, the colour of night. Hung casually at its middle, like a pendant on a neck chain, is a full moon, which has lighted my footsteps since breakfast.

Behind me, the eastern ranges burn orange like a lantern, a layered aura that seems to flow through a crack in the hills at Emily Gap, about 7 kilometres east. It is there, say the Eastern Arrernte, that giant caterpillars, the so-called Creation Ancestors, rose from the earth to create the world as they marched southwards, calling into existence the hills and rivers and valleys. Anzac Hill, or Untyeyetweleye (Onjeea-toolia), has its own Dreaming stories, but since Anzac Day 1934 it has also been the town's most visited landmark, where is commemorated the region's wartime dead and others who fought in conflicts the world over. I have seen a thousand-strong crowd—black and white—pack this hill for the dawn service.

Despite broad-scale changes wrought over the 150 years since white settlement and a history of frontier violence, many Aboriginal people still see the landscape viewed from Anzac Hill as overlain with criss-crossing story tracks, the songlines, mental maps of sacred sites and important food and water sources, invisible to the unknowing eye. Many such stories and memories are now hidden beneath the town, cloaked by a wink of streetlights that rule over the grid of Alice Springs roads and lanes that are only just waking to the day, as expectant as an unmade bed. The town is built over the floodplain of the Charles Creek and the Todd River; river red gums, some of them sacred, line the banks of the dry streambeds; other varieties feed off irrigation and came with the settlers.

In the words of the academic Edward Said, culture is two things: that which we practise, and a reservoir of all that is known. People draw on such a reservoir for a range of social, cultural and environmental components with which to construct a sense of home. The relationship between humans and Nature is, nonetheless, one of unrest or restlessness, a vexed choice of whether to go or to stay vividly reflected in a European compulsion to progress, as well as the mobility of an Aboriginal relationship with Country and line over some tens of thousands of years, all of which helped Aboriginals to weather a long immigrant journey, several ice ages and innumerable droughts.

Australian novelist David Malouf, in retelling Plato's story of Protagoras, poses Man as 'man-the-maker', whose mission it is to 'turn wilderness into a fruitful landscape and lay down roads to move on'.[2] The key is the sense of shaping the landscape, for self and family, for a better life. While it appals many that Western modernity is usurping and erasing an emplaced and ecologically masterminded huntergatherer lifestyle, this does not negate the fact that the same basic intent permeates both Aboriginal and settler worldviews: to make a place in the world, to dwell, to nest, to make a home. For as human beings we cannot fail to dwell, inasmuch as dwelling is ultimately the 'existential core of human being-in-the-world from which there is no escape'.[3] In the words of local author Jo Dutton, Alice Springs happens to be one place where the wheels of colonisation have failed to run over an ancient culture. The songlines are a resilient symbol of a culture before, a resistant mark in time that simply won't be rubbed out.

~

Birds circle Anzac Hill in laps now, the glow from the east glancing from their wings. Grey birds with peach-like faces, they flash a rich black against the yellow of the wattles and the lilac of the ptilotus flowers feathering the rock edge of the hillslope, which in turn falls away from the cenotaph towards the town: lest we forget. The glow of the horizon conspires with the full moon and street lighting to wash the entire landscape in what for all the world looks to be an internally generated glow; even in the dead of night, the hills still take on this seemingly self-perpetuating hue.

Many kilometres to the west the ranges collapse into a scatter of boulders and disappear into the plains of the desert to the south. To my mind and ears comes the imagined voice of the Australian explorer Ernest Favenc, part-historian, part-poet, a man fascinated by the Centre, its strong loneliness and hidden mystery. The country calls to him, he once wrote. My friend Pat, an Eastern Arrernte woman, says the same whenever she goes south to visit family: 'I had to come back, I could hear those hills calling to me'. Perhaps in some way, they call to many of us. 'To pass a night alone in the desert spinifex country,' Favenc writes, 'is to feel as much cut off from the ordinary life of the world as one could feel if transplanted to another sphere.'

It is easy enough to imagine it was morning when Favenc wrote this. For mornings and just before night falls are when Central Australia— and the world inside one's own mind—are seen most clearly. It's the light, especially in the winter, from about May on, but, to more or less an extent, throughout the year and across the seasons. I can't recall another place where the heavens have seen fit to so illuminate a landscape so clearly deserving of mood lighting.

The whole of the range now lights up in a rush, as the sun seems to fall over its own lip. Mount Gillen slips further into deep red and the rest of the ranges are ushered into crisp relief. The Western Macs crank up another notch on a sliding scale of Namatjira purple, and the whole topography appears to sigh and come to rest on a more three-dimensional footing. Twilight's shadows are annihilated between dawn's first rays and a solar ball that reveals itself to the waking town.

In these moments, and in the countdown to sunset, Central Australians are daily treated to a light show for which there is perhaps no parallel. I couldn't count the times I have stopped driving to pull over and park on the side of the street simply to gape at a staggering blaze of pinks and reds, gold-tinged clouds melting across the ranges that themselves have deepened from brown through so many reds to rest in purple-black. No matter what the working day has been like, such a sight gives grounding and perspective, reminding us of our ant-like place in the universe.

Many argue a sense of place takes generations to develop. My experience suggests it can happen in a blink: sometimes the place claims the person, rather than the other way around. Elsewhere I have argued Alice Springs is a litmus test for Australia, a bold proving ground of reconciliation, where black and white must learn to live together on the same red dirt. But a prerequisite to this is the acknowledgement that both groups have a right to belong. To imagine anything else is to doom the town to failure.

A sense of belonging in place is tied to neither ownership nor length of residency; rather it is an existential opportunity that presents itself to all. Of course, this would make belonging independent of origin: the Muslim migrant, the fifth-generation pastoralist or the Arrernte woman from Central Australia all have a right to a connection with the place they choose to live. Understanding between the cultures, however, takes time. And understanding is the only thing that might ever lead to a shared sense of place.

The late Wenten Rubuntja, a strong advocate of Aboriginal Law and traditional owner of Alice Springs, said all children born in the town, both Aboriginal and non-Aboriginal, are spiritually connected to the Ayeparenye Caterpillar Dreaming. Rubuntja understood the town 'as both an Arrernte place and a white place', even though there were many reasons for him to take a harder line, and clearly spaces of racial exclusion remain.

This is not to imagine that settlers or immigrants might have any form of legal 'right' of claim, but more that such flexibility points to a shared articulation of the idea of 'home'. And it would seem to substantiate the perception that contemporary Aboriginal society is not so much embracing a modernist worldview, as updating a traditional worldview, assigning new meanings to the objects of modernity they now find dotting their world (including whitefellas).

Make no mistake regarding Rubuntja's meaning, however, for he also says that when the Europeans came and found Aboriginal people living in Australia, they 'put their cities and culture all over our country. But underneath this, all the time, Aboriginal culture and laws stay alive'.

Insofar as it is ever possible, I have tried to bring an objective eye to the examination of the stories retold in this book. However, I remain undeniably entranced by the poetry of the Centre, its lands and people. For the poet, words express something of the world around us through the sounds they make and images they evoke; they can even move the soul with their sense of melody. Yet there are times gazing at the MacDonnell Ranges when words fall away to nothing, and I am left with only a deep, deep silence. Paradoxically, it is in this silence that I hear most clearly Favenc's call.

And with that call comes the knowledge that something of this landscape's tectonic mystery may never be grasped, perhaps not by walker, writer, artist, scientist or photographer. Instead, the answer to its riddle must remain bundled and impenetrable, locked deep within the rock like a family secret. For maybe such knowledge is not ours to hear, and, as Henry David Thoreau once wrote, it is merely our own true natures we measure by gazing into earth's eye. If that be the case, a last line in the poem of the Centre may never be written.

MAP REFERENCES

Marlpwenge
Adapted from an original map published on p. 23 of the story '*Artweye erlkwe Marlpwenge*: A Man from the Dreamtime' in Turpin, M., *Growing Up Katetye: Stories by Tommy Kngwarraye Thompson*, Jukurrpa Books, Alice Springs, 2003, pp. 20–37.

Stuart
Adapted from *Plan of Discovery by John McDouall Stuart*, created s.n. 1861? MAP RM 4077, retrieved April 2017 at http://nla.gov.au/nla.obj-232420876/view

Strehlow
Adapted from information in Strehlow, T.G.H., *Songs of Central Australia*, Angus & Robertson, Sydney, 1971, and provided by courtesy of The Strehlow Research Centre, Alice Springs.

Groom
Adapted from the journey map as published in Groom, A., *I Saw a Strange Land: Journeys in Central Australia*, Angus & Robertson, Sydney, 1959 (original work published 1950).

Chatwin
Constructed using information about Chatwin's real journeys during 1983 and 1984 as discernible from letters and biographical information contained in Chatwin, E. and N. Shakespeare (eds), *Under the Sun: The Letters of Bruce Chatwin*, Vintage, London, 2011; and Shakespeare, N., *Bruce Chatwin*, Vintage, London, 2000.

Hogan
Constructed using Alice Springs street maps and information contained in Chapter 2, 'The Gap', in Hogan, E., *Alice Springs*, NewSouth Publishing, Sydney, 2012.

BIBLIOGRAPHY

Primary sources

Chatwin, B., *The Songlines*, Picador, London, 1988 (original work published 1987).

Groom, A., *I Saw a Strange Land: Journeys in Central Australia*, Text Publishing, Melbourne, 2015 (original work published 1950).

Hardman, W. (ed), *Explorations in Australia: The Journals of John McDouall Stuart During the Years 1858, 1859, 1860, 1861, and 1862, When He Fixed the Centre of the Continent and Successfully Crossed it from Sea to Sea*, Saunders, Otley and Co, London, second edition 1865. The online version of the fourth journal, adapted from this second edition, was retrieved from <johnmcdouallstuart.org.au/expedition-four> (viewed 21 August 2014).

Hogan, E., *Alice Springs*, NewSouth Publishing, Sydney, 2012.

Strehlow, T.G.H., *Journey to Horseshoe Bend*, Rigby, Sydney, 1978 (original work published 1969). Reissue 2015 by Giramondo Publishing.

Thompson, T.K., 'Artweye Erlkwe Marlpwenge: A Man from the Dreamtime', in Myfany Turpin (ed), *Growing Up Kaytetye: Stories by Tommy Kngwarraye Thompson*, Jukurrpa Books, Alice Springs, first edition, 2003, pp. 20–37.

Suggested reading

On walking

Amato, J.A., *On Foot: A History of Walking*, New York University Press, New York, 2004.

Harper, M., *The Ways of the Bushwalker: On Foot in Australia*, UNSW Press, Sydney, 2007.

Macfarlane, R., *The Old Ways: A Journey on Foot*, Penguin, London, 2013.

Nicholson, G., *The Lost Art of Walking: The History, Science, and Literature of Pedestrianism*, Riverhead Books, New York, 2008.

Shehadeh, R., *Palestinian Walks: Forays into a Vanishing Landscape*, Scribner, New York, 2008.

Sinclair, I., *Lights Out for the Territory: 9 Excursions in the Secret History of London*, Penguin, London, 1991.

Solnit, R., *Wanderlust*, Vero, London, 2001.

Thoreau, H.D., 'Walking', *The Atlantic*, June 1862.

Woolf, V., 'Street Haunting: A London Adventure', *The Death of the Moth, and Other Essays*, University of Adelaide, 2015; original edition, San Francisco: Westgate Press, 1930; <ebooks.adelaide.edu.au/w/woolf/virginia/w91d/chapter5.html>.

On Aboriginal culture

Donovan, V. and C. Wall (eds), *Making Connections: A Journey Along Central Australian Aboriginal Trading Routes*, Arts Queensland, Brisbane, 2004.

Kerwin, D., *Aboriginal Dreaming Paths and Trading Routes: The Colonisation of the Australian Economic Landscape*, Sussex Academic Press, Eastbourne, 2012.

Myers, F., *Pintupi Country Pintupi Self: Sentiment, Place and Politics among Western Desert Aborigines*, University of California Press, Berkeley, 1986.

Nicholls, C., 'Dreamings and Dreaming Narratives: What's the Relationship', *The Conversation*, 6 February 2014. <theconversation.com/dreamings-and-dreaming-narratives-whats-the-relationship-20837> (viewed 4 July 2014).

NT Writers Centre, *This Country Anytime Anywhere: An Anthology of New Indigenous Writing from the Northern Territory*, IAD Press, Alice Springs, 2010.

Turner, M.K., *Iwenke Tyerrtye—What it Means to Be an Aboriginal Person*, IAD Press, Alice Springs, 2010.

On the Red Centre

Finlayson, H.H., *The Red Centre: Man and Beast in the Heart of Australia*, Angus & Robertson, Sydney, 1935.

Haynes, R.D., *Seeking the Centre: The Australian Desert in Literature, Art and Film*, Cambridge University Press, Melbourne, 1998.

Hill, B., *Broken Song: T.G.H. Strehlow and Aboriginal Possession*, Vintage Books, Sydney, 2003.

Kimber, R.G., *Man from Arltunga: Walter Smith Australian Bushman*, Hesperian Press, Carlisle, 1986.

Latz, P.K., *Bushfires and Bushtucker: Aboriginal Plant Use in Central Australia*, IAD Press, Alice Springs, 1995.

Moss, R., *The Hard Light of Day*, University of Queensland Press, St Lucia, 2010.

Traynor, S., *Alice Springs: From Singing Wire to Iconic Outback Town*, Mile End, South Australia, Wakefield Press, 2016.

Glenn's picks

Davidson, R., *Tracks*, Jonathan Cape, London, 1980.

—— 'Return of the Camel Lady', *Griffith Review*, no. 9, Spring 2005, pp. 128–39.

Giles, E., *Australia Twice Traversed: The Romance of Exploration, Being a Narrative Compiled from the Journals of Five Exploring Expeditions into and through Central South Australia and Western Australia from 1872 to 1876 by Ernest Giles*, two volumes, Sampson Low, Marston, Searle and Rivington Ltd, Fleet Street, 1889.

Plowman, R.B., *Camel Pads*, Angus & Robertson, Sydney, 1933.

Rubuntja, W. and Green, J., *The Town Grew Up Dancing: The Life and Art of Wenten Rubuntja*, Jukurrpa Books, Alice Springs, 2002.

Russell, A., *A Tramp Royal in Wild Australia: 1928–29*, Jonathan Cape, London, 1934.

Van Dyke J.C., *The Desert: Further Studies in Natural Appearances*, Johns Hopkins University Press, Baltimore, 1999. Originally published by Charles Scribner's Sons, New York, 1901.

Other publications mentioned in the text

Austin-Broos, D., *Arrernte Past, Arrernte Present: Invasion, Violence and Imagination in Indigenous Central Australia*, University of Chicago Press, Chicago, 2009. <www.australianreview.net/digest/2010/10/nungarrayiprice.html> (viewed 28 November 2014).

Baudelaire, C., *The Painter of Modern Life and Other Essays*, trans. J Mayne, Phaidon Press, 1970 (original work published 1860) <www.columbia. edu/itc/architecture/ockman/pdfs/dossier_4/Baudelaire.pdf> (viewed 9 February 2015).

Bechervaise, J.M., 'Camera Supplement: Ayers Rock, Northern Territory', *Walkabout*, January 1949, pp. 21–38.

Benjamin, W., 'The Paris of the Second Empire in Baudelaire', in *Charles Baudelaire: A Lyric Poet in the Era of High Capitalism*, trans. H. Zohn, NLB, London, 1973.

Carter, P., *The Road to Botany Bay: An Exploration of Landscape and History*, University of Minnesota Press, Minneapolis, 2010 (original work published 1987), p. 73.

Clift, C., 'The Centre', *The World of Charmian Clift*, Collins, Sydney, 1983, pp. 203–6.

Davidson, R., 'Robyn Davidson Introduces *I Saw a Strange Land*', *Text Publishing Blog*, posted 17 June 2015, retrieved 31 May 2017 at <https://www. textpublishing.com.au/blog/robyn-davidson-introduces-i-saw-a-strange-land>.

Dutton, J., *From Alice With Love*, Allen & Unwin, Crows Nest, 2013.

Favenc, E., *Voices of the Desert*, Elliot Stock, London, 1905.

Griffiths, T., 'Journeying to the Centre', in *Hunters and Collectors: The Antiquarian Imagination in Australia*, University of Cambridge Press, Melbourne, 1996, pp. 176–92.

Kelham, M., cited in Hogan, E., *Alice Springs*, NewSouth Publishing, Sydney, 2012, pp. 140, 169.

Krien, A., 'Booze Territory', *The Monthly*, September 2011, pp. 22–32.

Mulvaney, D.J., 'The Chain of Connection: The Material Evidence', in Peterson, N. (ed), *Tribes and Boundaries in Australia*, Australian Institute of Aboriginal Studies, Canberra, 1976, pp. 72–94.

Newbury, P., 'Perspectives of Identity in Being Australian', *Griffith Review, Edition 36: What is Australia For?*, 2012

Platzer, M., 'Sensing Belief Systems. Review of *Broken Song: T.G.H. Strehlow and Aboriginal Possession* by Barry Hill', *The Culture Mandala*, vol. 7, no. 2, 2007.

Poe, E.A., '"The Man of the Crowd", in *The Works of the Late Edgar Allan Poe 1850–1856'*, *Griswald Edition*, vol. 2, 1850, pp. 398–40 <www.eapoe.org/works/tales/crowdd.htm> (viewed November 2013).

Price, B.N., 'We Need to Change Our Law', *Australian Review of Public Affairs*, address by Bess Nungarrayi Price to the Australian Lawyers Alliance National Conference in Alice Springs, 22 October 2010.

Roth, W.E., *The Queensland Aborigines*, vol. 1, Hesperian press, Victoria Park, W.A. 1984 (original work published 1897).

Said, E., *Culture and Imperialism*, Vintage Books, New York, p. xii.

Smith, T., 'Blurring Distinctions: Autobiography and Identity in Bruce Chatwin's *The Songlines'*, *Bucknell Review*, vol. 47, no. 2, 2003.

Sutton, P., 'On a Mission: John Strehlow's Tale of Frieda Keysser', *The Monthly*, April 2012 <https://www.themonthly.com.au/issue/2012/april/1339558171/peter-sutton/mission> (viewed 31 May 2017)

Weil, S., *The Need for Roots*, Routledge Classics, London, 2003 (original work published 1949).

Wild, P., 'The Desert as Literature: A Survey and a Sampling', *The Deserts in Literature*, no. 35, Spring/Summer, 1994 <ag.arizona.edu/oals/ALN/aln35/Wild.html> (viewed January 2016).Notes

NOTES

Author's note

1   The APY Lands is a local government area in the remote north-west of South Australia, home to about 2500 people of the Pitjantjatjara, Yankunytjatjara and Ngaanyatjarra language groups. Governed from Adelaide, the APY lands are closer to Alice Springs, and many services are provided from there.

1   Marlpwenge

1   Ultimately, the case deepened from a nation-wide manhunt to a lengthy and controversial police investigation, and a murder conviction prompting newspaper headlines from London to New York. For more information, see Paul Toohey's *The Killer Within: Inside the World of Bradley John Murdoch*, Allen & Unwin: Crows Nest 2007.

2   Rubuntja, W. and J. Green, *The Town Grew Up Dancing: The Life and Art of Wenten Rubuntja*, Jukurrpa Books, Alice Springs, 2002, p. 29; see also Hartwig, M.C., *The Coniston Killings*, University of Adelaide, 1960, p. 50.

3   Central Land Council, 'Barrow Creek', <www.clc.org.au/land-won-back/info/barrow-creek> (retrieved 6 February 2015).

4   Turpin, M., *Growing Up Kaytetye: Stories by Tommy Kngwarraye Thompson*, Jukurrpa Books, Alice Springs, 2003.

5   Determined to work from collected stories so as to give everyday context for the language she was documenting, Dr Turpin started recording some of Thompson's stories. The stories were subsequently translated—a joint effort by many different Kaytetye speakers—and later published.

6   See her 2014 series for popular current affairs website *The Conversation*.

7   Norris, Ray P. and Bill Yidumduma Harney, 2014, 'Songlines and Navigation in Wardaman and other Australian Aboriginal Cultures', *Journal of Astronomical History and Heritage*, vol. 17, no. 2, pp. 1–15.

8   As Stuart Rintoul reported for *The Australian* in 2012, a million-dollar project chronicling two songlines in Central Australia, called 'Alive With the Dreaming: Songlines of the Western Desert', was brought almost to a standstill

over a disagreement about whether or not some important knowledge should be made public.

9   Gibson, Ian W., 'Preserving Cultures through Written Story: An Introduction to the Writing of Kuloin (Audrey May Evans), Aboriginal Australian', in Tonya Huber (ed), *Storied Inquiries in International Landscapes: An Anthology of Educational Research*, Information Age Publishing, 2010, p. 171.

10 See Morrison, G., 'A Flâneur in the Outback: Walking and Writing Frontier in Central Australia', *New Scholar: An International Journal of the Humanities, Creative Arts and Social Sciences*, vol. 3, no. 3, 2014, pp. 51–72.

11 As the story states: 'She was the wrong skin for him [an Ametyane]. They were both Kaytetye and were related as father and daughter, but they were married'.

12 The English translation of the Aboriginal concept was first used in the nineteenth century by Alice Springs Telegraph Station master Frances (Frank) Gillen, then popularised by anthropologist Baldwin Spencer's inclusion of it in the 1894 report of the Horn Expedition. In the Arrernte language, the Dreamtime is called *Altyer* or *Altyerrenge*, and in languages of the Western Desert, *Tjukurrpa*. By contrast, Arrernte author M.K. Turner refers to narratives of the Dreaming simply as 'Traditional Country Stories'.

13 For the Mparntwe Arrernte culture, David Wilkins describes similar circumstances pertaining to a *pmere* (significant place).

14 For more on this recent research see the journal article, Malaspinas, A.S. et al., 'A Genomic History of Aboriginal Australia', *Nature*, vol. 538, 2016, pp. 207–14.

15 As recently as the turn of the twentieth century it was thought that Aboriginal people had lived in Australia for only about 400 years. By the 1960s, the length of inhabitation had been put back to 8000 years. Such underestimates would change suddenly late one afternoon in 1974, when researcher Jim Bowler stumbled upon a skeleton in a sandhill at the edge of a dry lake bed in south-west New South Wales. Carbon dating would put the age of the skeleton at about 23,000 years. The bones were those of a woman, later called Mrs Mungo for the lake where she was found. All at once, Mrs Mungo had tripled estimates of how long Aboriginals had been in Australia. In 1989, work by Rhys Jones, Mike Smith and Bert Roberts at Malakunanja II in Arnhem Land put the timing back again to 50–55,000 years. Estimates of the Aboriginal occupation of Australia now mostly hover around 60,000 years.

16 Hamm, G. et al., 'Cultural Innovation and Megafauna Interaction in the Early Settlement of Arid Australia', *Nature*, vol. 539, pp. 280–3.

17 Brooks, D., *A Town Like Mparntwe: A Guide to the Dreaming Tracks and Sites of Alice Springs*, Jukurrpa Books, Alice Springs, 2003, p. 6.

18 Elkin, A.P., *Aboriginal Men of High Degree: Initiation and Sorcery in the World's Oldest Tradition*, Traditions International, Vermont, 1994, p. 113; original work published by UQ Press 1977.

19 Kevin, T., *Walking the Camino: A Modern Pilgrimage to Santiago*, Scribe, Carlton North, 2007, p. 187.

20 In the 1940s, Charles Mountford mapped the Winbaraku songline in the West MacDonnell Ranges near Alice Springs, a place described in some detail in Cowan, J. and C. Beard, *Sacred Places in Australia*, Simon & Schuster, East Roseville, 1991, pp. 136, 140. Anthropologist David Brooks describes some of the Dreaming tracks of the Alice Springs township in Brooks, D., *A Town Like Mparntwe* (2003). Work at the Strehlow Research Centre at Alice Springs to map Western Arrernte songlines of the Finke region is underway under the direction of anthropologist Adam McFie and Western Arrernte man Mark Inkamala. Also, the Ngintaka Songlines Project in the remote deserts south and west of Uluru, led by anthropologist Diana James, and published as James, D., 'An Aboriginal Ontology of Place', in Vanclay, F., M. Higgins and A. Blackshaw (eds), *Making Sense of Place: Exploring Concepts and Expressions of Place Through Different Senses and Lenses*, National Museum of Australia Press, Canberra, 2008.

21 The routes converge on the well-known ochre deposits of Pukardu Hill near Parachilna in the Flinders Ranges of South Australia. Annual ritual journeys followed this strictly prescribed way. McBryde assesses the possible heritage value of traditional trade routes or songlines, citing for international comparison UNESCO's World Heritage Listing of the El Camino de Compostela and arguing the ochre Dreaming trail constitutes a similarly valuable heritage resource.

22 The first European mention of *pituri* is in the diaries of Burke and Wills. Sole survivor of the expedition John King notes that *pituri*'s effects were equivalent to 'two pretty stiff nobblers of brandy'.

23 A guide to pilgrimage can be found in Davidson, L.K. and D.M. Gitlitz, *Pilgrimage: From the Ganges to Graceland—An Encyclopedia*, ABC-CLIO, Santa Barbara, 2002. Also, for a comparison of non-Christian pilgrimages, see Chélini, J. and H. Branthomme, (eds), *Les chemins de Dieu. Histoire des pèlerinages chrétiens des origines à nos jours*, Hachette, Paris, 1982.

24 James, D., 'An Aboriginal Ontology of Place'.

25 In *Narrative as Social Practice*, Daniele Klapproth tells a story about a group of Pintupi telling stories as they are driven to Warlungurru, west of Alice Springs in the Kintore Range. Her narrator is a white man in Richmond, NSW, who simultaneously tells Klapporth *his* story as a way to construct an identity for himself. Both parties map themselves into landscapes physical and cultural to establish who they are. See Klapproth, D.M., *Narrative as Social Practice: Anglo-Western and Australian Aboriginal Oral Traditions*, Walter de Gruyter GmbH & Co, Berlin, 2004.

26 The Enlightenment can be thought of as a number of social, political and cultural changes occurring near the end of the eighteenth century. The

Enlightenment emphasised bringing light to the Dark Age, based on a core belief in human progress and the 'power of reason to improve human society'. In his essay *Was ist Aufklärung*, Immanuel Kant argues Enlightenment is man's emergence from a self-imposed immaturity.

27 Fighting between Warlpiri and Waringari hunter-gatherers reached the level of 'pitched battles' with a 'score or more dead', and took place in order to 'occupy' and monopolise wells, among other reasons. Of the red ochre expeditions, historian Dick Kimber writes that while 'cordial relationships' were mostly sought, fighting while travelling was common. An entire party barring one man was ambushed and killed about 1870. Then in 1874, all but one of a group of thirty were 'entombed in the [ochre] excavations'.

28 The Bungalow was a series of corrugated iron sheds operated by the Australian Government in Alice Springs where up to fifty half-caste children and ten adults were housed, reportedly in appalling conditions by modern standards; they slept on the floor or outside with one standard-issue blanket per year to see them through the winter, sometimes in sub-zero temperatures. The sheds had replaced a tent, originally set up by a local policeman in 1914. In 1932, the Alice Springs Telegraph Station closed and for a while it became home to the relocated Bungalow. Despite a great deal of controversy, the Bungalow operated there until 1942 when it was closed, the children evacuated and the site turned into a native labour camp. For more, see 'History of the Bungalow 1914–1929', File No.1, National Archives of Australia, A1/15, 1927/2982; and 'About Alice Springs—History', <Alicesprings.nt.gov.au>, 31 August 1933 (retrieved 30 May 2011).

29 Tommy Thompson's skin name, for example, is Kngwarraye.

30 Peterson, N., 'Myth of the Walkabout', in Bell, M. (ed), *Population Mobility and Indigenous Peoples in Australasia and North America*, Routledge Research in Population and Migration, Routledge, London, 2004.

31 Tindale, N., *Aboriginal Tribes of Australia*, University of California Press, Berkeley, 1935.

32 Elkin, A.P., *Aboriginal Men of High Degree: Initiation and Sorcery in the World's Oldest Tradition*, Inner Traditions International, Vermont, 1994, p. 4.

2 Stuart

1 Buffel grass (*Cenchrus ciliaris*) is an introduced perennial grass that came to Australia with camels in the 1860s and has sprouted along the route of the Overland Telegraph Line since. Being strong and deeply rooted as well as drought hardy, the seed was spread after World War I and trials begun for cattle in the North during the 1920s. A cultivar called 'American' was spread near Alice Springs to control dust storms in the 1950s and 1960s and also sewn on

cattle stations round this time. In South Australia it is now a declared weed, but in the Territory there is still no clear policy.

2   See Hardman, W. (ed), *Explorations in Australia: The Journals of John McDouall Stuart During the Years 1858, 1859, 1860, 1861, and 1862, When He Fixed the Centre of the Continent and Successfully Crossed it from Sea to Sea*, Saunders, Otley and Co, London, second edition, 1865. The online version of the fourth journal, adapted from this second edition, was retrieved from <johnmcdouallstuart.org.au/expedition-four> (viewed 21 August 2014). Other versions abound: In the South Australian parliamentary papers (J.M. Stuart, *Mr Stuart's Exploration in South Australia*) and as a stand-alone volume (J.M. Stuart, *Fourth Expedition Journal*). Individual journals are also available online (see 'John McDouall Stuart Society'), and there is the compilation volume of all of Stuart's journeys (W. Hardman), which are cited widely.

3   For an interesting interview with owner of the lease John Chambers, see '"A Chat with an Old Colonist", Interview with John Chambers, by our Special-Reporter', *South Australian Register* (Adelaide SA: 1839 1900), Wednesday, 11 January 1888. Viewed at: <trove.nla.gov.au/newspaper/article/46867360>.

4   For a more in-depth introduction to the men I suggest a 2011 paper by historian Rick Moore for the John McDouall Stuart Society, 'Stuart, Kekwick, Head: The Character of the Men'. Viewed at: <issuu.com/johnmcdouallstuart/docs/stuart_kekwick__head_-_the_character_of_the_men>.

5   For more on walking in the colony, see Harper, M., *The Ways of the Bushwalker: On Foot in Australia*, UNSW Press, Sydney, 2007.

6   Elliot's comments and Strehlow's analysis can be found in Strehlow, T.G.H., *Comments on the Journals of John McDouall Stuart*, Libraries Board of South Australia, Adelaide, 1967.

7   From Giles, E., *Australia Twice Traversed: The Romance of Exploration, Being a Narrative Compiled from the Journals of Five Exploring Expeditions into and through Central South Australia and Western Australia from 1872 to 1876 by Ernest Giles*, two volumes, Sampson Low, Marston, Searle and Rivington Ltd, Fleet Street, London, 1889, pp. 39–40.

8   'Beautiful View Calms Outback Stroke Victim', ABC Alice Springs, posted 31 July 2009, 3:17 pm AEST. Updated 31 July, 2009, 3:37 pm AEST.

9   Trust in camels, which would later become a regular feature of Australian exploratory expeditions, was still uncertain as Stuart planned his fourth expedition. And despite widespread and continued faith in horses, walking persisted as a means of purposeful travel throughout the colonial era and beyond, bouts on foot featuring episodically but significantly throughout Stuart's expedition record.

10 Suggested reading: Melissa Harper explores walking in Australian history in *The Ways of the Bushwalker*.

11 It is worth noting that some literary specialists treat explorer journals as travel writing, as if written by a tourist in search of pleasure. This is ultimately misleading. Admittedly, Charles Sturt, who vied for Central Australia with Stuart in 1844, once wrote he had never 'been happier than when roving through the woods'. And it is certainly plausible that Stuart and his men took breaks for a pleasurable walk, especially at well-watered camps such as the Finke River. But Stuart does not report this. Even if the explorers did go for pleasurable walks it would not have suited Stuart's purpose to report the fact. A pleasant walk might have broken the spell Stuart weaves, of the suffering explorer as Romantic hero. To be fair, he *was* suffering in his effort to cross country his lack of knowledge rendered undeniably harsh. However, comparing the journeys of the Central Australian explorers to a European walking tour and further blurring the lines between exploration, travel and tourism trivialises the severity of the explorer's physical experience, and militates against the dire political consequences of the colonialist imperative for Aboriginal people.

12 Geographers now consider there is no true centre of Australia. Nonetheless, there are at least five methods for determining such a location. All fail to agree, but a plaque was erected in 1988 at the centre point calculated by director of the National Mapping Office Bruce Phillip Lambert. It is near Kulgera, NT, 275 kilometres south of Alice Springs. For more on this topic, see Morrison, G., 'Seeking the Centre', *Australian Geographic*, Mar/Apr 2016, no. 131, p.130.

13 Cultural historian Paul Carter argues that geographical knowledge is really personal knowledge, and for explorers this was often subject to mood and reflected in the names given to the places they map and the descriptions they give. Consider the names given by explorers to Cape Catastrophe, Mount Misery, Retreat Well and Cape Disappointment. This is the land to which the convicts of the First Fleet were sent. On the other hand, in the naming by Matthew Flinders carried out during his circumnavigation of the coastline and documented in *A Voyage to Terra Australis*, there is a unique sense of home. Flinders reduces the unknown coastline to the proportions of the human body, a house, with names such as Elbow Hill and Backstairs Passage. There is a warm sense of embodiment.

14 Gerritsen, R., 'A Post-colonial Model for North Australian Political Economy? The Case of the Northern Territory', in Gerritsen, R. (ed), *Political Economy of Northern Australia: Issues and Agendas*, CDU Press, Darwin, 2010, pp. 18–40.

15 Indeed, until 1967 they were considered part of the nation's flora and fauna.

16 Historian Russell McGregor notes as much while exploring Doomed Race Theory in *Imagined Destinies: Aboriginal Australians and the Doomed Race*

Theory, 1880–1939, Melbourne University Press, Carlton South, 1997. By associating savagery with indolence, Tench invokes the Enlightenment.

17 Tench, W., 'A Complete Account of the Settlement at Port Jackson, 1793', in Tench, W., *Sydney's First Four Years*, Angus & Robertson, Sydney, 1961, pp. 78–94. Tench's viewpoint suggests a further motivation for Stuart's mission: to bring the benefits of progress to Aboriginal people. But it is clear there is an ambiguity in this representation of Aboriginals, in turn imparting ambivalence to the journal's textual constructions of the frontier. Indeed, a diversity of opinion on such matters was commonplace: based on the same Enlightenment thinking, judge advocate David Collins concludes that Aboriginals are incapable of becoming civilised and useful members of society. The great chain of being and other representations had imagined nature as a hierarchy of differently developed creatures arranged in sequence, from inanimate matter through to the simple organism, with man high in the rankings and God crowning the collection at its apex. Europeans had soon filled the gap between man and monkey with black races situated closest to the simian at the base of the human sector. For more, see McGregor, R., *Imagined Destinies*.

18 Strehlow (1967), p. 7.

19 See Kimber, R.G., 'Message Sticks and Yabber Mail', in Donovan, C. and C. Wall (eds), *Making Connections: A journey along Central Australian Aboriginal Trading Routes*, Arts Queensland, Brisbane, 2004, pp. 29–33.

20 Strehlow (1967), p. 8.

21 By 1830, Doomed Race Theory was secure in the colonial imagination and still prevailed at the time of Stuart's expeditions. Such ideas may explain his continued reluctance to accept the signs of water indicated by the presence of Aboriginal travellers. Doomed Race Theory held that Aboriginals were destined for extinction; combined with humanist thought, the role of the coloniser ranged from helping to hasten this process as the kindest thing to do, to easing their suffering towards the inevitable. Such ideas also colour any appraisal of the ability of Aboriginal people to civilise. English missionary Lancelot Threlkeld and colonial magistrate William Hull, for instance, believed Aboriginals to be the degraded remnants of a formerly civilised people, Threlkeld arguing that Indigenous populations were on the decline before the colonists arrived. In 1858, Hull suggested it was providence that an inferior race would perish ahead of a superior race, since 'we have occupied the country, the Aborigines must cease to occupy'.

22 An entire party barring one man was ambushed and killed about 1870. Then in 1874, all but one of a group of thirty was 'entombed in the [ochre] excavations'. See Kimber, R., 'The End of the Bad Old Days: European Settlement in Central Australia 1871–1894', *Occasional Paper No. 25: The Fifth Eric Johnson Lecture*, State Library of the Northern Territory, Darwin,

1990, p. 163; see also p. 26 of Gat, A., 'The Human Motivational Complex: Evolutionary Theory and the Causes of Hunter-Gatherer Fighting. Part I: Primary Somatic and Reproductive Causes', *Anthropological Quarterly*, vol. 73, no. 1, 2000, pp. 20–34.

3 Strehlow

1 Strehlow, T.G.H., *Journey to Horseshoe Bend,* Rigby, Sydney, 1978 (original work published 1969). Reissue 2015 by Giramondo Publishing.

2 T.G.H. Strehlow describes his parents' residence as 'roofed only with slim desert oak saplings which supported a top layer, some three inches thick, of lime concrete', *Journey to Horseshoe Bend*, p. 9.

3 Chlanda, E., 'Widow Cities and Rural Bliss: A Diverse Electorate', *Alice Springs News*, 5 June 2016, <www.alicespringsnews.com.au/2016/06/05/widow-cities-and-rural-bliss-a-diverse-electorate>.

4 William Henry Willshire was a police officer born in Adelaide in 1852. Posted to Alice Springs in 1882, he was swiftly promoted to constable first-class and soon gained a reputation for effective 'dispersal' of Aboriginals. In 1886 he established the police station at Heavitree Gap and built an outpost at Boggy Hole near Hermannsburg. By 1890 he had been officially associated with the death of thirteen Aboriginals. Complaints by missionaries led to Boggy Hole being abandoned after three 'escaping' Aboriginal prisoners were shot in the back. In his published accounts of the period, Willshire portrayed himself as a heroic frontiersman.

5 T.G.H. Strehlow concedes, upon reflection, that the officer his father had dressed down that day, thereby saving many of those captured, may not have been Wurmbrand at all.

6 The Strehlow's farewell inspired a cantata composed by Andrew Schultz and later performed by John Stanton and others, the Sydney Symphony Orchestra and the Ntaria (Hermannsburg) Ladies Choir, at the Sydney Opera House on 28 and 29 May 2003. A film called *Cantata Journey* by Hart Cohen was also adapted from the text, which is the subject of two recent projects of note: a web-based multimedia database and research project by the University of Western Sydney, and another by Western Arrernte elder Mark Inkamala in conjunction with the Strehlow Centre at Alice Springs, which aims to map the songlines of the Finke region.

7 Now kept at the Strehlow Research Centre in Alice Springs, it is in German, with an English translation available.

8 Strehlow's studies of Aboriginal languages led to the publication of several seminal texts, including *Aranda Phonetics and Grammar* (Sydney, 1944) and *Aranda Traditions* (Melbourne, 1947). *Songs of Central Australia* (Sydney, 1971), which many consider his *magnum opus*, came much later.

9   Only a small critical literature of Strehlow's text has emerged, from an earlier 1981 biography of Strehlow by Ward McNally to the more recent *Broken Song: T.G.H. Strehlow and Aboriginal Possession*, Vintage Books, Syndey, 2003 by Barry Hill. A flurry of contemporary essays coincided with the book's reissue in 2016, perhaps the best being Paul Galimond's critique 'To Know is to Live' in the *Sydney Review of Books*, 13 July 2016.

10 The subject of Kimber, R.G., *Man from Arltunga: Walter Smith, Australian Bushman*, Hesperian Press, Carlisle, 1986.

11 From: Russell, A., *A Tramp Royal in Wild Australia 1928–1929*, Cape, London, 1934, pp. 254–5.

12 Strehlow obtained much of his botanical knowledge of the landscape much later, during his university studies, and subsequent years of research in Central Australia. The psychological framework set up in the younger Strehlow, however, complements the studied experience of the older, delivering a rich texture of place. The result, a mixture of natural and postcolonial themes, may be viewed as a form of nature writing, which US nature writer Barry Lopez explains is concerned with the 'evolving structure of communities from which nature has been removed, often as a consequence of modern economic development'. In such stories 'the fate of humanity and nature are inseparable', and so such a literature searches for a human identity that lies 'beyond nationalism and material wealth'. See Lopez's 1997 essay, 'A Literature of Place', *Portland Magazine*, Summer, <arts.envirolink.org/literary_arts/BarryLopez_LitofPlace.html> (viewed May 2011).

13 See Gregory, J.W., *The Dead Heart of Australia: A Journey Around Lake Eyre in the Summer of 1901–1902, with Some Account of the Lake Eyre Basin and the Flowing Wells of Central Australia*, John Murray, London, 1906.

14 According to a paper by Kathleen Strehlow (Strehlow's second wife) the *iliaka njemba* were 'grim emu-shaped phantoms that stalked over the sandhill wastes at night and devoured the children who dared to move too far away from the campfires of their parents'. Strehlow, K.S. 'The Operation of Fear in Traditional Aboriginal Society in Central Australia', The Strehlow Research Foundation, *Traditional Australian Aboriginal Culture*, 1970 retrieved 31 May 2017 at http://www.aboriginalculture.org/uploads/3/4/9/5/34950296/operation_of_fear.pdf

15 In his essay 'A Walk to Wachusett', which describes an 1842 hike to Mount Wachusett, Thoreau compares the naturalist Alexander Von Humboldt's modern-day excursion of the Andes with the ancient journeys of Virgil and Homer. Humboldt travelled extensively in Latin America at the turn of the nineteenth century, describing it for the first time from the scientific viewpoint. Thoreau wrestles a suspicion that his comparison with Humboldt is disingenuous, that in forging a link to such ancient worlds he reaches in

reality for a lost utopia. In fact, in 'A Walk to Wachusett', Thoreau's destination appears only as a 'hovering presence', a reference point for 'imaginative projections of purpose', adding myth and authority to the journey.

16 As Barry Hill has noted, the Arrernte themselves had no word for map, but rather they were 'in the map, and their conception of their habitat was a matter of continuous enactment of the map's meaning'.

17 Schultz, A. and G.K. Williams, *Journey to Horseshoe Bend: A Cantata Based on the Novel by T.G.H. Strehlow*, music by Andrew Shulz, libretto by Gordon Kalton Williams. Performed by Sydney Symphony Orchestra, 2003, <www.australianmusiccentre.com.au/work/schultz-andrew-journey-to-horseshoe-bend> (viewed 10 February 2015).

4 Groom

1 Correspondence from Arthur Groom to the Superintendent Hermannsburg Mission, dated 3/3/46. Courtesy of Finke River Mission Collection—Old Lutheran Church History Collection, copy kindly loaned to the author by Olga Radke, of Friends of the Strehlow Research Centre.

2 Jarrott, J.K., 'Groom, Arthur (1904–1953)', *Australian Dictionary of Biography*, <adb.anu.edu.au/biography/groom-arthur-6496/text11139> (viewed 12 March 2014).

3 For Groom's conservation ideals, worth a look is Groom, A., *One Mountain After Another*, Angus & Robertson, Sydney, 1949.

4 In May 1930, Groom founded the National Parks Association of Queensland, which in 2013 erected a monument at Binna Burra to his 'love and understanding of the bush'.

5 The walk is described in 'Voice of the Ages', the sixth chapter of *I Saw a Strange Land*, although I also draw liberally from the book in its entirety.

6 Companies include Wilderness Australia and Truly Australia. As for Uluru, to the Anangu it is sacred, and the area round its base hosts a variety of pools, waterholes, rock caves and paintings important for cultural reasons. According to Parks Australia, Anangu say they prefer tourists learn about their culture than climb the Rock. However, for some of the more than 400,000 visitors who come to the park each year, climbing it remains the dream of a lifetime. In 1990, 74 per cent of visitors climbed the rock, but by 2012 that figure had fallen below 20 per cent. Nonetheless, in 2016, then NT Chief Minister Adam Giles called for Anangu to 'get behind the climb'.

7 From Thoreau's essay *Walking*, first delivered as a lecture in 1851, then many times after, but published as the essay by *The Atlantic Monthly* only after his death in 1862.

8 Alexander Sutherland and John Le Gay Brereton are the subject of research by historian Melissa Harper, and published in *The Ways of the Bushwalker: On Foot*

in Australia (2007), as well as in her journal article 'Sensuality in Sandshoes: Representations of the Bush in the Walking and Writing of John Le Gay Brereton and Percy Grainger', *Australian Historical Studies*, vol. 31, no. 115, 2000, pp. 287–303.

9   Jillian Barnes has undertaken a history of tourism in the Centre, published as Barnes, J., 'Tourism's Role in the Struggle for the Intellectual and Material Possession of "The Centre" of Australia at Uluru, 1929–2011', *Journal of Tourism History*, vol. 3, no. 2, 2011, pp. 147–76.

10 See Clary, A., 'Mark Twain in the Desert', *The Journal of Ecocriticism*, vol. 3, no. 1, 2011 pp. 29–39; this quote from p. 29.

11 For Raymond Williams' full treatment, I suggest 'Ideas of Nature', in Jonathon, B. (ed), *Ecology, the Shaping Inquiry*, Longmans, London, 1972, pp. 146–64.

12 The first quote is from literary scholar Lawrence Buell, who cites a range of meanings of 'wilderness', whereby undisturbed areas such as mountains are seen as symbols of undomesticated nature. The second quote is from critic Raymond Williams, who describes Nature variously as 'the primitive condition before human society', through the sense of an 'original innocence from which there has been a fall and a curse'. It might also convey the requiring of redemption, or the 'special sense of a quality of birth as in the Latin root; through again the sense of the forms and moulds of nature which can yet, paradoxically, be destroyed by the natural forces of thunder'. Or finally, it is that 'simple and persistent form of the personified goddess, Nature herself'. The meaning of Nature may range from the essential essence of a thing, to Mother Nature, to a mystical force at odds with a monotheistic God.

13 The Australian landscape was declared *terra nullius* in 1835 after New South Wales Governor Richard Bourke quashed an attempt to purchase Port Phillip land from the Aborigines there via a treaty. After this time, anyone found occupying the land without authority was considered to be trespassing.

14 In Australia, the term 'wilderness' eventually evolved a range of meanings suited to specific interest groups (for example, The Wilderness Society). In the US, such definitions are entrenched in the 1964 Wilderness Act, usually specifying an area that is remote, of substantial size and relatively undisturbed by humans.

15 Reginald Ernest (Rex) Battarbee (1893–1973) was an artist and former farmer credited with having introduced the techniques for watercolour landscapes to Albert Namatjira. He moved to the Centre from Victoria in 1940 and ran classes in painting for Aboriginals at Hermannsburg.

16 Brady, E.J., *Australia Unlimited*, George Robertson, Melbourne, 1918, p. 588.

17 See Langton, M., Boyer Lectures 2012, *The Quiet Revolution: Indigenous People and the Resources Boom,* HarperCollins, Sydney, 2013.

18 Van Dyke, J.C., *The Desert: Further Studies in Natural Appearances*, Johns Hopkins University Press, Baltimore, 1999. Originally published by Charles Scribner's Sons, New York, in 1901.

19 Such correspondence between inner and outer worlds is a hallmark of nature writing—a genre one is tempted to use to describe Groom's writing—and yet it is a device Groom so rarely enlisted.

20 Gammage, B., *The Biggest Estate on Earth: How Aborigines Made Australia*, Allen & Unwin, Sydney, 2011. Langton, p. 108.

5 Chatwin

1 See Chatwin, E. and N. Shakespeare (eds), *Under the Sun: The Letters of Bruce Chatwin*, Vintage, London, 2011, p. 353.

2 Chatwin had long suspected he had HIV. Reading a copy of *Time* magazine in 1982, he stumbled upon an article that mentioned the 'gay plague' and told his wife he thought it applied to him. For more, see Susannah Clapp's entertaining memoir *With Chatwin: Portrait of a Writer*, Vintage, London, 1998.

3 In his 2000 biography *Bruce Chatwin*, Nicholas Shakespeare introduces Chatwin as an Englishman carrying a rucksack and walking boots who strides into a bungalow in the Irene district of Pretoria. This impression of the archetypal walker remains the popular conception of Chatwin the man: 'six feet tall, with fair hair swept over a huge forehead and staring blue eyes'.

4 Clapp, S., *With Chatwin*, p. 238

5 Even before Chatwin's arrival in Australia his ideas about humanity's walking nature 'approached the level of a secular religion'. As Paul Theroux writes in *The Tao of Travel*, Houghton Mifflin Harcourt, New York, 2012: 'Walking defined him … [he was] one of the great walkers in travel literature', moreover he believed 'walking defined the human race—the best of it'. In *The Songlines*, walking traces a pathway to Chatwin's grand narrative of the human condition, that man will be better off once he returns to his nomadic roots. And while many walking narratives are concerned with a 'journey against great odds', Chatwin's challenges are social rather than geophysical: how to get past the gatekeepers to the 'real' Aborigines, and on to a deciphering of the mysterious songlines.

6 For a thorough treatment of Bruce Chatwin's themes of nomadism, see Chatwin, J.M., '"Anywhere Out of the World": Restlessness in the Work of Bruce Chatwin', PhD thesis, University of Exeter, 2008, <https://ore.exeter.ac.uk/repository/bitstream/handle/10036/41273/ChatwinJ.pdf?sequence=2> (viewed 15 January 2015).

7 See Morphy, H., 'Behind the Songlines', *Anthropology Today*, vol. 4, no. 5, 1988, pp. 19–20. Conversely, Strehlow biographer Barry Hill in *Broken Song* judges Chatwin's rendering of the songlines quite harshly as being plain wrong. Only recently have a number of neglected themes of the book been retrieved.

8 Brown, R., '*The Songlines* and the Empire that Never Happened', *Kunapip,* vol. 13, no. 3, 1991, pp. 5–13.

9 Similarly, Sydney critic Stephen Muecke quips: 'The book's walking is confined to the English garden path. It ends up, after a slightly sordid adventure with the Other, back home in time for high tea'. Most journeys in the text are, in fact, by car, with Bruce's walks confined to short sojourns at prominent locations. Even so, Chatwin completed a number of walks in Alice Springs and elsewhere that, while not appearing in the text, are influential. And though examples are piecemeal, walking in *The Songlines* remains key to unlocking many of the themes of Chatwin's narrative.

10 The result is a familiar split between 'the West' as superficial and materialist modernity, and Aboriginal culture as something wiser, a simpler, more authentic—and by implication preferable—nomadic primitivism, attractive to those disenchanted with the West.

11 The description 'rough and ready' is by Baron Alder in 'The Australian Legend 50 Years On', *Quadrant*, September 2008, <www.quadrant.org.au/magazine/ issue/2008/9/the-australian-legend-fifty-years-on>; for thoughts on Russel's attention to the existence or otherwise of Aboriginals, see Angela Woollacott's 'Russel Ward, Frontier Violence and Australian Historiography', *Journal of Australian Colonial History*, vol. 10, no. 2, 2008, pp. 23–36, and Henry Reynolds' *Why Weren't We Told*, Penguin Books, Ringwood, 2000.

12 Political scientist Jeff Archer makes the most serious attempt at unpacking walking in the text, in Archer, J., 'Australian Indigeneity and Political Literature: Bruce Chatwin and Australian Politics', *Australasian Political Studies Association Conference*, University of Newcastle, 2006, <www.newcastle.edu.au/ Resources/Schools/Newcastle20Business20School/APSA/ANZPOL/Archer-Jeff.pdf> (viewed 30 June 2012).

13 In an interview with Michael Ignatieff published in *Granta*, Chatwin says of the genre question: 'As a category it's indefinable'. But he later adds that 'With *Songlines*, if I had to tot up the inventions, there would be no question in my mind that the whole thing added up to a fictional work'. Ignatieff, M., 'An Interview with Bruce Chatwin', *Granta*, vol. 21, Spring 1987, pp. 23–37.

14 Such trips serve a narrative purpose by introducing Bruce to remote communities and the 'real' Aboriginals he so wants to understand. In this fashion, the journey and its events might well be considered fiction, but it is important to remember that *The Songlines* also produces slabs of reportage of Central Australia during the 1980s and in this way should also be closely examined as non-fiction. Importantly, many of Chatwin's readers may never have met an Aboriginal person, and so his representation of Aboriginality takes on far greater significance.

15 This is certainly a common understanding among certain groups in Alice Springs, and has been my personal experience. Melbourne author Eleanor

Hogan, who spent time in Alice Springs, makes a similar observation in Hogan, E., 'Thinking Too Much', in Hutchinson, J. (ed), *Fishtails in the Dust*, Ptilotus Press, Alice Springs, 2009.

16 'Gin' is offensive slang for an Aboriginal female.

17 Again, in the Ignatieff interview, Chatwin says: 'I was impressed by that essay of Walter Benjamin in which he says the ideal book would be a book of quotations, and then there's a wonderful commonplace book by Hofmannsthal. I also had the remains of an essay on nomads, about the metaphysics of walking'.

18 Here Chatwin refers to D.H. Lawrence, who resided briefly in Western Australia, where he wrote of the landscape.

19 Anthropologist Francesca Merlan's work near Katherine produced similar results regarding ways of seeing a landscape. She walked repeatedly in the same hills over a long period with some Aboriginal friends, noting that, over time, 'I began to feel that I was learning something of my companions' mode of absorption.' 'Over months, the experience became an increasingly subtle one for me, as I learned about some of the things they were watching for and learned something of the layers of the past to which those markers belonged and of the people with whom they were associated.' A good introduction to Merlan's work is Merlan, F., *Caging the Rainbow: Places, Politics and Aborigines in a North Australian Town*, University of Hawaii Press, Honolulu, 1998.

20 In the Michael Ignatieff interview, Chatwin admits: 'I handed in this book—which is, above all, about walking—and the day after I couldn't walk across the hotel bedroom. I wrote that last chapter about three old men dying under a gum tree, when I was just about to conk myself. It was done with great speed'.

6 Hogan

1 A version of this incident appears originally in my weekly newspaper column under the title 'Cliches cut deep', *Rural Weekly NT*, 23 October 2015, p. 6.

2 There have been many suggested motivations for the NT Intervention. Critics say the move was to secure land tenure ahead of expected growth in Australia's rich mining industry, others that it signalled a rollback of land rights for Aboriginal people. Attitudes on the Intervention remain mixed and volatile and lie at the heart of much of the discontent in Northern Territory politics.

3 Madigan M., S. Strutt and G. Morrison, 'Troops Begin War Against Abuse', *Herald Sun*, 28 June 2007.

4 Wheeler Centre, 'Writing Alice Springs: An Interview with Eleanor Hogan', 24 October 2012, <www.wheelercentre.com/notes/500b7d64ca77> (viewed 8 June 2013).

5 Finnane, M. and K. Finnane, 'A Death in Alice Springs', *Current Issues in Criminal Justice*, vol. 23, no. 2, 2011, pp. 255–71.

6 Finnane, K., 'Bleak Tunnel Vision in New Book on Alice Springs', *Alice Springs News Online*, 10 September 2012, <www.alicespringsnews.com.au/2012/09/04/bleak-tunnel-vision-in-new-book-on-alice-springs> viewed 12 December 2014).

7 *Alice Springs* is structured around the Arrernte calendar with each of its six sections bearing an epigraph describing prevailing climatic conditions during each of the section's chapters. Hogan's recollections are then arranged according to the time of year they occurred, together constructing a 'year in the life of the town'. Season-wise, the book begins in *Uterne mpepe* when 'Hot winds begin to blow from the north west. We call that the bad wind, making people tired and irritable'. Hogan then assembles a memoir of place that gathers history, media reports, interviews with locals, and observations during walks.

8 Whether the Strehlow Research Centre is best to return these secret-sacred objects to Country, or continue to act as the modern-day *mukka mukka* it seems to have become, is unclear. An increasing number of Aboriginal people visit the centre to learn about genealogy, cultural heritage, songs, sacred sites and ceremony. The items themselves and the knowledge they represent are, nevertheless, still important to Law and ceremony and some who loaned them out for safe keeping or know their meaning are still alive.

9 See p. 12 of McDonald, W., 'Tricky Business: Whites on Black Territory', *Australian Author*, vol. 29, no. 1, 1997, pp. 11–14.

10 Recent research suggests that reference to ethically published Aboriginal Dreaming stories may greatly assist the writing of place in the Centre and elsewhere. For more on this, see Morrison, G., 'In the Footsteps of the Ancestors: Oral Fixations and Ethical Walking on the Last Great Songline', in Strange, S., P. Hetherington and J. Webb (eds), *Creative Manoeuvres: Making, Writing, Being*, Cambridge Scholars Publishing, Newcastle-upon-Tyne, 2014, pp. 33–52. For a fascinating ethnography, see also Bowman, M. (ed), *Every Hill Got a Story: We Grew Up in Country*, Central Land Council, Hardie Grant Books, n.d.

11 By way of contrast, local novelist Jo Dutton captures such complexity more resolutely in her recent work of fiction *From Alice With Love*. But Dutton's novel does this without squibbing on the many intractable issues of life in the Centre—alcohol, welfare dependence and cultural obligations—that often run counter to Western expectations.

12 Giacometti, M., 'Two Cultures Can Hold Each Other', *Meanjin* blog, <meanjin.com.au/articles/post/two-cultures-can-hold-each-other> (viewed 14 July 2014).

13 'The Right to Drink in Alice Springs', *Inside Story*, 9 May 2013, <inside.org.au/the-right-to-drink-in-alice-springs> (viewed 27 June 2014).

14 Nowra, L., *Bad Dreaming: Aboriginal Men's Violence Against Women and Children*, Pluto Press, Melbourne, 2007.

15 Walker, B.W., D.J. Porter and I. Marsh, 'Fixing the Hole in Australia's Heartland: How Government Needs to Work in Remote Australia', September 2012, remoteFOCUS, Desert Knowledge Australia, <www.desertknowledge.com.au/Files/Fixing-the-hole-in-Australia-s-Heartland.aspx> (viewed December 2014).

16 A similarly polemical approach recently led a pair of international academics mistakenly to render the Alice Springs town camps as 'spaces of respite and survival', whereas, in fact, black-on-black violence is widely experienced and reported on the camps. The misleading representation was pilloried as serving to 'reproduce a stereotype of Aboriginal people as victims, lacking agency'. For more on this, see Finnane, M. and K. Finnane, 'A Death in Alice Springs', 2011, where they deal with the paper, Perera, S. and J. Pugliese, 'Death in a Dry River: Black Life, White Property, Parched Justice', *Somatechnics*, vol. 1, no. 1, 2011, pp. 65–86.

17 Both quotations are from Finnane, M. and K. Finnane, 'A Death in Alice Springs,' 2011.

18 In their application to the Aboriginal Benefit Account, Lhere Artepe stated that in obtaining the three licences they would 'be able to contribute to combating problems of excess alcohol consumption in Alice Springs'. Actions contained within the strategy that have been implemented include removal of cask wine and clean-skin bottled wine, introduction of a *de facto* floor price on wine and spirits, and provision of education material in the bottle shops.

19 Davidson, R., 'Return of the Camel Lady', *Griffith Review*, no. 9, Spring 2005, pp. 128–39.

20 Trigger, D., 'Place, Belonging and Nativeness in Australia', in Vanclay, F., M. Higgins and A. Blackshaw (eds), *Making Sense of Place*, 2008, pp. 301–9.

21 A growing body of right-wing research and opinion by think tanks such as The Bennelong Institute, and periodicals such as *Quadrant* and *Viewpoint*, looks for the roots of Aboriginal violence in precolonial cultural practices. Yet in representing this in a literature of place, or a text like Hogan's, it is important to remember Moss's warning that it is 'easy to present the camp life around town as dysfunctional: just take a photo of litter, dogs and snotty-nosed kids'. In Rod Moss's estimation, it is vital to note 'Aboriginal-inspired initiatives as a counter-balance'.

22 Kapferer, B., 'Caging the Rainbow: Places, Politics, and Aborigines in a North Australian Town by Francesca Merlan (Review)', *Oceania*, vol. 70, no. 2, 1999, pp. 184–6.

Epilogue

1 Parts of this epilogue are drawn from two articles previously published: Morrison, G., 'Favenc's Call', *Territory Quarterly*, Sprout Creative, Darwin,

2014, pp. 104–5, and Morrison, G., 'No Direction Home: Race and Belonging in a Frontier Town', *Northern Territory Literary Awards 2013*, NT Library, Darwin, 2013, pp. 70–9, <artsandmuseums.nt.gov.au/__data/assets/pdf_file/0005/160637/NTLA-publication-2013.pdf> (viewed September 2013).

2 Malouf, D., 'The Happy Life', *Quarterly Essay*, issue 41, 2011.

3 Paraphrased from geographer David Seamon and based on ideas of the German philosopher Martin Heidegger.

ACKNOWLEDGEMENTS

To those who helped bring this book to fruition, my heartfelt thanks.

Parts of the work have appeared elsewhere, published by the Australian Association of Writing Programs, Cambridge Scholarly Publishing, in the journal *New Scholar* and online journal *Neo*. Reference is made to material previously published in my weekly newspaper column for APN's *Rural Weekly*, as well as magazine articles and essays for *Territory Quarterly*, book reviews in the *Sunday Territorian*, various news reports, and two personal essays published by the Northern Territory Library.